The Truth-Seeking Heart

Other titles in the *Canterbury Studies in Spiritual Theology*

Glory Descending: Michael Ramsey and His Writings
Douglas Dales, John Habgood, Geoffrey Rowell and Rowan Williams

Firmly I Believe: An Oxford Movement Reader
Edited by Raymond Chapman

Forthcoming

The Sacramental Life: Gregory Dix and His Writings
Edited by Simon Jones

To Build Christ's Kingdom: An F. D. Maurice Reader
Edited by Jeremy Morris

Holiness and Happiness: A Traherne Reader
Edited by Denise Inge

CANTERBURY STUDIES IN SPIRITUAL THEOLOGY

The Truth-Seeking Heart

Austin Farrer and His Writings

Edited by
Ann Loades and Robert MacSwain

First published in 2006 by the Canterbury Press Norwich
(a publishing imprint of Hymns Ancient & Modern Limited,
a registered charity)
9–17 St Albans Place, London N1 0NX

www.scm-canterburypress.co.uk

British Library Cataloguing in Publication data

A catalogue record for this book is available from the British Library

ISBN 1-85311-712-9/978-1-85311-712-1

Typeset by Regent Typesetting, London
Printed and bound in Great Britain by
MPG Books Ltd, Bodmin, Cornwall

Contents

Part 3 Reason

Preface

In preparing this volume for publication, we are gratefully aware of some considerable debts. First of all, to Christine Smith of SCM-Canterbury Press, who suggested the idea of including an Austin Farrer reader in the series 'Canterbury Studies in Spiritual Theology'. Second, to the Farrer Estate for granting copyright permission, and to the previous publishers – especially SPCK – for allowing us to reprint Farrer's texts.

Third, all readers of Farrer are in debt to his earlier posthumous editors, namely Leslie Houlden, Charles Conti and Richard Harries. Although a comprehensive reader of this sort has never before appeared, Conti is responsible for initially gathering many of Farrer's far-flung essays in philosophy, theology and biblical studies into *Reflective Faith: Essays in Philosophical Theology* (SPCK, 1972) and *Interpretation and Belief* (SPCK, 1976), thereby earning a permanent place in Farrer scholarship.

Fourth, we are indeed grateful for that community of scholars who have kept the flame of Farrer's legacy alive. While several more could be named, we particularly thank Diogenes Allen, David Brown, Charles Conti, the late Philip Curtis, Jeffrey Eaton, Rodger Forsman, Julian Hartt, Brian Hebblethwaite, Charles Hefling Jr, David Hein, Edward Hugh Henderson, Michael Goulder, Basil Mitchell, Michael McLain, Helen Oppenheimer and Robert Boak Slocum.

Fifth and finally, we are of course most deeply indebted to Austin Farrer himself. The title of this reader was inspired by a passage in one of his sermons about John Keble. It has been remarked that this passage is an equally good (if not better) description of Farrer, and aptly captures his abiding importance for Christian theology:

> After all the detection of shams, the clarification of argument, and the sifting of evidence – after all criticism, all analysis – a man must

> make up his mind what there is most worthy of love, and most binding on conduct, in the world of real existence. It is this decision, or this discovery, that is the supreme exercise of a truth-seeking intelligence. ('Keble and His College', in Austin Farrer, *The End of Man* [SPCK, 1973, p. 157])

Our concept for this reader was to gather together in one volume some of Farrer's classic writing on Scripture, tradition and reason. The contents are drawn from sermons, essays and chapters from his books. We have endeavoured as far as possible to select texts which may be presented entire, just as Farrer wrote them, with a minimum of editorial intervention. Some, however, have been edited for length: abridgements within texts are indicated by bold ellipses, and any material cut from the beginning or end has been acknowledged in the brief introductions which accompany each selection. And some texts have been very lightly revised to make them more accessible to a contemporary audience. Farrer wrote before a time when language was consciously inclusive or exclusive and we have mostly retained his use of such terms as 'mankind'. Our hope in preparing this volume is that Austin Farrer's profound integration of the truth-seeking intelligence and the truth-seeking heart will again inspire a new generation to seek the One who is the Truth.

Ann Loades and Robert MacSwain
Durham, England
April 2006

Introduction

Like several other great Anglican theologians – such as Joseph Butler, F. D. Maurice and Michael Ramsey – Austin Marsden Farrer (1904–68) had the very good fortune to be born into a Nonconformist family. Nonconformity in England had long been associated with serious commitment to education and learning, and this particular family was no exception. His father taught Scripture and Church History in a Baptist establishment for the training of ministers, originally in London but now located in Oxford. Austin was the middle of three children (with two sisters), and the whole group enjoyed a lively and stimulating home life, with the parents attempting to do justice to the considerable talents of each of them.

Times, of course, were hard. Farrer was fortunate to have been born on a date which kept him clear of service in the appalling conditions of the First World War battlefields, though only the most privileged in Britain escaped the privations inescapable in wartime in respect of food and fuel. Comparable privations were to continue during the period after the war, with a General Strike in the UK and the economic slump that followed it. Europe was to be in turmoil for much of his life, with the Russian Revolution and the advent of Communist governments, and the almost indescribable menace of the rise of National Socialism and Fascism. To follow were the horrors of the Second World War, with systematic mass murder, aerial bombing of civilians, including the saturation bombing of German cities by the Allies, and a tragic culmination in the atomic bombing of Hiroshima and Nagasaki in the Far East.

Farrer also escaped military service in the Second World War. He had been ordained in 1929 and was ensconced in Oxford. Oxford, however, was anything but isolated from what was going on, as the terrible war memorials in its college chapels vividly remind us, quite apart from the presence as undergraduates of the young men who returned to begin or complete interrupted degrees. There were, too, survivors of the First World War battlefields among Oxford dons, C. S. Lewis for one, with anguished memories expressed in such books as his autobiography, *Surprised by Joy*, and on which he drew in *The Problem of Pain.*

So in attending to Farrer's career and his writings it is important to keep this overall background in mind, for it is certainly echoed in his texts, even if he did not harp on it. His primary responsibilities, in any case, were the teaching and pastoral care of undergraduates and other members of his Colleges, not to the broader political scene directly, though many of those he taught would take on significant and serious commitments in public life after leaving Oxford.

Farrer himself won a place at St Paul's School in London where he received a thoroughgoing literary and classical education, thriving in academic achievement, and with a marked taste for more, as one might expect from someone moving from St Paul's to Balliol College, Oxford. Both at school and at college he became thoroughly familiar with the worship of the Church of England, and its inheritance of the 'King James' or 'Authorized' version of the Bible, and the prose and poetry of the Book of Common Prayer. Both Bible and Prayer Book were produced for public readings, and for those who attended to them their metaphor and imagery became part and parcel of their own speech and imaginative, intellectual and emotional worlds. Add to this Farrer's access through his classical education to the Western Church's Latin tradition and devotion, and we have some understanding of how he developed a prose style and a manner of writing sermons which has as yet to be matched by anyone else. He also had the singular advantage of having had years of listening to Nonconformist preachers, concentrating as they were most likely to do on scriptural texts. His preaching style was thus a fusion of these diverse elements.

As it happened, during his undergraduate years Farrer not only became a member of the Church of England, but discovered in himself a vocation for ordination. That vocation was examined and approved by the Church and explored during a period at what was then Cuddesdon Theological College, just outside Oxford. A friend and fellow student at Cuddesdon was Michael Ramsey (1904–88), the future Archbishop of Canterbury. Like Farrer, Ramsey too was drawn towards the High Church wing of the Church of England. This encouraged both of them towards a sacramental vision that stressed God's positive endorsement of his creation, not least in the incarnation.

After ordination, Farrer served a curacy in Dewsbury, Yorkshire. He learned German – very wisely, given the major impact of German-speaking theology of all kinds on international theological scholarship, though he never became an unqualified enthusiast for the work of such major figures as Karl Barth or Emil Brunner. Farrer returned to work at St Edmund Hall, Oxford as Chaplain and Tutor (1931–35), moving to Trinity College, Oxford as Chaplain and Fellow for what turned out to be a long stint in that position (1935–60). These were good years for Farrer, despite the background of social, economic and political distress in Europe as a whole. This background had an inevitable impact on everyone's life. Despite having escaped invasion, hardship prevailed in Britain for some years although there were major post-war achievements with public provision of schooling, healthcare, transport and pensions as economic recovery continued.

Marriage to another Oxford graduate, Katharine Newton in 1937, and the birth of their one child in 1939 brought some domestic happiness, notwithstanding the immense pressures on those who held college posts in some very difficult years. Farrer had his disappointments too – not being made Regius Professor of Divinity in Oxford – but he was ultimately appointed as Warden of Keble College from 1960 until his early and unexpected death in 1968. During these years he made some forays to the USA where his work had been admired in some circles since the 1940s.

Farrer himself was a man with an unequalled intellectual and imaginative range, at least among his English contemporaries. In the Preface to his second book, *The Glass of Vision* (1948), he famously wrote: 'Scripture and metaphysics are equally my study, and poetry is my pleasure. These three things rubbing against one another in my mind, seem to kindle one another, and so I am moved to ask how this happens' (p. ix). Given that Scripture and metaphysics and poetry rarely 'rub together' in the same mind, this quotation speaks volumes about the range of Farrer's interests. However, in this Reader we have adopted the rather more conventional Anglican triad of Scripture, Tradition and Reason. For Farrer indeed made important contributions to our understanding of each, and also to how they should interact in Christianity theology.

His 'short' Bible is a masterly presentation of crucially important and inter-related texts, quite apart from its introduction. Belonging as he did to a generation of 'professional' theologians who were ordained to preach as well as to celebrate the sacraments, he necessarily had to reflect on scriptural texts as a matter of course, and relate them to the pattern of the liturgical year. Although we tend to categorize Farrer as belonging to the 'Catholic' side of the Church of England, we misjudge him and indeed others if we neglect the importance they attached to the exposition of Scripture, and to the contribution such teaching and preaching made to the coherence of their appreciation of doctrine and tradition – it all came together in one piece, as it were, over the course of time.

Yet Farrer by no means repeated conventional wisdom about what was involved in public responsibility for Christian faith on the part of an ordained person such as himself. The Reader's chapter from *The Glass of Vision* ('Images and Inspiration') exhibits him as one capable of thinking with much independence of judgement about revelation, not least in reflecting on Christology as expressed in certain dominant images, such as sacrifice, communion, expiation, covenant, kingdom, and Son of Man. Drawn from human life, without which they could not be intelligible to us, these images were also inspired by the Holy Spirit and given to us in conjunction with crucial events – Christ's baptism and his last supper with his disciples in particular. Image and event coinciding with one another reveal God to us. Such revelation continued in the apostolic life of the early Church, and on into the life of the Church during subsequent centuries, manifest most clearly in the lives of the saints, and the experience of believers in their liturgies, prayers, and personal devotion and practical commitments.

In his commentaries on the books of Mark, Matthew and Revelation, Farrer ventured into reflections almost unique for a Church of England theologian, particularly in regard to his theories about the biblical authors' creative literary and theological activity. Clearly Farrer had little time for the kinds of biblical scholarship which left the texts in shreds, or was merely preoccupied with their narrowly 'historical' import, rather than sustaining a Trinitarian and Easter-centred faith. Farrer's strong and sensitive 'reformed' roots, however, never let him suppose that the Christian tradition was incorrigible, however authoritative and central some of its convictions. Precisely because he believed that the Church's role in this life was to incorporate humanity into the life of the ascended, still-incarnate God, he held that it was a Christian's responsibility to detect and reject both 'period junk' and betrayal – whatever would hinder, confuse and restrict such incorporation. As he put it, 'We must have no bogus history.'

In his approach to the traditions of the Church, Farrer is much concerned to make these live, as well as stress the fallible context of their creators. So, if on the one hand he can appear quite fierce in his critique of any pretensions to church or papal infallibility, on the other hand he is resolute in insisting on divine guidance of the Church. It has the glorious role of ultimately incorporating us into the very life of the Trinity. If these two aspects sound inconsistent, he attempts to make sense of this by insisting that an indispensable element to the incarnation was God entering into human limitations. Jesus knew *how* to be the Son of God, even if he did not know *that* he was the Son of God. Particularly impressive is Farrer's constant aim of integrating doctrine and prayer. The Creed was for him no abstract list of formulae to which subscription was demanded, but a series of prayerful commitments which should truly animate the Christian's whole life.

Farrer had many intellectual challenges on his doorstep, too, as one might expect, given the impact of so many twentieth-century developments in the natural and social sciences, and in philosophy – such as, for example, the logical positivism of A. J. Ayer's *Language, Truth and Logic*, first published in 1935. This book, which remains immensely readable, implied (even where it did not robustly and straightforwardly state) that much of what counted for authority in knowledge, morals and belief was simply nonsense. This sort of challenge was further developed and debated in an influential collection edited by Anthony Flew and Alasdair MacIntyre (*New Essays in Philosophical Theology*, 1955). Farrer, however, was equal to the challenge, with the publication of a formidably difficult book, *Finite and Infinite* (1943).

There is no easy way of summarizing even the main points of this text, but basically he writes about the way in which God relates to 'being-as-activity' (substance) and therefore attends in detail to the analogies which make possible a sort of climbing of an inner 'scale' within ourselves which yields knowledge of God. In another philosophical work, *The Freedom of the Will* (1958), he explored something very important to him, namely that central to being a human person is the freedom to become what we will. Then in his *Faith and Speculation* (1967) he considered faith and reason, grace in relation to free will, and re-visited the relation between revelation and rational theology, as well as the significance of history. These themes are developed in a more accessible way in the chapters, sermons and essays which comprise the third and final section of this Reader – particularly the proper role of reason in relation to religious belief. This section also includes some of Farrer's seminal reflections on the problem of evil, as found in his book, *Love Almighty and Ills Unlimited* (1961).

Works such as these secured him the abiding respect and affection of some distinguished figures in the post-war years. His friendship with Archbishop Michael Ramsey has already been mentioned. Another colleague was Eric Mascall of Christ Church Oxford and King's College London, who shared Farrer's interest in appropriating the work of St Thomas Aquinas for Anglican theologians. And one of Farrer's closest friends was C. S. Lewis: they worked together in Oxford's Socratic Club, and Lewis dedicated his book *Reflections on the Psalms* to both Austin and Katharine. (Katharine was, incidentally, a figure in her own right: translator of Gabriel Marcel, author of detective stories, and correspondent with Dorothy Sayers.) When Lewis married Joy Davidman, the Farrers witnessed their vows and the two couples became mutual friends. Later, Austin would sadly perform the funeral services for both Joy and 'Jack'.

A group convened by Eric Mascall, called 'The Metaphysicals', began to meet after the Second World War and became Farrer's primary intellectual community. In addition to Mascall and Farrer, it included I. M. Crombie, Michael Foster, R. M. Hare, G. C. Stead, J. R. Lucas, Ian Ramsey and Basil Mitchell. Iris Murdoch was an original member, but eventually left as her Christian faith faded. She was soon replaced by Helen Oppenheimer, one of the most distinguished writers on Christian ethics in the post-war period. A book edited by Mitchell and titled *Faith and Logic* (1957) collected some of the papers presented within this high-powered set of Christian philosophers. But Farrer was their acknowledged leader.

In conclusion, Austin Farrer was a brilliant yet idiosyncratic Anglican priest and scholar, deeply at odds with the prevalent modes of biblical criticism, theology, and philosophical reasoning of his day. But he simply got on with the job of trying to interpret the Bible and tradition in the light of reason, properly understood. He saw that Scripture and tradition needed critical interpretation and constant re-appropriation if they were not to stultify; and that reason was both deeper than mere logic and yet also limited in the face of divine mystery. In retrospect, it seems that in many ways Farrer was a prophetic figure, for certain recent developments in all three of these disciplines can find parallels in his work. For example, literary approaches to the biblical text, the revival of Trinitarian theology, the re-engagement of contemporary philosophers with the contribution of ancient and medieval thought to Christian doctrine, not to mention the increased interest in linking theology and spirituality – all of these trends were prefigured in Farrer and are manifest in the contents of this Reader.

One goal of this volume is that it may thus provide a useful introduction to the three disciplines of biblical study, theological reflection and philosophical reasoning. Those who read its contents will find themselves taught by someone who was a master of each discipline, and gently but clearly led to new, often challenging – yet also moving and edifying – understandings of all three. But our primary hope in preparing this book is that Christians in general – and Anglicans in particular – may find in Farrer a model for the faithful union of heart and mind. Perhaps what is most striking about Farrer is his combination of rigorous intellectual *honesty*, deep personal (and corporate) *humility*, and yet also great *confidence* in the truth and reliability of the Christian gospel. At a time of increasing polarization among Christians – with some retreating into fundamentalism and others surrendering all claims to divine revelation and truth – Farrer's witness is more relevant now than ever before.

Part One
Scripture

'Introduction' from *A Short Bible*

Published in 1957. Farrer wrote this introduction to a selection of readings from the Authorized Translation, published in England as A Short Bible *and in the United States as* The Core of the Bible. *These passages were chosen and arranged by Farrer to provide those unfamiliar with the Scriptures with what he regarded as their essential distillation. But this brief essay is also valuable in its own right. Charles Hefling says that it is 'by far the best popular statement of his position on scripture as a whole, and it is to be regretted that it is not more widely known'.* Here Farrer not only explains to a general audience the most basic facts about the Bible, but also provides some insight to its contents and some guidelines to its interpretation. Obviously, the intervening fifty years have called some of Farrer's dates and details into question, but his basic picture has weathered remarkably well. Moreover, his theological understanding of Scripture still bears careful consideration. For example, against the widespread assumption that in order to be the Word of God the Bible itself must be inerrant, he makes the intriguing claim that:*

> *The scripture expresses the whole work of God – what his work does, what it works with, and what it works against, all are there; sin and error appear beside truth and holiness, fantasy and idealisation beside the unflinching delineation of failure, and, as we all know, Satan quotes nothing but the Bible. If Christ were not there to set Satan right, we should not know what to think.*

---

* Charles Helfling, 'Farrer's Scriptural Divinity', in David Hein and Edward Hugh Henderson (eds), *Captured by the Crucified: The Practical Theology of Austin Farrer* (New York/London: T & T Clark International, 2004), pp. 149–72 [172 footnote 7].

The last paragraph of the Introduction, which concerns specific details of the book's format, is not included.

The Bible is not a book but a library of books, descending from an age when writers used fewer words than they do now. A complete Bible comprises in one volume almost all that survives of the literature of Israel between 1,000 and 250 BC or of Christian writing in the first Christian century.

To write an introduction to the Bible would be like writing an introduction to English poetry from King Alfred to Queen Victoria. How could you do it, without writing a whole history of the intervening ages? All the same, there is a difference. Anyone who tried to make out that the value of English poetry over so many centuries lay in the expression of a single theme, would be supporting an artificial fancy. That the Bible is valued and read for the sake of a single theme is no ingenious paradox, but sober fact. The Scriptures of the Old and New Testaments are included under a single name for no other reason than this, that through them the persona and work of Jesus Christ are understood. The New fulfils the Old, the Old is indispensable for understanding the New.

The unity of the Bible can be best appreciated from within; we must plunge in somewhere. Let it be into the Epistle to the Galatians. Here is a letter of which no one in his right senses has doubted the genuineness. A sharp and unguarded polemic thrown off to meet an emergency, it opens the heart of its author and reveals the painful discords of the first Christian days. The writer, it appears, has himself converted to a new faith some inhabitants of the Roman province called Galatia. He has taught them that in virtue of their faith they are members in the true Israel of God; though few of them have a drop of Jewish blood in their veins, they take over the destiny of the Chosen People. But now the writer is outraged at the news of a second mission following up his own. The new missionaries say that while it is a fine thing to have been grafted into Israel by faith in Israel's King, it would be a finer thing still to complete the process by acceptance of the Israelite way of life and all its customs, beginning with ritual circumcision.

The new missionaries say that in offering such advice they have the backing of the original apostles or representatives of their common

Master, Jesus, the spiritual King of Israel; if St Paul says otherwise, he is going back on his superiors, the men who gave him his gospel. No, says St Paul, God gave me the gospel and sent me to preach it in the non-Jewish world. I have no superiors, though I have several seniors. But my contacts with my older fellow-apostles have been few. I have not taken their orders; I have made sure that my gospel was the same as theirs and that they acknowledged me for a colleague. They were to preach to Jews, I to non-Jews, as I was already doing; that was the agreement. Jews should be Jews, non-Jews should be neither Judaized nor circumcised. If they are now saying differently it is they who have gone back on me, not I on them. And it is no personal matter; the Gospel is at stake. If non-Jews accept circumcision and the Jewish customs, they cannot single-mindedly believe that the true Israel is constituted by acceptance of the Messiah, and by that alone.

In illustration of his plea the Apostle sketches his career. He is writing some little while after the sixteenth year of his conversion to Christ, and, as we gather from other indications, some twenty or more after Christ's crucifixion. He has been in the new movement almost from the start. The common ground of the preaching places salvation here and hereafter in adherence to Christ, in obedience to him, and in a supernatural share of his life and Spirit, a gift bestowed on his followers through death and resurrection. St Paul does not say that he places salvation in these things while the more Jewish-minded apostles place it in something else. He says they all place it in these things, but that he is consistent, while they, with their recommendation of circumcision to non-Jewish converts, are not.

In the twentieth-or-so year of Christianity the best debating argument already was: 'Christ is all. You know it, for you live it; and my doctrine is the doctrine which can best uphold it.' Such is the argument St Paul presses upon St Peter himself in the second chapter of Galatians. Here is our earliest evidence; there is no reason for thinking that there had ever been a different Christianity from this. Galatians contains all the high doctrine of Christianity in germ; and Galatians was written by a contemporary of Christ when he had outlived him in this world for a score or so of years and reached about the fiftieth of his own age.

A reader who knew nothing of biblical religion and who read Galatians would be left asking a large number of questions; and the unity or common purpose of the Bible may be said to lie in this, that it contains the evidence necessary for answering them.

Our first question will probably be about Jesus Christ as a historical character. St Paul and his fellow-apostles say that he is the Lord's Anointed, for which 'Messiah' is the Jewish term and the Greek 'Christ'. That is to say, he is the promised king who revives the glory of Israel and establishes the empire of God. He is Son of God by birth; his followers, through union with him, become sons of God by adoption. Such is the faith; about whom is it held? Galatians says no more of Jesus Christ than that he had a human mother, lived within the Jewish system, died by process of law, being crucified, and was raised from the dead. We learn more from St Paul's next surviving letter, the First to the Corinthians.

Some few years after writing Galatians St Paul met an equally painful emergency with a letter equally unsparing. In recalling his Corinthian converts to the standards of Christian life he has occasion to remind them of the first things they learnt about Jesus Christ, pieces of stereotyped catechism which St Paul derived from his own conversion and handed on to them at theirs. Jesus Christ died for our sins as the scriptures had promised, and was buried. But he rose again the third day after, likewise according to scriptural promise, and showed himself first to Peter, then to the Twelve; after that, adds St Paul, to a large number of others, among whom I was myself the last. Another piece of catechism described how, on the night in which he was betrayed to his death, Christ had instituted the sacrament of the Supper. The Epistle cites two other pieces of common knowledge about Christ. He had instituted apostles and given exact directions about their maintenance, and he had forbidden the marriage of the divorced.

St Paul's Epistles are our earliest evidence for Christ's life. They do not tell us about an exemplary reforming rabbi, but about the Son of God, the institutor of the Apostolate and the Supper, who died and who rose, thereby fulfilling the scriptures, and who made at least one novel and severe demand on his disciples' virtue. The teaching of St Paul, and of other apostolic leaders, may be followed out in the remaining Epistles. But for any considerable increase in our information on Christ's life, we must turn to the Gospels.

St Paul's letters were called out by various emergencies in the Churches. No such emergency seems to have called for an early casting of the tradition about Christ's words and deeds into literary form. When written accounts did appear they were anonymous. The four Gospels do not contain their authors' names, though there are hints in St John and in St Luke's second volume, the Acts of the Apostles. The traditional names were added very early. It is not at all likely that any of the four was written in St Paul's lifetime. 68 AD is a fair guess for St Mark's date, towards 90 for St Matthew and St Luke, soon after 100 for St John. St Matthew and St Luke each knew St Mark; St John very likely read all his predecessors, but if so, he did not choose to reproduce them closely.

The Evangelists were not ignorant men; they possessed scripture-learning in various degrees. But of course they had no idea of historical biography as we now conceive it. A comparison of their work shows that they arranged many of the traditional anecdotes about Christ according to subject, not according to any order of actual occurrence. Certain incidents, being the turning-points of the history, keep their true historical positions. For the rest we must be in large measure content not to know what followed what.

Such an admission carries with it no disparagement of the Gospels as authorities for what their writers wished to say. They give us a picture of Christ's person and teaching which, though greatly expanded, holds the same balance as St Paul's sketch. Did the Christ of St Paul correct rabbinic teaching on the subject of divorce? According to the Gospels he corrected it on many points besides, yet, as St Paul says, remained within Jewry to the day of this death. Was his resurrection a supernatural event according to St Paul? The Gospels tell us it was not the first, but the climax of many miracles. Are the death and resurrection, and the world-wide church, the substance of the Gospel as St Paul proclaims it? Christ, say the Evangelists, had himself concentrated his disciples' minds on these things before they came to pass, and exerted himself to make them intelligible beforehand.

The Evangelists fill in St Paul's outline. Their marked disagreements raise many historical puzzles, but they are puzzles about the Church's memory towards the end of the century, and cannot possibly weaken the plain apostolic testimony which is so much more direct, and which, indeed, carries us back into the very heart of the events. In Galatians the voice of St Paul appeals to the faith of St Peter, the chief companion of Jesus throughout his ministry. The men whom I Corinthians recalls to the fundamentals of their religion had listened to St Peter as well as to St Paul.

Jesus Christ in the Gospels, and St Paul in his several epistles are concerned with the action of God in their own time, through which his love for mankind takes practical effect. It is all the more remarkable that what they have to say is so largely expressed by means of allusion to the Old Testament. That spiritual realities can often be best conveyed by allusion to other things, is a principle sufficiently illustrated by Christ's own use of parables; but the one great complex living parable of the New Covenant is the Old.

The relation of the one to the other finds expression in a special and strange use of the word 'true'. The Church is the 'true' Israel, Jesus is the 'true' Anointed King, his death is the 'true' sacrifice. The opposite of 'true' in this way of speaking is not (as we might expect) 'false' but 'literal and prefigurative'. The Israel of King David was a literal Israel, prefiguring the true; David himself was a literally Anointed King, prefiguring the true Christ; and so on. You might suppose that, once possessed of the 'true' things, we could afford to forget the literal prefigurations of them. But this is not so. If you do not know what the love of a literal father is like, it will be useless to talk about the true paternal love of God, and if you cannot discover what literal sacrifices were once thought to be, you will gain no light on the death of Christ from hearing it called 'the true sacrifice'. Nor will it do to rummage the ancient world at large for your information, when Christ is set forth as the true sacrifice. It is not of Greek or Babylonian rites that he is called the 'truth'.

The divine way of teaching is certainly different from the human. When we ask for guidance about God and our relation to him, we are given no philosophical generalities, we are shown a typical action which God himself has once for all performed in human life, incarnate, dying, rising; an action which he will extend to us and work out in us, with endless adaptations to our circumstances, yet always the same. And when we ask for help with the understanding of a divine act productive of such infinite consequences, we are still not given cool, luminous abstractions, but flesh-and-blood parables; and not even then only parables picked at random, as we expect them to be, one from the lilies, another from the sparrows, but a single living mass of parable, the spiritual being of a nation, deployed through centuries of time, voiced by inspired utterance and fixed in written letters, the Old Testament.

The Old Covenant is the parable of the New, but not the mere parable. Christ and his Apostles did not, as by a lucky accident, lay their hands on a traditional literature which supplied the fund of parables they happened to require. They were themselves, humanly speaking, the product of the culture they drew upon. The divine truth born in the New Testament is the divine truth with which the Old Testament travails, and towards which it works as pregnancy works towards birth.

If we use the language of belief, and call God the true author of both Testaments, we are using 'true' as we defined it above by contrast with 'literal'. God is the true author, but his authorship is not executed with pen and ink, nor simply by the direct inspiration of literal penmen. His materials are the whole stuff of history and his hand is Providence. His 'writing' of the scripture is just as much his creation of the life which finds expression in the words, as his guidance of the expression. The scripture expresses the whole work of God – what his work does, what it works with, and what it works against, all are there; sin and error appear beside truth and holiness, fantasy and idealisation beside the unflinching delineation of failure, and, as we know, Satan quotes nothing but the Bible. If Christ were not there to set Satan right, we should not know what to think.

No formula will do justice to the divine authorship of every text; the manner and the directness of spiritual control vary so greatly. The words of a prophet, treasured and recorded by his disciples, are the very instrument of the divine Spirit in the making of Israel, and the prophet's own belief was, that the words were given him. A scribe recording traditional histories of legal rules might, on the other hand, have no notion of his own inspiration. If his words are written by the finger of God, it is because the matter which dictates the expression shows the hand of Providence.

There are two ways in which to regard the Old Testament, and they must not be confused. On the one hand it is a body of writings which existed for Christ and his Apostles much as it does for us. It provided the intellectual and imaginative universe which, no less than the real world, Christ died to transform. I can read it over the shoulders of St Paul or St John, I can listen to it in synagogue with the child Jesus. On the other hand it is evidence for the reconstruction of two thousand Israelite years: not a fresco on one plane, but a series of fragmentary pictures, of inscriptions half defaced, set back one behind another into a haze of distance. Where the apostle contemplated the landscape of the past, the historian walks into the country. He tries to think not with St Paul or St John, but say with a nameless man writing of Moses in Hezekiah's reign. Then, by a still more hazardous advance, he stands before the glowing bush on Sinai, and looks through Moses' eyes.

Of the two approaches we have distinguished, it is the apostolic approach which more obviously concerns the ordinary reader, and it is an approach which he can make without the portentous machinery of critical learning. If the Bible is taken as a first-century book, the Twentieth-century man can read it, not without risk of misunderstanding, but with great enjoyment and substantial profit. The other approach, the historical, is a technical inquiry and the amateur is helpless without professional assistance. His views on the way in which King Josiah met his end, or on the facts behind the saga of the exodus from Egypt, will be worthless.

The Bible as such, that is, as a sacred collection, belongs to the apostolic approach, not the historical. The New Testament is the body of Christian writings which were being read out as carrying apostolic authority in the Church of the second century. The Old Testament is what the synagogues were already reading in the two centuries before Christ. In both collections there were a few disputed items of marginal importance, on which a final decision was not reached until somewhat later.

In all essentials our Old Testament was the Bible of Christ and of St Paul. But no part of the old Jewish world placed all the scriptures on a level. The scripture par excellence was the reputed work of Moses, the first five books of our Old Testament, and called in Hebrew 'Torah', a term conventionally but inadequately translated 'Law'. This was the canon within the canon; Moses, and Moses alone, was the religion of Israelites.

The Torah alone was read straight through in the synagogues, continuing on each sabbath where the previous sabbath had left off. The reading and hearing of Torah was the great ceremony of synagogue worship. You went to synagogue to hear the voice of God, as Israel had heard it on Mt Sinai on their way from the Red Sea to the Promised

Land. The voice still spoke through Moses, the appointed mediator: Moses transferred from flesh and blood to ink and papyrus, Moses declaimed in his own Hebrew, and rendered by a second speaker in the language of the people.

So far as the Service went, the rest of the Bible was a mere quarry from which to dig Second Lessons illustrative of the Mosaic portion for the day. Most of the Bible was never read at all and what was read was often repeated. Certain parts of Isaiah, for example, were worked especially hard. Even in theory the choice on ordinary days did not embrace the whole of what was not Moses. It should be taken from 'the Prophets', a title describing not only twelve minor prophecies and three major, Isaiah, Jeremiah, Ezekiel, but six histories as well, Joshua, Judges, and the two double books of Samuel and Kings.

On certain festivals and set occasions, however, lessons were admitted from 'the Scrolls', that is, from the books additional to 'Moses and the Prophets'. The Psalms stood technically among the Scrolls, but they were not read, for they were being sung continually. They were the hymnbook of the synagogue, borrowed from their original home, the Temple.

Though little used for lessons, the Scrolls were in the synagogues, anyhow in the greater and richer synagogues, for the use of the learned. After the second sabbath-lesson there was usually a preacher, and there was hope that he might be a learned man. If so, his audience might hear much quotation from unfamiliar scriptures, and even from writings which were not 'scripture' at all. They might also hear a deal of Oral Tradition, the customary interpretation of scripture passed from rabbi to rabbi.

The arrangement of our complete Bible, bound up in a majestic continuity of books, confirms the bent we receive from our historical education, and inclines us to view scripture as a record of God's dealings with mankind, interspersed with various illustrative pieces. The Jew did not think like this. His scriptures were on separate scrolls of papyrus kept in three distinct parts of the cupboard. They arranged themselves in his imagination as their synagogue usage suggested. 'Moses', the revealed will of God, was the citadel of truth; the Prophets formed an outer wall, protecting Moses from the danger of misunderstanding. The Scrolls were a third line of defence, the unwritten Tradition was a fourth and last palisade. Moses was the text; concentric rings of interpretation surrounded him. Everything must be in Moses, even though without his inspired interpreters Israel would not know how to find it there.

St Paul shared the rabbinic view; it is plain that to him the Bible is 'the Law', buttressed by its traditional outworks. If, in his view, the Old Testament did anything, it imposed a Law, and this was God's purpose for the while. But now the Law has fallen foul of Christ, crucifying him as a law-breaker. So much the worse for the Law; its reign is at an end, and the old Covenant or Testament gives place to the New. Indeed, if we look carefully at the Law, we see that it carries in it the mark of its own provisional character and the promise of what will supersede it. Not that the servants of God are henceforth lawless; they do what the Law requires, not through conformity to Law, but through devotion to Christ.

The suggestion of something like a civil war between the two Testaments which we meet here and there in St Paul belongs to his defence of an infant Church against reabsorption into legal Judaism. The danger quickly passed, leaving St Paul's followers free to develop the less polemical side of his thought, and to nourish themselves on the riches of the Scripture. They exploited it, not only for edifying examples and sound maxims, but for seeds and prefigurations of the salvation to which it led.

In compiling the very short Bible which follows we have paid some regard to the facts we have just been explaining. The Old Testament pieces which we have put together are not an anthology of the most uplifting passages the ancient scripture contains. They are the background to the New Testament mind. For this reason 'Moses' occupies the principal place. 'Moses' is the substance of the ancient faith; here is mankind created as the flower of the world, fallen in the person of Adam, called to renewal in Abraham, delivered from bondage under Moses and formed into a holy nation.

What the Jews called 'the Prophets' contained the after-history of Moses' great foundation: a record of many ups and downs, and a setting for the work of the prophets properly so named; inspired preachers sent to recall a back-sliding people to its God-given privileges. As the kingdom of David foundered, prophecy turned more and more to future hope. The sons of David had failed, but a Son of David would yet arise to establish not so much his empire, as God's. We have contrived to give some sort of continuous outline from Joshua to the great prophets by inserting passages from later parts of the Bible, written by men who look back and summarise. We have used the same device already for joining together our selections from 'Moses'.

To 'Moses and the Prophets' we have added seven psalms – the Bible contains twenty times as many. But we have hoped to give the reader some idea of what is meant when on the last page of St Luke's Gospel the Risen Christ recalls to his disciples 'all things written in the Law of Moses and the Prophets and the Psalms' concerning himself.

We have chosen St Luke to tell the gospel story, and printed him entire. We have continued his narrative through 'Acts' as far as the setting out of the first organised apostolic mission. We have added from St Matthew and St John further discourses of Jesus which no one could endure to omit. Of Epistles we have printed only two, both virtually entire. And we have added the visions in which St John's great Revelation of the invisible future culminates.

The Inspiration of the Bible

Broadcast by the BBC on 29 June 1952, first published in Interpretation and Belief. *This piece follows from the first one by moving from a discussion of the actual text of Scripture to the nature of its inspiration. Inspiration does not mean that the Bible is free from human error or bias, but rather that it is not invalidated by such imperfection. Farrer says, 'People will always ask why God gives us his truth in such a mixed form; just as they will always ask why God made the world such a mixed affair.' Although it may not satisfy those who wish for an infallible source of divine revelation, Farrer's answer to this dilemma is given through a moving parable of a soldier who writes a letter to his wife on the eve of a battle. While Farrer was not an existentialist, this view of the nature and inspiration of the Bible strikes an existentialist chord which resonates far more deeply into the life of faith than fundamentalist inerrancy.*

They say the Bible makes good reading, but unless you are concerned for the everlasting salvation of mankind, you will prefer to look for your reading elsewhere. It is a sort of sacrilege to recommend the Bible as culture or amusement. The story of David and Absalom is a better piece of literature than Matthew Arnold's *Sohrab and Rustum*; but that has nothing to do with the reasons for which we read the Books of Samuel. Christ promised many additional blessings to those who put the kingdom of God first, and readers who listen for the commands of a divine King in Scripture will enjoy all sorts of incidental satisfactions. But that is on the side, and if you read the Bible otherwise than as the word of God, you will yawn over most of it.

Christians read the Bible because they want to listen to God.

Sentimentalists and moralizers find God a handsome subject to make speeches about, but true believers would rather hold their tongues and let God speak. Here am I speaking about God at this moment; if, by a miracle, you could change the wavelength and hear God himself, I take it that you would turn me off. And so Christians in all ages have turned from the theologians and philosophers who write about God, to the Bible in which they hope to meet God's Spirit.

You will say to me: Yes, that's what Christians have done; that's what my great-aunt did; I know that without being told. Christians used to be able to do that because they were as simple-minded as children, but now we have grown up, and we can't do it any more. My great-aunt read Isaiah or St Paul, and said, 'These are the words of God.' But I (you will say) read the same texts, and I say 'These are the words of a couple of ancient Jews, giving their ideas about what God wants, warns against, or promises.' Now which of us is right, my great-aunt or I? Did God put St Paul, or Isaiah for that matter, into a trance, and make them do automatic writing under his control; or did these men stay awake and write their books by the use of their own wits, like any one else?

Well, if I am to try and answer the question, I will begin by saying that Christians do not believe, and never have believed, that the Bible writers were out of their ordinary senses when they composed, except where they tell us themselves that they are undergoing visions or ecstasies, and that is not often. But in the second place I shall say that it is a disastrous mistake to suppose that God can only make men his instruments by suspending their normal consciousness and wagging their tongues and hands for them as a showman does for his puppets. If that were so, God would be no better than a puppet-master, and the obedience of faith would be no better than a dance of dolls. By that doctrine you don't make nonsense of Bible inspiration only, you make nonsense of religion altogether. For what does religion amount to, if we cannot even do what the children do, and ask God to make us kind or brave? How do you expect him to make you kind and brave, except by inspiring and heightening and guiding your mind and conduct? When God inspires us, he does not make us any less ourselves, he makes us twice the men we were before. And St Paul does not cease to be St Paul, he is twice the Paul he was, when the Spirit of Jesus possesses his pen.

There is, of course, a great difference between the inspiration God gives us and the inspiration he gave St Paul. I do not merely mean that St Paul's inspiration was stronger than ours, or that he obeyed it more completely, though no doubt both those things are true. I mean that what he was inspired to do was something different. We are inspired to care for good things and to do good actions; we are not inspired to speak to our fellow men the words of God, as St Paul was. We may be inspired to embrace what St Paul revealed: he was inspired to reveal it. We may be inspired to expound what he taught: but he was inspired to teach it. Inspired, not manipulated: he spoke for God and he remained himself.

But if so, surely the practical result for the Bible-reader remains perplexing. For, when God inspires us to do a good action, and, as I was saying, makes us twice the men we were in the doing of it, is there anyone alive clever enough to put our good action through a filter, strain out all the part of it which is merely ours, and isolate the part of it that is purely divine? And, similarly, if God inspires St Paul to speak, how are we to strain out St Paul, so as to be left with the pure word of God? We do not want St Paul's national prejudices or personal limitations, which, good man as he was, he could not wholly escape, no one can, it is like trying to jump off one's own shadow. How then are we to draw the line between the Apostle's oddities and the word of God?

It would save us a lot of trouble if we could find a cut-and-dried answer to that question; but cut-and-dried answers to spiritual questions are always false, and in the special matter of understanding God's word Christ rules such answers out. 'He that hath an ear to hear, let him hear', said he. We cannot hear the voice of God in Christ's words, let alone in St Paul's or Isaiah's, unless we have an ear attuned. After we have done our best to understand the words by the aid of mere honest scholarship, there is still something to be done, and that is the most important thing of all: to use our spiritual ears. If we do not believe that the same God who moved St Paul can move us to understand what he moved St Paul to say, then (once again) it isn't much use our bothering about St Paul's writings. 'God is his own interpreter, and he will make it plain.'

'God is his own interpreter.' Does that mean that each of us is to take any given text to signify just what we happen to feel about it at the moment of reading? Certainly not. God is his own interpreter, but he does not interpret himself only by speaking in the single reader's mind, he interprets himself by speaking in the Church, the whole organized body of Christian minds; we are not alone, we have the mind of Christendom, the Catholic Faith, to guide us. God is his own interpreter in another way, too: he gives us one text by which to interpret another. The God who spoke in St Paul spoke also in St John, he who inspired one page of St John also inspired the next page, and the one will cast light upon the other. And above all lights, most clear and most brilliant, is the light of Christ.

People used to talk about the *verbal* inspiration of Scripture, that is, the inspiration of the actual words. In one sense that is absolutely right, but in another sense it is misleading. Verbal inspiration is a misleading expression, if it means that every word is guaranteed to be free from human error or bias, so that (for example) St Luke's dates, St John's history, and St Paul's astronomy are absolutely beyond criticism. That is not so: St Paul's astronomy is (as astronomy) no good to us at all. St Luke appears to have made one or two slips in dating, and St John was often content with a very broad or general historical effect, and concentrated more on what things meant than just the way they happened. It does not matter. God can and does teach us the things necessary to our salvation in spite of these human imperfections in the texts.

But in another sense *verbal inspiration* is a proper expression; indeed it stands for the very thing we need to think about most. It is not true that every word is guaranteed, but it is true that the inspiration is to be found in the very words and nowhere else. What God inspired St Paul to do was to use the very words he used, just as, when God inspires you to do a good action, the action itself is what God inspires. He doesn't put some sort of vague blue-print for action into the back of your head, and leave you to carry it out according to your own ability. He inspires the action, and if we want to see God's spirit expressed in the lives of his true servants, we don't look for it in any general ideas, policies, or attitudes they may have, but in the particular things they do. Every detail counts; the tone of the voice, the gesture of the hand can make the difference between social hypocrisy and Christian kindness. So too it is in the detail of expression, in the living words of divine Scripture that we hear the voice of the divine Spirit, not in any general (and therefore dead) ideas. We are listening to the voice of

God, not reading a text book of theology; we must attend, therefore, to the homely phrases, the soaring poetry, the figures of speech, the changes of mood; for these are the alphabet of the divine utterance.

I take up the Bible and I read. Here are a million or so printed words, in which divine gold and human clay are mixed, and I have to take the gold and leave the clay. Is there clay everywhere mixed with the gold, does no part of the text speak with a simple and absolute authority? Indeed it does in some part, for some part of it is the voice and recorded action of Christ, and in Christ the divine does not need to be sorted from the human, the two are run into one, for here is God in human nature by personal presence. Christ is the golden heart of Scripture. Indeed, if he were not there, the rest would not concern me. Why do I read St Paul? Because he sets Christ forth. Why do I read the Old Testament? Because it is the spiritual inheritance Christ received, it is what he filled his mind with, it is the soil in which his thought grew, it is the alphabet in which he spelled, it is the body of doctrine which he took over and transformed. So whenever I am reading the Old Testament I am asking, 'What does this mean when it is transformed in Christ?' and whenever I am reading the New Testament I am asking, 'How does this set Christ forth to us?'

There is no part of the Bible which is not inspired, because there is no part that does not either illuminate, or receive light from, the figure of Christ. But obviously not all parts are equally important and some of them are more the concern of theologians than of laity. Begin from the most important parts, read the Gospels and Epistles, read Genesis, Exodus, Deuteronomy, Psalms, and Isaiah, and when you are full of those, spread your net wider.

People will always ask why God gives us his truth in such a mixed form; just as they will always ask why God made the world such a mixed affair. And those who are looking for excuses to live without God will say that, until God speaks more clearly, they cannot be bothered to listen; but people who care about God will listen to him here, because this is where he can be heard and because it's a matter of life and death. What is the Bible like? Like a letter which a soldier wrote to his wife about the disposition of his affairs and the care of his children in case he should chance to be killed. And the next day he was shot, and died, and the letter was torn and stained with his blood. Her friends said to the woman: The letter is of no binding force; it is not a legal will, and it is so injured by the accidents of the writer's death that you cannot even prove what it means. But she said: I know the man, and I am satisfied I can see what he means. And I shall do it because it is what he wanted me to do, and because he died next day.

Images and Inspiration

Published in 1948 as the third chapter of The Glass of Vision, *the Bampton Lectures preached that year in St Mary's, the University Church of Oxford. Very different from the first two texts, which were shorter and for a general audience, this chapter is only part of a larger argument and is far more subtle and sophisticated. If the first essay in this Reader was mostly on the text of the Bible, and if the second was on its inspiration, here Farrer moves to consider not only inspiration but also the nature of divine revelation in Holy Scripture. He attempts to develop an understanding of revelation which is neither the old-fashioned* propositional *theory, nor the then-fashionable view that revelation was only through* events, *not texts. Farrer's famous suggestion is that we should think of revelation in terms of* images; *or, more exactly, the 'interplay' between image and event. Thus, he says that 'the thought of Christ Himself was expressed in certain dominant images' – such as the kingdom of God ('the image of God's enthroned majesty'), the Son of Man ('the dominion of a true Adam'), and Israel ('the human family of God'). Christ taught through such images, and these 'living images' also inhabited and were further developed by the 'apostolic mind'. Thus, Farrer says, 'The great images interpreted the events of Christ's ministry, death and resurrection, and the events interpreted the images; the interplay between the two is revelation.' For example, 'If we want to find the Divine Trinity in the New Testament, we must look for the image of the Divine Trinity.' And he finds that image first of all in the baptism of Christ, with the voice of the Father and the descent of the Spirit upon the figure of the Son. This is an enormously rich and evocative chapter, but again it is only part of Farrer's overall investigation in* The Glass of Vision *into 'the form of divine truth in the human mind'.*

Thou hast known the sacred writings which are able to make thee wise unto salvation. Every scripture is inspired of God.
2 *Timothy* 3.15–16

We have considered the mere idea of supernatural action in the mind, and especially in its knowledge of God. Such knowledge bestows an apprehension of divine mysteries, inaccessible to natural reason, reflection, intuition or wit. Christians suppose such mysteries to be communicated to them through the scriptures. In particular, we believe that in the New Testament we can as it were overhear men doing supernatural thinking of a privileged order, pens in their hands. I wish to make a fresh examination of this phenomenon. For I am not content simply to believe that supernatural thinking takes place, nor simply to accept and contemplate what it reveals, according to my own capacity. I desire to know something more in particular about the form and nature of that supernatural thinking. I may be told that it is sectarian of me to limit my study to the Christian Scriptures. But a man must limit his study to something, and it is as well to talk about what one knows, and what one, in fact, thinks most important. I speak of the Christian Revelation as Revelation *par excellence,* as Revelation simply and without qualification, for such I believe it to be. The degree in which other faiths have something of revelation in them, and the manner in which they are related to Christ's revelation, are matters which I well know to be worthy of discussion, but I beg leave not to discuss them.

No doubt the inspiration of the Scriptures will seem to many people a topic so old and so wearisome that it can be no longer endured. But if so, it will either be because they have no interest in the Scriptures themselves, or because they have not discovered what the Scriptures are good for. Anyone who has felt, even in the least degree, the power of these texts to enliven the soul and to open the gates of heaven must have some curiosity about the manner in which the miracle is worked. And, looking about him, he will quickly realize that interests more vital than those of curiosity are at stake. The prevalent doctrine about scriptural inspiration largely determines the use men make of the Scriptures. When verbal inspiration was held, men nourished their souls on the Scriptures, and knew that they were fed. Liberal enlightenment claims to have opened the scriptural casket, but there appears now to be nothing inside – nothing, anyhow, which ordinary people feel moved to seek through the forbidding discipline of spiritual reading.

In taking up the topic of scriptural inspiration, we should like to attach ourselves to the thought of the ancient Church: but this, we are told, is just what we have not to do. For, it is said, pre-modern thought on the subject was vitiated by a single and cardinal false assumption – the assumption that revelation was given in the form of propositions. The sacred writers were supposed to have been moved by it matters not what process of mind to put down on paper a body of propositions which, as they stand on the paper, are *de facto* inerrant. These propositions, interpreted by the light of one another and apprehended through the Church's supernatural faith, gave an account of the saving mysteries as perfect as the condition of earthly man allowed him to receive.

This being the assumption, the question of inspiration could be opened up in two directions. Either one might ask, what sort of control was exercised by the Divine Spirit over the writer, to get the propositions safely down on to the page. Or one might take up the propositions themselves, and ask in what sense they truly signified supernatural realities – whether literally or spiritually; whether univocally or analogically.

It is now impossible, we are told, to get anywhere from here. We now recognize that the propositions on the scriptural page express the response of human witnesses to divine events, not a miraculous divine dictation. The ancient theory, it might appear, gave a senselessly duplicated account of revelation. The primary revelation, on any showing, was Christ, his life, words, passion, resurrection; and Providence was careful to provide fit witnesses of these events. But now, it appears, the occurrence of the events in the presence of the witnesses is of no practical importance, nor are they allowed to report according to their natural abilities: a few of them are seized by the Spirit, to be made the instruments of a supernatural dictation; and that is what the world will read for ever. It is as though a number of shorthand writers had been solemnly engaged to take down a supposedly extempore oration, and then the orator's secretary were to come round after its delivery and say that as a matter of fact he had got a complete text of the speech in manuscript, and would dictate it to them slowly, so that they could write it in long hand: for his employer had no faith in them, and was convinced from previous experience that they would have jumbled their notes.

Revolting from such absurdities, we say that the revelation was the fulfilment of the divine events in the presence of sufficient witnesses: as for the Scripture, it is just the record of the witnesses', or their successors', reaction to the events. It is what St Luke couldn't help fancying someone's having said he thought he remembered St Peter's having told him: or it is the way St Paul felt about what Christ meant to him. As for the terms in which St Paul expressed it – well, there you are – he used any sort of figure that came to hand: he picked a rhetorical metaphor from a cynic preaching in the market; he turned a commonplace of the synagogue pulpit inside out. He would have been amazed to learn that subsequent generations would make such stuff the foundation of dogmas. We should strip off the fashions of speech; but keep the substance, of course. But what is the substance? It has an uncanny trick of evaporating once its accidents of expression are all removed. Still, let us not acknowledge defeat. At the very least we can safely conclude that Christ had for St Paul a supremely high numinous and ethical value; that he inspired him with new ideals, curing his bad habits, inhibitions and worries. What more does a Christian need to know? Let the modern believer nourish his soul on that. Yes: but to do it, does he really need to read St Paul? He usually thinks not, and it is difficult to refute him.

It does not seem as though the theory of revelation by divine events alone is any more satisfactory than the theory of dictated propositions. At a pinch it will suffice for an account of the historical aspect of Scripture. The events occurred, and we get some sort of usually second-hand report about them with which we must make do. But what did the events mean? It is about this that St Paul and St John have been taken as inspired authorities. The theory we are considering makes them authorities for no more than the way they and their contemporaries were feeling about what God had done. It denies that they were inspired at all, in the technical sense. No doubt they had the Spirit, but then, have not we all? They were inspired as St Francis or St Bernard or John Wesley was inspired. The New Testament is not *uniquely* inspired (though some of its pages may be supreme in this kind). It is, however, uniquely informative, because through it the divine events, and their impact on their age, are made known to us. No other writings can replace it as the channel through which the revealing events come to us.

It does not seem good enough to say that the Scriptures are uniquely informative, but not uniquely inspired, for two reasons. It gives us bare historical events, which by themselves simply are not the Christian revelation, and says they are our only revelation; denying authority to the apostolic interpretation of the events which alone can make them a revelation. And it denies to the text of St Paul and St John the supernaturally revealing character which Christian experience has constantly found in it.

Let us now attempt to construct some account of scriptural inspiration from first principles. This at least in modern thought upon the subject is true: the primary revelation is Jesus Christ himself. When we were talking previously about supernatural knowledge of God, we attempted to define it metaphysically by reference to the primary and secondary causality operative in man's existence. From one point of view, my active existence is exercised by me, its second cause: from another point of view by its first cause, God. My natural mind is identified with the operation of the second cause. In so far as I am made to see things in any degree as from within the operation of the first cause, my mind performs a supernatural act: and this cannot happen by my exertion, but by God's supernaturalizing action. Now the Person of Christ, in the belief of Catholic Christendom, is, as it were by definition, the height of supernaturality: for in it the first and second causes are personally united, the finite and infinite centres in some manner coincide; manhood is so taken into God, that the human life of Jesus is exercised from the centre of deity so far as a human life on earth can be, without ceasing to be a human life on earth: for in him also the general maxim is verified – the supernatural enhances and intensifies, but does not remove nature.

Thus, as a matter of faith, we believe that the revelation of deity to manhood is absolutely fulfilled in Christ himself: in him, man exercises not a supernatural act only, but a supernatural existence, in perfection; he both knows and enacts deity in all his life and thought. To speak so of Christ is to give a deceptively precise description of an unfathomable mystery. We define him, as we define deity itself, by a coincidence of opposites. Deity, for example, is defined as Timeless Life, though with us all life is temporal process and cannot be imagined otherwise, and all that is timeless is lifeless abstraction and cannot be imagined otherwise. In much the same manner we define Christ by the coincidence of supernaturalized manhood and self-bestowing deity, though with us even supernaturalized manhood merely aspires after the infinite transcendence of deity and cannot be imagined otherwise, and even self-bestowing deity is the infinitely distant goal of human aspiration and cannot be imagined otherwise. Christ's Person defeats our intellect, as deity defeats it, and for the same reason, for deity is in it. So the sheer occurrence of Christ's existence is the perfection of revelation to Man, but it is not yet the perfection, or even the beginning of revelation to us, unless we are enabled to apprehend the fathomless mystery which his manhood is.

The first thing to be said of Christ's self-revelation to us is that it is by word and deed, where 'doing' is taken to embrace the action of Christ's will in his *sufferings* also. If we are allowed this gloss, we may be content with St Luke's formula: 'the things that Christ did and taught' are the subject-matter of the gospel.

The actions of Christ's will, the expressions of his mind: these, certainly, are the precious seeds of revelation, but they are not the full-grown plant. Everything that grows must grow from them: but the growth is as necessary as the seed, if there is to be any fruit. It would be abstractly possible to conceive that Christ should have given in his teaching a sufficient exposition of the saving mystery of his being and his act: but even in a context of *a priori* argument we must deign to acknowledge facts. The facts to be considered are two. First, the New Testament itself tells us that the words of Christ in the days of his flesh were not, without comment, sufficient to reveal salvation. Second, our own historical study of the New Testament leads to the conclusion that we cannot separate from apostolic comment a body of Christ's sayings which by themselves surely and sufficiently determine saving truth. So the apostolic church tells us that we cannot do without what the Spirit revealed to the Apostles: and by study of the New Testament we discover that we are lost, without what the Spirit revealed to the Apostles.

Such is the situation. It is often misleadingly expressed in a distinction between 'the fact of Christ' and 'the inspired apostolic comment', as though Christ has said nothing, and the apostles had done nothing. Christ both performed the primary action and gave the primary interpretation: the apostles, supernaturalized by the Spirit of Pentecost, worked out both the saving action and the revealing interpretation of Christ. As his action underlies theirs, so his interpretation underlies theirs. It is not my reading of the biblical evidence that the luxuriant growth of apostolic teaching is impenetrable – that it utterly hides Jesus, the root from which it springs. I will freely confess, for my own part, that unless I thought myself honestly led to recognize in Christ's historical teaching seeds of the doctrine of his divine person and work then I should not believe. I cannot take these things simply from St Peter and St Paul, as their inspired reaction to 'the fact of Christ'. But I can accept St Peter's and St Paul's inspired comment as the absolutely necessary guide to what I may recover of the Lord's own oracles. Again, if I did not, in my own judgment, consider that the Lord's oracles bore out the apostolic comment, I should not believe. But that does not mean that apart from the apostolic record, I could from the bare oracles make out the apostolic doctrine for myself. I could not.

The work of revelation, like the whole work of Christ, is the work of the mystical Christ, who embraces both Head and members. But, as in other aspects of his work, the action of the Head must be central and primary, it must contain in epitome all that the members fulfil and spread abroad. The primacy of the Head in revelation is seen in two things. First, the self-giving of the divine mind to man is fully actualized in the personal existence of Jesus Christ. Secondly, the communication to mankind in general of the human-divine mind of Jesus Christ is begun by Jesus Christ, who by that beginning lays down the lines of all further development. Development is development, and neither addition nor alteration. The first and decisive development is the work of the Apostolic age.

The interpretative work of the Apostles must be understood as participation in the mind of Christ, through the Holy Ghost: they are the members, upon whom inflows the life of the Head. As the ministerial action of Christ is extended in the Apostolic Mission, so the expressed thought of Christ is extended in the Apostolic teaching. Now the thought of Christ Himself was expressed in certain dominant images. He spoke of the Kingdom of God, which is the image of God's enthroned majesty. In some sense, he said, the regal presence and power was planted on earth in his own presence and action: in some other sense its advent was still to be prayed for: in some sense men then alive should remain to witness its coming. Again, he spoke of the Son of Man, thereby proposing the image of the dominion of a true Adam, begotten in the similitude of God, and made God's regent over all the works of his hands. Such a dominion Christ claimed to exercise in some manner there and then: yet in another sense it was to be looked for thereafter, when the Son of Man should come with the clouds of heaven, seated at the right hand of Almightiness. He set forth the image of Israel, the human family of God, somehow mystically contained in the person of Jacob, its patriarch. He was himself Israel, and appointed twelve men to be his typical 'sons'. He applied to himself the prophecies of a redemptive suffering for mankind attributed to Israel by Isaiah and Jewish tradition. He displayed, in the action of the supper, the infinitely complex and fertile image of sacrifice and communion, of expiation and covenant.

These tremendous images, and others like them, are not the whole of Christ's teaching, but they set forth the supernatural mystery which is the heart of the teaching. Without them, the teaching would not be supernatural revelation, but instruction in piety and morals. It is because the spiritual instruction is related to the great images, that it becomes revealed truth. That God's mind towards his creatures is one of paternal love, is a truth almost of natural religion and was already a commonplace of Judaism. That God's paternal love takes action in the gift of the Kingdom through the death of the Son of Man, this is supernatural revelation.

The great images interpreted the events of Christ's ministry, death and resurrection, and the events interpreted the images; the interplay of the two is revelation. Certainly the events without the images would be no revelation at all, and the images without the events would remain shadows on the clouds. The events by themselves are not revelation, for they do not by themselves reveal the divine work which is accomplished in them: the martyrdom of a virtuous Rabbi and his miraculous return are not of themselves the redemption of the world.

The interplay of image and event continues in the existence of the apostles. As the divine action continues to unfold its character in the descent of the Spirit, in the apostolic mission and in the mystical fellowship, so the images given by Christ continue to unfold within the apostolic mind, in such fashion as to reveal the nature of the supernatural existence of the apostolic church. In revealing the Church, they of necessity reveal Christ also, and the saving work he once for all performed. For the supernatural life of the Church can be no more than the exposition in the members of the being of their Head. If they understand their life-in-grace, they understand the grace by which they live, and that grace is Christ's saving work. St Paul, for example, sees that his own life in Christ is a continual death and resurrection: and in understanding so his own living exposition of Christ's redemption, he of necessity understands the redemption of which it is the exposition.

In the apostolic mind, we have said, the God-given images lived, not statically, but with an inexpressible creative force. The several distinct images grew together into fresh unities, opened out in new detail, attracted to themselves and assimilated further image-material: all this within the life of a generation. This is the way inspiration worked. The stuff of inspiration is living images.

It is surely of high importance to know what is to be looked for in Scripture. The Mediaeval Scholastic mind, it would seem, was (in theory, at any rate) on the hunt for theological propositions, out of which a correct system of doctrine could be deduced by logical method. If we set about the quest in that way, we close our ears to the voice of Scripture. The modern tendency is to seek after historical record, whether it be the record of events, or of spiritual states in apostolic minds: it is not surprising if it fails to find either the voice of God, or the substance of supernatural mystery. We have to listen to the Spirit speaking divine things: and the way to appreciate his speech is to quicken our own minds with the life of the inspired images.

I have heard it wisely said that in Scripture there is not a line of theology, and of philosophy not so much as an echo. Theology is the analysis and criticism of the revealed images: but before you can turn critic or analyst, you need a matter of images to practise upon. Theology tests and determines the sense of the images, it does not create it. The images, of themselves, signify and reveal.

Let us take an example of the way in which a matter of divine truth is contained in Scripture under the form of images. It is a famous question whether, and in what sense, the doctrine of the Trinity is in the New Testament. The answers which we get follow from our methods of putting the question. The old scholastic way was to hunt for propositions which declare or imply the doctrine in its philosophical form. It is possible to make out a case along these lines, but then along these lines it is possible to make out a case for most things. Then there is the new scholastic way, the method of the research-degree thesis. We painfully count and classify the texts in St Paul or St John in which the Heavenly Father, the Divine Son and the Holy Ghost are mentioned, either severally or in connexion with one another. We inquire whether the texts about the Second and Third Persons talk of them as personally presenting deity, or not: and what is implied of their relation to the First Person and to one another.

This method, since it starts from statistics and lexicography, exercises the usual fascination of those techniques over our minds: but it is false in its assumptions and inconclusive in its results. It is false in its assumptions, because it supposes that St Paul or St John is, after all, a systematic theologian. A very unsystematic systematic theologian, no doubt, too impulsive and enthusiastic to put his material in proper order or to standardize his terminology. Still, what of that? Anyone who has a decent modern education can do it for him: we, for example, will be rewarded a research degree for doing it. We will draw into the light the system which was coming to birth in the Apostle's mind. But suppose there was no system coming to birth in the Apostle's mind at all – not, that is, on the conceptual level? Suppose that his thought centred round a number of vital images, which lived with the life of images, not of concepts. Then each image will have its own conceptual conventions, proper to the figure it embodies: and a single over-all conceptual analysis will be about as useful for the interpretation of the Apostle's writings as a bulldozer for the cultivation of a miniature landscape-garden. The various images are not, of course, unconnected; in the Apostle's mind, they attract one another and tend to fuse, but they have their own way of doing this, according to their own imagery laws, and not according to the principles of conceptual system.

The method of the research-degree thesis is inconclusive in its results, because it attempts to find the Trinity as a single scheme behind the many images. But here we break down for lack of evidence. It is obvious, before we start, and without the statistics or the lexicography, that St Paul's several imagery statements speak of personal divine action in the Father, the Son, and the Holy Ghost, and further, that St Paul was not a polytheist. But whether he regards the Son and the Spirit as instrumental modes of the Father's action, or as divine Persons in their own right, can be determined only by a subtle and risky construction of inferences. Just because St Paul writes in images, we fall into absurdity at the first inferential step. Have we not been taught that images can be trusted only to express what he who speaks them intends by them, and that if we syllogize from them in the direction of our own questions which are not his, our process is completely invalid: like that of the man who asks what is the meaning of details in a parable having no bearing on what the speaker has used the parable to say. 'Straightway he puts in the sickle, because the harvest is come.' The reaper is the Son of Man, the corn is the faithful: what does the sickle represent? . . .

If we want to find the Divine Trinity in the New Testament, we must look for the image of the Divine Trinity. We must look for it as a particular image, here or there. Most of the time other images will be occupying the page: we must be content if we can find it anywhere. Our next endeavour, after we have found it, must be to isolate it and distinguish it from other images, not to show that other images are really expressed in terms of it, for they are not. The Trinity is one of the images that appear, it is not a category of general application. When we have isolated the image of the Trinity, and studied it in itself, we can then proceed to ask what place it occupies in the world of New Testament images – whether dominant or subordinate, vital or inessential: and how other images are affected by it. After that we can, if we like, go on to ask what metaphysical comment the New Testament image of the Trinity provokes, and which subsequent theological conceptualizations do least violence to it.

But is the image of the Trinity in the New Testament? The image we have to look for is that of a divine Son pre-existing in heaven and bound to his Heavenly Father by the Father's Spirit. Such an image can certainly be found. It is, indeed, a pre-Christian image, except that the Son is neither divine nor really pre-existent, in the pre-Christian form of it. We may start with the eleventh chapter of Isaiah, in which we read of an anointed king, whose anointing is not with oil, but with the Spirit of the Lord, resting sevenfold upon him. Here are the elements of the Trinitarian image. We may take as the next step forward a text which overlays the idea of spiritual anointing with the idea of divine sonship. A famous Jewish writing, known to the principal New Testament authors, is 'the Testaments of the XII Patriarchs'. This book looks forward to a supreme anointed head, of whom it writes: 'For him the heavens will be opened, and there will descend hallowing upon him, with the Father's voice as from Abraham to Isaac.' The author goes on to set forth the hallowing as the Holy Spirit, in words which are a direct allusion to the eleventh chapter of Isaiah. 'The Father's voice as from Abraham to Isaac' is the voice of the Father upraised in blessing upon an only and beloved Son: 'only and beloved son' being the unforgettable and repeated designation of Isaac in the most memorable history about him. We may now advance into the New Testament itself, to see the whole image become fact in the baptism of Jesus Christ. The heavens are now opened indeed, the voice of the Father audibly designates a divine Isaac as his beloved Son, and the spirit of hallowing descends visibly as a dove.

This is what we read in St Mark. The son is now divine, but is his association with the Father through the Father's Spirit yet seen as pre-existent and heavenly? What St Mark describes takes place at the baptism of Christ: it is an earthly and historical event. Yes: though St Mark, I do not doubt, saw the historical event as the temporal manifestation of a state of things older than the world. But this does not become explicit in his Trinitarian image. For explicit development we must look elsewhere.

There is no doubt, anyhow, that the Son of the Johannine writings was Son before the world began. St John sees him in his Apocalypse like a Lamb standing as slaughtered, having seven horns and seven eyes, which are the seven spirits of God; they are the Holy Ghost, manifested as sevenfold vision and sevenfold strength. There is once more a plain allusion in the wording of the vision to Isaiah's oracle on the prince endowed sevenfold with the Spirit of the Lord. But, what is more significant, St John has himself a few lines before described to us the same sevenfold Spirit of God as a cluster of seven flames burning before the Father's throne. The sevenfold light of the Holy Ghost burns before the Father's majesty, it blazes also in the eyes of the mystical Lamb. The Father's sevenfold plenitude of Spirit is bestowed upon the Son: 'he giveth not him the Spirit by measure.' The Father, the sevenfold Spirit before his throne, the Son on whom the whole Spirit is bestowed – this is the divine Trinity of Names wherewith St John blesses, when he blesses in the Name of God: 'Grace to you and peace from the IS, WAS, and COMETH, and from the Seven Spirits that are before his throne, and from Jesus Christ, the Faithful Witness. . . .'

St John simply sets forth the image of the Trinity as representing the mystery of divine love into which we are taken up. It is there before we are taken up into it: it belongs, it would seem, to the nature of things. It is plain that the seer does not intend to talk about the form of his own religious experience, but about a transcendent mystery which is simply there. It is because it is simply there, that it gives form to his experience. St John is content to set forth the image. He does not speculatively determine the relation of the Son to the Father. Later theology was to conclude that there is no real meaning in the absolute priority and essentiality of Christ's sonship, if he is himself a creature. He must be himself of the deity. It must be that by an unfathomable mystery, Godhead itself moves round to face in filial devotion the paternal throne of Godhead, and to receive the indwelling of the Father through his inbreathed Spirit.

But that is to go beyond St John, and beyond any New Testament text. We have in St John simply the *image* of the Father, Son and Spirit, placed by relation to us and our salvation in the transcendent place he assigns it. We can argue if we like that it is no more than an hyperbole for the unique spiritual eminence of the man Jesus Christ: we can argue as we will: in any case the image is there, and it is the image out of which the dogma of the Trinity historically grew. . . .

The theologian may confuse the images, and the metaphysician may speculate about them; but the Bible-reader will immerse himself in the single image on the page before him, and find life-giving power in it, taken as it stands. He reads how we were bondmen until God 'sent forth his Son, born of a woman ... that we might receive the adoption of sons': and how, to confirm our sonship, there was a second mission: 'God sent forth the Spirit of his Son into our hearts, crying Abba, Father.' The Christian who reads this considers the perfection of unique divine sonship, and stirs his heart to gratitude for the amazing gift of a share in it: he awes his mind with the thought that he is possessed by the Spirit of God, and is, in reality and in God's eyes, Christ towards his God and towards his neighbour: he deplores the darkness which commonly veils what now he sees in the clarity of faith, and the sin which falsifies it in act. He throws himself on the love of the Trinity, more patient with him than he is with himself, and silently operative to produce in him even such penitence and vision as now he has. All these motions of the soul take place within the field of the image: they do not pass out of it into the thin upper air of definition and speculation, nor down onto the flat ground of mere penitence and self-management.

Now it will be said, and rightly said, that however vital a place great images hold in the text of the New Testament, they by no means fill it all. Thus, to say that the apostolic mind was divinely inspired by the germination there of the image-seeds which Christ had sown, is not to give a plain and uniform account of the inspiration of the text of Scripture, comparable with the old doctrine of inerrant supernatural dictation. But this, surely, is no blemish. For a doctrine of the unchallengeable inspiration of the whole text is a burden which our backs will no longer bear. What is vital is that we should have such a doctrine of Scripture as causes us to look for the right things in reading Scripture: above all, that we should look for the life-giving inspired word, and make the proper use of it when we have found it. There is a great deal else in Scripture. If we want a single formula to cover the unique value of it all, then it seems we must call it not 'inspired' but 'revealing', in the sense of 'informative about saving facts': for it contains historical matter, and matter which, not itself historical, is of predominantly historical interest to us: for example, St Paul's direct discussion of certain practical problems which have no close analogy in our own world, but cast a vivid light on the primitive community.

Yet, as soon as we have made the distinction between the 'informative' and the 'inspired', we feel inclined to retract it. For the effects of inspiration are widely seen over the historical paragraphs, and anything which suggests the fencing-off of non-inspired areas is to be abhorred. For example, it used to be thought, some twenty years ago, by people who ought to have known better, that St Mark's gospel is informative rather than inspired, that it is a patient and somewhat unhandy compilation of traditions, rather than an inspired interpretation. We know better now. Inspired image and historical memory are so fused in this oldest of our gospels, that it is virtually impossible any more to pull them apart. Or to take St Paul's discussions of practical problems, now obsolete. How long does he ever remain on the simply practical plane? Do not we, as we read, suddenly perceive that the apostle's feet have gone through the floor and his head through the roof, and that he is speaking in the large dimension of inspired vision? Presently, in the authority and the spirit of a great image, he returns to settle the matter in hand.

It might do justice to the facts as we see them, if we described Scripture as 'a body of writings uniquely informative, and a field in which inspiration works'. And that description may stand, even though we must proceed to take a further distinction within the work of inspiration. Where, we may ask, does the act of inspiration take place? Does it take place in the mind of the biblical writer as he composes, or rather at other times, say in prayer and worship, or even in other men, for example, in prophets and possessors of various 'spiritual gifts'? And if so, is the biblical writer to be regarded as retailing inspiration in the images he employs, rather than undergoing it there and then?

We cannot return a simple answer to this question. On the one hand, we cannot think of reviving the old biblicist error, always, perhaps, more common as an unexamined assumption than as a consciously held belief. We cannot say that the primary instrument of the Pentecostal Spirit was the Bible. No, it was the apostolic Church, of which the apostles and prophets were the sensitive organs. If the biblical books had not been taken to express the apostolic mind, they would not have been canonized: and we shall rightly suppose that the dominant images of the New Testament were the common property of the teaching Church. But it would be mistaken to infer that direct and immediate inspiration played a small part in the composition of the books. It may be that the decisive shaping of the images took place elsewhere. But the images are still alive and moving in the writers' minds, not fixed or diagrammatic. They continue to enter into fresh combinations, to elaborate themselves, to beget new applications. The composition of the books may be on the fringe of the great process of inspired thinking, but it is still inspired thinking, much of it as vivid and forcible as anything one could well conceive.

We have to remember that the business of writing about sacred matters was viewed by the Jew with a solemnity which we cannot easily recover. There was for him only one primary body of writings, the sacred scriptures of the Old Testament: any other writing must be regarded as a sort of extension of Scripture, and he who composed it must attempt to draw out the substance of Scripture by spiritual aid. The New Testament writers are given a position of greater independence through the new revealing acts of God, but will not alter at once the spirit in which they approach their task. St Mark's and St John's Gospels, and St John's Apocalypse, are, by their very *genre*, sacred writings, mysteries. It is often said that it would have amazed these writers to learn that their books would be viewed as 'Scripture'. I believe this to be true only in so restricted a sense, that it is, if taken without qualification, a pernicious error. They would have been surprised to see their books treated as *primary* Scripture, and placed on a level with the Old Testament. But that they were writing books of the *nature* of sacred Scripture, they did not doubt: they had no idea of doing anything else. And so it is virtually certain that, if they were men capable of inspired thinking, they did it then, with their pens in their hands.

The case of the Epistles, or anyhow of those Epistles which really were letters written upon particular occasion to a particular address, is not quite the same: but to suggest that they were simply letters of the sort one writes every day, is grossly absurd. They are at the very least instruments of sacred teaching and authoritative apostolic direction. If St Paul invoked the spirit of prophecy when he spoke mighty and burning words in the congregation, so he might when he composed the letter which was to be read out as his voice's substitute. In fact he records the opinion of some, that he was weightier with his pen than with his lips. Nor would he suppose for a moment that the Corinthian or Philippian Church, after reading his inspired admonition, would toss it into the fire. They would keep it by them (as they did) to be an enduring guide. Many students of Scripture might incline to judge that the breath of high inspiration blows more unevenly in St Paul's true Epistles than anywhere else in the New Testament. When it comes upon him, he achieves sublimities nowhere else found: when the mood or the subject is more pedestrian, so is the level of his writing.

The New Testament books may not be at the centre of the process of Pentecostal inspiration, but they are our only direct clue to its nature, and if we neglect the evidence they supply, we shall know nothing about it. It is the constant experience of him who studies the records of the past, that he begins by reading ancient books for the light they cast on the minds of those about whom they write, and then comes to realize that the only mind with which they bring him into immediate and satisfying contact is the mind of their author. We may read the New Testament for what it tells us about prophetic inspiration through the Spirit of Pentecost, in the hope of constructing some account of the phenomenon. But what we learn is little but externals: that the

Spirit appeared to act compulsively, that prophets had difficulty in withholding their utterance until suitable occasion, that they supposed themselves to be the heirs of the Israelite prophets and imitated their behaviour, that it was taken for granted by all that they were really possessed, that tests were applied to prove whether their possession was of God or Beelzebub, that some of their utterances were particular predictions, and others of them rebukes which laid bare the innermost thoughts of their hearers. All this is of interest so far as it goes, but it does not tell us what sort of yeast it was that worked in those exalted minds: indeed, we are tempted to complain that the primitive Christians were too much impressed by the froth. No doubt what they called prophecy was often frothy enough. But the true substance of inspiration was surely everywhere one: the most histrionic of the prophets, if they had any breath of real inspiration in them, were under the pressure of supernatural mysteries speaking through living images. If we want to know anything of the nature of the process, we must see how the minds of the sacred writers are moved as they write, in their passages of high inspiration.

Through the secret act of God by which the Apostles were inspired there came upon us in imaged presentation the shape of the mystery of our redemption. It possessed and moulded their minds, it possesses and moulds ours: we are taken up into the movement of the life above all creatures, of the Son towards the Father in the Holy Ghost. *Now therefore and always be ascribed as is most justly due all might, dominion, majesty and power to the Unity indivisible, the Trinity of sovereign love.*

Messianic Prophecy

Preached in St Mary's Oxford during the Hilary Term of 1951, published in Theology, *Volume 54, 1951, and then reprinted in* Interpretation and Belief. *This sermon deals with the difficult question of finding Christ prefigured in the Hebrew Bible or Old Testament, and thus raises the issue of Jewish/Christian relations. It is a beautifully poetic sermon but ventures into potentially dangerous territory. Farrer clarifies his position at the end when he says that although the 'founder of this sermon particularly desired that his preacher should address himself to refuting the cavillings of Jewish commentators', Farrer himself has done so 'in the only sense in which any person of good will would wish to see it done'. That is, although Christians may legitimately see Christ prefigured in the Old Testament where Jews do not, this is not because Jews wilfully misread their own Scriptures. Rather, Farrer says, 'There is no place for any dispute on points of detail between Jewish scholarship and our own. Whenever Christians and Jews fight for the possession of a single text ... the two parties are arguing at cross-purposes.' Different understandings of the Messiah mean that in fact there is 'no dispute between the Jews and ourselves on the exegetical level'.*

My subject is messianic prophecy, that is to say, the predictions of Christ in the Old Testament. No one speaks from the pulpit for any other purpose but to publish the truth of God; and it is with the aim of knowing God himself that we must speak of messianic prophecy. We have sufficient warrant. We are Christians, and for us to know God is to know Christ. And Christ made himself, his work, and his glory known to men by an appeal to messianic prophecy. The beginning of wisdom is to acknowledge Christ as what he claimed to be, that is, as Christ, the Messiah, the Lord's Anointed. And if the Old Testament had not taught to Israel the expectation of Messiah, the foundation on which Christ built would not have been there.

It is unquestionable, therefore, that the Spirit of God effectively proclaimed the Messiah through the Old Testament. The whole sense of Scripture, working by the power of the Spirit on believing minds, revealed the messianic promise. That is a simple matter of history. And it is important to distinguish this plain historical fact from a whole range of secondary questions which admit of doubt. It is clear that, through the whole sense of Scripture, God taught the Messiah to the Jews. It is not necessarily so clear that this and that scriptural text was messianic to the prophet who originally conceived it or wrote it down. The fact of messianic prediction is proved by Messiah's having been effectively predicted, and not by any dogmatizing about the original sense of 'A virgin shall conceive' or 'Behold my servant whom I uphold'. The original senses of Old Testament texts are the objects of a praiseworthy historical curiosity, but the inspired word of God for us Christians is the instrument through which God taught that Israel among whom Christ came.

I said that our purpose here is to understand God himself, his action and his ways, how he has bestowed himself and spread abroad his grace through messianic prophecy. Now God is his own interpreter: we understand one field of his action best by comparing it with another field of the action of the same God; the two will cast light upon one another, and so upon the God who is displayed in both. And what I shall do here is to draw out the parallel between God's self-revelation in prophecy and his self-revelation in nature. Scripture itself makes the comparison *Caeli enarrant* – 'The heavens declare the Glory of God'; but also in the same psalm, a little below, 'The testimony of the Lord is sure, giving wisdom unto the simple.' And the prophet makes the comparison more directly: 'I am the Lord thy God, that stirreth up the sea, that the waves thereof roar; the Lord of Hosts is his name. Moreover, I have put my words into thy mouth, and covered thee with the shadow of my hand; that I may be he who planteth the heavens and layeth the foundations of the earth, and saith to Zion, Thou art my people.'

The first point I will make about revelation by prophecy and revelation in nature is the inadequacy of anything like argument or proof to set forth the form of either. There was a time when theologians argued confidently from the works of nature to prove that their author was divine, and supposed the proof to be logically cogent. And in the same way, and with the same mind, the same men argued from the miraculously exact predictions of Jesus Christ in the Old Testament, and drew the supposedly inescapable conclusion that he was the Incarnate Word. Both arguments can be broken and refuted by consistent unbelief, and for the same reason. If the whole thought and conception of a divine author and first cause is eradicated from a man's mind, then the very questions to which the creator is given as the answer can be rejected as superfluous or illegitimate. All reasoning from nature towards God is the recognition of God displayed in his handiwork; it is a reasoning from God to God, from God seen in nature to God considered in himself. If God is not seen, or half seen, in the beginning of the argument, he will not be seen at the end of it either. As with the light of the sun. From the manifold reflections and radiations of his light, from the world of colour spread over the whole face of things, a child may learn to appreciate the power of the sun; and apart from these tokens, the sun might seem nothing but a hurtful and stabbing point isolated in the blue expanse. But all this reasoning from the reflections to the original presupposes the sun actually there and diffusing his light. Blot out the sun himself, and there are no reflections by which the knowledge of him can be recovered. And so it is with our mental picture of the world. If the divine idea is utterly blotted from the mind, it is no longer reflected in anything, and all evidence perishes. But, happily, it is not so easy as some persons suppose to exclude every vestige of the divine idea from every level of the human soul.

As the reflections of God in nature point back to and enliven and confirm our idea of the first cause and primal bounty, so the shadows of Christ in prophecy point the Christian back to Christ. But here again the same condition holds: the shadows of Christ in prophecy can only be seen as such if we have the body and substance of Christ in the gospel. Blot Jesus Christ out of the Scripture and the messianic anticipations bear no longer any clear or single sense. There remains nothing but a conflicting pile of hopes and images, some beautiful, some barbarous and strange; pictures of Israelite world empire, of a new David, of a jewelled city floating from the sky; motives of sacrificial piety and of bitter self-vindication. True, we may speak, as we did speak, of God's Spirit drawing this matter together and preaching Messiah to the Jews before Messiah came. But that spiritual preaching needed to be fixed and clarified by the actual coming of Christ. Without the Christ of flesh and blood, the Jewish foresight of him is a flickering and transitory gleam. It is in the light of Christ himself that all messianic prophecy is understood.

I will continue the comparison between Christ foreshown in prophecy and God displayed in nature by taking a further point, namely this: that in both fields revelation moves from multiplicity towards unity. The image of the sun and of its radiations will serve us here once more. The whole power and glory of the sun is in the sun, but gathered and concentrated in such a simplicity of incandescent splendour as to baffle our eyes. We turn from the sun, and range over the variety of his innumerable effects, the universe of warmth and growth and light. We gather and collect our impressions, we carry them back and up into their source, and so we enrich our perception of the power of the sun. And thus it is with our knowledge of God through the works of nature. The dazzling simplicity of his being is extended and shaded and pluralized through the variety of his works, and we gain some conception of his glory by gathering the effects of God's act and drawing them back into his act; into the simplicity of absolute power in which they are all prefigured.

So it is again with the many figures of messianic anticipation and the one Christ. Christ has the intense and blinding simplicity of God. Every circumstance of his life, every word and action, is clear, simple, and meaningful without end. In his death and resurrection all divine truth is summed within a few events. Here is too much light, too much truth, too much reality drawn into a point. But it was never the intention of God that this blinding simplicity should confront the unprepared mind. He had extended and shaded and scattered the truth of Christ in the manifoldness of the messianic images; and those who saw and believed Christ were inspired to draw together into him all this universe of anticipated meaning. What had the promise of a new temple signified? What but the flesh of Jesus Christ, wherein God truly inhabited? Who else but he was the marvellous child, the token of deliverance and bearer of the name *God-with-us*? All the atoning blood that ever ran down under the altar of Solomon, what had it been but a shadow of the death of Christ? And so one could continue endlessly. It is no mere speculation or construction on our part to say that the disciples of Christ understood Christ by seeing his glory scattered in the Old Testament, and by gathering all those scattered lights into his divine splendour. This is no speculation of ours; it is what the men of the New Testament, and Christ himself, manifestly did. The legal and controversial type of mind has misinterpreted the New Testament, just as it has misinterpreted the vision of God in his works. We look upon the works of God to see God, not to prove him; and the primary purpose of the apostles, say of St Paul, when they looked into the Old Testament, was not to demonstrate Christ thence, but to see Christ there. Certainly when they saw Christ in the Scripture it had the force of evidence, for seeing, after all, is believing; and they laboured to show him to others there, that they too might believe. They gathered, or collected, Christ from the Old Testament by the light of the Holy Ghost, and they called upon others to submit to the same illumination. It was not, of course, the manhood of Christ that they collected from the Old Testament. The man stood before them; they took him in with their eyes and ears. It was the supernatural act and being of God in Christ that they sought in the ancient text, where all the images of divine action and divine indwelling were displayed. It is the Godhead that dazzles and blinds, that drives our eyes from the centre towards the circumference, to judge of the centre from there; to judge of him that sits upon the throne from the rainbow that surrounds his majesty.

I shall advance a third point of comparison between knowing God from his works and knowing Christ from the prophetic shadows of him. I will show that what is called the coincidence of opposites occurs in the second no less than in the first. How is it that a certain coincidence of opposites arises in a conception of God collected from his works? It arises through our inability to see how the diversity of the creatures is prefigured in the simplicity of the Godhead. We find several similitudes of God in the world, and we run them all back to their source in God, and we say that God is that very point in which these several lines of glory meet and are united in a single being. Certain things in the world, and certain aspects of the world, suggest to us the ideal of changeless permanence, of exemption from the tyranny of process, sequence, time. Other things, and very different things, present us with the ideas of consciousness and life. Nothing here below, nothing that we can remotely conceive, can combine life and changelessness in a single being. The changeless does not live; the living changes by the very act of living. Nevertheless we define God by the coincidence of these opposites; he is that changelessness which lives, or he is that life which does not change. And this coincidence of opposites in God is not a difficulty about the idea of God; it is the idea of God. It is not something to be cleared up in a philosophical footnote; it is something to be set in the middle of the theological page, and proclaimed as the hallmark of Deity. God is God, God transcends our world and our conceiving; therefore his being holds together in unity what neither our world nor our mind can truly unite.

Ascending, then, from the creatures to God, we fall into a coincidence of opposites. But so we do in advancing from messianic anticipations to Jesus Christ. Christ is seen to be God incarnate and no bare creaturely fulfilment of the prophetic types, by everywhere forcing opposites into an undreamt-of union. To take a famous example. The story of Abraham's sacrifice is wholly based on the distinctness and oppositeness of the two sacrificial victims, Isaac and the ram caught in the thicket. Isaac was a moral sacrifice, not actually offered. The ram was a slaughtered sacrifice, but morally no more than a token. Isaac is human obedience and self-oblation; the ram is divine mercy and providential redemption. Isaac is the only or Beloved Son: the beast is the Lamb of God which takes and bears the sin, the indebtedness, of man, that man may live. The whole meaning of the story, in its Old Testament dress, turns on the distinction between these two figures. The New Testament, again and again, points to the ancient story, but only to show that in Christ the opposites have coincided; the beloved son and the Lamb of God are one. The merciful redemption and the willing self-oblation, human devotion and divine deliverance, death and the exclusion of death – all these are one, when the Son of God is also the Son of Mary, and voluntary death achieves resurrection.

Another example, and one more obviously prophetic, more obviously messianic. Daniel predicted and Enoch elaborated the deliverance of the suffering saints by the advent of the Son of Man. The sufferings were referred to Israel in this age, the glory of the Son of Man to the advent of King Messiah. This was the pathos of the picture: the sufferers looked for a deliverer; and the deliverer came in power divine and irresistible. But Christ, gathering up all things in himself, taught this lesson to St Peter: 'The son of Man must suffer', the sufferings are his as well as the glory, he is both the martyrdom which calls forth the intervening mercy, and also the mercy which intervenes.

The coincidence of opposites in Christ differs for us in a marked way from the coincidence of opposites in the being of God above all worlds. Both are marvellous, but the one marvel is enacted, as it were, before our eyes; the other is invisible. We have not seen the beatific vision, we have not appeared before the face of God nor traced all the rays of glory back to their coexistence in the substance of glory. But the work of Christ is revealed, it is what we have heard, what we have seen with our eyes, says St John, what we have surveyed, and what our hands have handled of the Word of Life. We have made the pilgrimage through the prophecies and arrived at Bethlehem and Calvary; but the pilgrimage through the creatures and through all worlds to the Throne of Glory we have not made; we have not finished it, that is; we are still upon the road. Even so, our thoughts outrun our feet, and aspire after the apprehension of our goal, that living unity who draws all the riches of diversity into himself.

I will take another point of comparison between nature pointing to God, and prophecy pointing to Christ, and I will call it 'signs' or 'indications' of deity. When we survey our natural environment, we encounter two sorts of things which speak to us of God, which I will call respectively signs and evidences. The evidences suggest God by way of reason, the signs by way of mere similarity. The orderliness of nature is *evidence* of the divine government, the existence of spiritual creatures is *evidence* of God's spiritual nature. There is a reasonableness about the appeal of such evidence, however wrong it may be to reduce such reason to the form of a hard demonstration. But the signs of deity do not appeal to reason in the same way at all. For example, the sun appears to us a most striking *sign* of deity, and I have already made several applications of it in this discourse. It is a sign of deity because there is (in our minds anyhow) a vivid similarity between the lordship of the sun in the kingdom of light and the lordship of God in the kingdom of being; and the devout mind is moved to adoration and wonder by a contemplation of the sun. But no theistic *evidence* can be found in the sun particularly; nothing is reasonably concluded about the creator from the fact that among his creatures there exists one large conglomerate of incandescent stuff.

Similarly in the realm of messianic prophecy there are both signs and evidences. The evidences are those texts which represent a serious anticipation of what Christ, when he came, proved to be. Thus the predictions of a Son of David or a Son of Man, or the Isaianic pictures of redemptive suffering conjoined with sanctity – such things as these are evidences of Christ. But there are also to the believing mind most striking signs, which are not evidences, and could scarcely form a part of any argument. How arresting, for example, are those phrases in the psalms which seem exactly to describe the psalmist crucified. 'They pierced my hands and my feet, they look, and stare upon me, they part my garments among them, and upon my vesture do they cast lots.' Such words move and astonish us, but they are plainly no part of a messianic prediction, except in so far as all innocent suffering faithfully borne is predictive of Calvary, and all righteous blood shed on earth, from the blood of Abel to the blood of Zacharias, speaks in the blood of Christ. No special messianic evidence can be collected from them, but they are nevertheless to us Christians a sign. And to regard them as such is not superstition. For all things are under the providence of God; the sacred text did not fall into the form it retains without the hand of God. It is the same with the signs exhibited by nature. If the sun is a sign of the divine bounty, it is not so without God's appointment. He made the sun, and he made our minds; he is the master of our thoughts. It is no accident, from the point of view of his contriving wisdom, that the sun signifies the deity to us; for, to the divine wisdom, nothing is mere coincidence.

But if we are speaking of the scriptural signs, the providential configurations of the sacred text, most striking of all, perhaps, is that which (if we are to believe St Justin) most moved the Jew with whom he disputed: I mean the position of the name of Jesus in the Old Testament. The matter is disguised from us by the use of Joshua in the Old Testament and Jesus in the New. But the names are one. Assimilate them, and what do you find? How is it that these words came to stand in the prophecy of Zechariah? 'The angel said, Be silent, all flesh, before the Lord, for he is waked up out of his holy habitation. And he shewed me Jesus the great Priest standing before the Angel of the Lord, and Satan standing at his right hand to be his adversary.'

Then, in the sequel, Jesus is justified and Satan condemned, and this is the salvation of all Israel. Or again, lower down in the same prophecy, 'Make crowns and set them on the head of Jesus ... and speak unto him, saying, Behold the Man, the Branch his name, and he shall branch up out of his place and build the temple of the Lord ... and he shall bear the glory, and shall sit and rule upon his throne ... and the counsel of peace shall be between them both.' No less wonderful are the significations that hang about the earlier Jesus, the son of Nun, whom we call Joshua, and after whom, presumably, our Saviour was principally named. For how surprising it is that Moses, the patron and the glory of the ancient law, was unable to fulfil his own work, or to bring the people to inherit the promises of God, but was obliged to leave all fulfilment and all victory to a successor, and that successor no other than Jesus. Moreover, this Jesus alone of Old Testament heroes is associated with the cross. For of him alone it is recorded that he crucified the potentates he overthrew. And this prompts St Paul, applying the principle of the *coincidentia oppositorum,* to reflect that the greater Jesus, by himself willingly accepting crucifixion, crucified the hostile powers in his own flesh. The bond that was against us, he says, he abolished, nailing it to the cross; he put off as a garment the principalities and powers, and publicly gibbeted them, triumphing over them on the tree. These surprising significations which follow the name of Jesus are not evidences, but signs only, but they are wonderful none the less, and they are the providences of God.

The founder of this sermon particularly desired that his preacher should address himself to refuting the cavillings of Jewish commentators. And I hope that my argument has done this, in the only sense in which any person of good will would wish to see it done. There is no place for any dispute on points of detail between Jewish scholarship and our own. Whenever Christians and Jews fight for the possession of a single text, we saying 'This points to Jesus Christ' and they denying it, the two parties are always arguing at cross-purposes. For by the phrase 'points to' the contestants do not mean the same thing. For us Messiah is God, for them he will be but a man. For us, therefore, that which 'points to' Messiah points to him as a created thing points to its creator: it points to a fulfilment which is transcendent, superexcellent, and joins opposites in unity. For the Jews there is none of this. What points to Messiah points to him as one creature points to another;

it points to a fulfilment which is literal, and lies in the same plane as itself. There is therefore no dispute between the Jews and ourselves on the exegetical level. They are showing what the prophecies mean in the mere sense in which they were uttered. We are showing how the prophets uttered more than they knew, and how that 'more' was wonderfully revealed and actualized by Jesus Christ. For in him it pleased the Father that all the fullness should dwell, and through him to reconcile all things unto himself, that they might ever so remain, tied in the cords of the Holy Ghost.

How to Read St Matthew

The first chapter of The Triple Victory, *the Archbishop of Canterbury's Lent Book for 1965. The book itself is concerned with the three temptations of Christ, but the first chapter sets the stage biblically, theologically and spiritually. Appearing only three years before his death, this mature work of Farrer's shows the deep integration of his mind. And while its title is 'How to read St Matthew', one could also add 'and St Mark, and St Paul, and Exodus, and Deuteronomy, and the Epistle to the Hebrews, not to mention "how to think theologically"'.*

My unbelieving friends tell me that it comes to the same thing whether God is taken to exist or not. For, say they, you must anyhow admit that his being is quite hidden away; that it lies far behind the surface of any world we can handle or know.

So they say, but faith contradicts them: God has laid bare to us his very heart. We do not, of course, know any other God than the God who acts upon us, and around us. But then there is no other God to know; his action is his being. His very nature is an inexhaustible creativeness. It has produced all this world of things, and us among them. Only, all these things are perishable. This world, or any other world there can be, is at best the secondary production of infinite Action. The product in which Eternal Power takes primary effect must be itself eternal. The heart of God's action is the ceaseless begetting of a life equal to his own; a life, a person worthy of his love, and able to return it. Hence comes the fellowship of Father and Son, tied in the bond of Holy Ghost.

Now this begetting and being begotten, this fellowship of love, is not an outside shown by God to us men, as though there remained some mystery behind, a mystery which is not or which cannot be shown. No; the life of the Trinity is not the portrait of Godhead, or even the face of Godhead; it is the heart.

Do not tell me that the poverty of human language prevents the heart of the divine life from being declared to us. The poverty of our language may indeed prevent us from talking perfectly about this, or any other given subject of our concern. It cannot oblige us to talk about some other subject instead. An imperfect story about God's heart is an imperfect story about his heart; it is not a story about his face.

Human language is, indeed, no better than human; yet no man in his right senses complains because the story he has to tell about anything is a human story, employing human words. What other words but human could a man hope to employ, or what other sort of story could he hope to tell? We do not complain of human speech except where it allows of improvement; and then it is better to set about the improving than to go on with the complaining. If God has taught us to speak of him as well as the resources of our language allow, we have nothing to complain of on that score. Are we to grieve that he has not taught us the tongues of angels? Our story would be a better story, and angels might be edified by our telling it – we should not; we should not know what we were saying. Angelic words would go through human throats like water through a pipe, leaving us unaffected.

We do, of course, complain of words, not for being human words, but just for being words. Only that is when something other and better than words is to be had. Words offer a poor and almost useless explanation of an unfamiliar ball-game or a piece of music never previously heard; we need to see the game played, or the music performed; still better to play or to perform ourselves. It is much the same with friendship. Words have their place; there is a satisfaction in being able to fix with a phrase the special charm or virtue of a friend we like; but the best chosen words would be a poor substitute for the friend. If we did not know him by direct acquaintance, and through the part of our life we share with him, the phrases we coin in his honour would have neither sense nor use.

So with the fellowship of Persons in blessed Trinity. It is life and action, which to be understood must be acted and lived. If God had given us nothing but diagrams of his three-person life, or nothing but general terms describing its quality, or images and comparisons (however apt), in which to view it, we should be little the better for the revelation. Happily that is not how God has dealt with us. He gave his Son to enter our sphere, and to live humanly, yet still in relation to his Father; so that the Society of Persons which is the heart of Godhead might have place among us, and be visible to us.

The story of Jesus is undeniably a drama in which one of the two main characters remains off the stage. The Son speaks to the Father, the Father answers by a voice and makes his presence continually felt. The whole play of the action turns upon him. He does not show his face. But here again, nothing that could be shown us is withheld from us. No man has seen, or can see, God at any time. The Father's countenance is reflected in the Son's eyes, conversing with him; and their mutual converse is the life of Godhead.

What we are saying is that God has given us a better revelation than by words, however apt; for by sending his Son he has brought the fellowship of Persons on our human stage. Well, but do we present-day Christians get anything but words, even so? Peter and John saw Jesus, they even heard him pray. Paul never did, unless it was in one blinding flash of vision; still less do we. We have the story in the Gospel, and what is the Gospel but words? Ah, but there is a wide difference between mere descriptions of divine love, and a human story of that love in action. Speaking of the heavenly love in its heavenly setting, we can do little but decorate it with handsome adjectives. It is pure, intense, mutual, infinite, inspired, no doubt; we may add a dozen other terms of praise, and remain as far as ever from entering into what it is we honour. But when we read the life of Christ, we enter into it. We too are men, we too have our being from a kind Creator. By sympathy and by a well controlled use of imagination we identify ourselves with Christ's act or attitude in the narrative before us.

Nor is that all. We do not simply enter into the recorded history of Christ, as we might enter into the destiny of a tragic hero, set before us on the stage. We make his action ours, or rather (as we think it truer to say) he takes our action into his own. Christ lives in every Christian; the life of the Blessed Trinity is revealed by being tasted, when we are made partners with the Son in his very Sonship to the Father.

What I have just written is, or ought to be, Christian commonplace. Our excuse for recalling such elementary articles of belief is the desire to focus attention on a single point. We have counted the steps in the process of God's self-revelation to us. We wish to concentrate on one of them – the entry of our mind into the action of the Gospel Christ, by the kindling of sympathy and imagination.

In the common case, when we read a human story either historical or fictional, we enter into it by the mere act of reading it. Beyond simple attention to what we read, no effort is required of us; it carries us away. And the Gospel narratives will often cast their spell unaided. No more would be required if all the Christian aimed at were the enjoyment of a story. But he aims at identification with Christ's act or attitude and so (to use the traditional language of religion) he meditates what he reads. He is not content to let the story flow over his mind; he tries to be Christ in the action or the thought which the narrative ascribes to Jesus. He tries to think Christ's thought, to adopt Christ's attitude. He tries, and of course he fails. The thought is still the man's, not Christ's. Even so, our thoughts, thought with good faith and by divine aid in the heart of Jesus, are likely to be better than any other thoughts we can think. They will fall short of truth, but they will point in a true direction.

Any Gospel scene may provide material for this sort of meditation just described. We can put into our own words what we conceive Jesus to be saying to his Father or feeling towards his neighbour – towards the sufferer who lies before him, or towards the enquirer who approaches him. We may be disappointed on a first view to note how little disclosure the Gospels afford of Christ's inward thought or sentiment. Further reflection will relieve our disappointment. We do not need special reports of Christ's inner mind, for Christ hides nothing. He is not sophisticated, not hypocritical like one of us, he is a person of entire straightforwardness. The inside and the outside of his life are all of a piece; his word is his thought, his act is his intention, his manner is his feeling.

Yet when we have acknowledged all this, we shall still attach a special value to those few verses which reveal the life of Jesus from within; and among such verses the account of his temptations hold a unique position. Nowhere else are we shown how Jesus found it difficult to be good – nowhere else, before we come to the garden of Gethsemane and see him face the most obvious of all trials, the acceptance of open failure and agonizing death. And so the temptations merit a quite special study.

St Mark, we have good reason to suppose, was the first to mention them; and he was content to give just that outside description of the event which the general character of Gospel story might lead us to expect. 'And it came to pass in those days that Jesus came from Nazareth in Galilee and was baptized by John in Jordan. Thereupon, coming up out of the water, he saw the sky part asunder and the Spirit descend upon him like a dove; and a voice came out of the sky, *Thou art my beloved Son, in thee I am well-pleased.* Then the Spirit drove him out into the wilderness. He was in the wilderness forty days, tempted by Satan. He was among the wild beasts; and the angels supplied his need.'

If St Mark were our contemporary, we should say that he had given us a crudely objective account of visionary experience, followed by bare statement: inward compulsion, he tells us, accepted as divine, drove Jesus into the desert. What purpose he saw in his journey, we are not told; only that, having gone there, he stayed there five or six weeks, undergoing trials of some kind, we are not told what. He was in a country of wild creatures, not of men. Being cut off from ordinary supplies, he was cared for by divine Providence – in what way, we are not told, either; only that the angels saw to it.

What we have just written about St Mark's story is not altogether fair. We have taken it in isolation. A great deal lies behind it in the writer's mind, and what his mind is can in large measure be seen from a study of his whole book, or from other scriptures. But when all's said and done it remains that he has left us without any inner account whatever of Christ's temptations. The evangelist we call Matthew felt the lack just as we do, and set out to make it good.

I hold it to be utterly pointless to discuss what evidence St Matthew had for the detail he supplies. It goes without saying that if there was direct evidence, Christ alone can have supplied it in the first place, and presumably in the course of conversation with his disciples. I can see no reason why he should not have done so. It has often been said that if he had, his account must have taken a form quite different from anything St Matthew records. But why? Apparently on the supposition that Christ's story would have had to be as literal as a police-report. And that is a very unreasonable supposition. Literal descriptions of inward experiences were not at all in favour with the Jews. Would not Christ have thrown his spiritual struggles into the pattern of a parable? Nothing seems more likely, always supposing that he chose to tell his friends anything whatever about his experiences.

Allowing for the moment that he did, we can go on to ask by what channels the story passed to our evangelist from those who had first heard it. Scholars have confidently believed that they could prove the existence of writings by older disciples now lost to us, on which the writer we call Matthew drew in various parts of his book, and especially in the part we are considering. I judge these scholars to have been wholly mistaken. We know nothing in particular about St Matthew's sources, beyond the fact that he had read St Mark. What we do know is that the Church was much concerned about the authenticity of Christian teaching; and that this Church accepted St Matthew's book widely, rapidly, and without question.

So then, the story of the temptations may for all we know rest on Christ's description of his early experiences; or, to take the opposite extreme, it may be St Matthew's dramatization in a single scene of trials which beset Jesus throughout his ministry – and what those trials were, St Matthew was in a far better position to judge than we are, whoever 'St Matthew' may have been. On either view, and indeed on any reasonable view, the temptation-narrative promises to cast a unique light on the heart and mind of Jesus.

There is only one way to begin estimating the value of the story, and that is by discovering first of all what it means. Here we find ourselves much more happily placed. Look in the direction of St Matthew's sources of information, and every door will slam in your face. Look in the direction of his meaning, or intention, and all the doors fly open before you. Nor is there anything in such a contrast to occasion surprise. For, as a casual reading will show, St Matthew is at no pains whatever to reveal his sources; whereas he does all he can to make his meaning plain. . . .

The first clue, and the most obvious, to take up is the parallel which St Matthew draws between Jesus in the wilderness and Moses in the wilderness. The most careless reader of St Matthew must have noticed his interest in the fulfilment of ancient prophecy, as witnessed by the recurrence of the refrain 'That it might be fulfilled which was spoken by the prophet, saying ...' Scarcely less striking than the recorded fulfilments of Old Testament prophecies are the hinted parallels with Old Testament events. Now to compare A with B involves taking a certain view of A. Those who called Edinburgh 'the Athens of the North' were telling us that Edinburgh clusters round a high citadel, stands just back from the sea, is largely built in classical style, is the capital of a small country where frugality prevails, and boasts a high level of intellectual life. By presenting Jesus in the wilderness as a new, or greater, Moses in the wilderness, St Matthew is suggesting a good deal more than this about Jesus and his wilderness-sojourn; for the comparison of Jesus with Moses is a far more fruitful parallel than that between Edinburgh and Athens.

That St Matthew does hint the parallel can scarcely be disputed: the hints are so broad. His phrase 'forty days *and forty nights,*' when added to his statement that Jesus fasted for the period, carries us straight to the fasts of Moses in the wilderness, as recorded in Deuteronomy 9.9, 18, 25. 'I abode in the Mount forty days and forty nights; I did neither eat bread nor drink water' ... 'I fell down before the Lord as at the first, forty days and forty nights; I did neither eat bread nor drink water, because of your sin that ye sinned, in doing that which was evil in the sight of the Lord, to provoke him to anger.' We shall see presently that St Matthew's parallel between Moses and Jesus extends far more widely than this; but before we pursue it further, let us glance at the significance which Deuteronomy attaches to Moses's fasts.

The text we have just quoted from Deuteronomy 9.18 makes it clear that Moses fasted in support of his intercession for sinful Israel. He fasted from bread, he fasted from water; his heroism was the direct opposite of the two sins the people committed before his first fast in mistrust of God and bitterness of spirit over these two things, bread (Ex. 16) and water (Ex. 17). We read that in pressing the demand for water, Israel committed the additional sin of putting God to the test, saying 'Is the Lord amongst us, or not?' In going without water all the days of his fast, Moses most plainly turned his back on any such temptation. He simply left it to God to sustain him in God's own way.

So in his first forty-day fast Moses stood in for Israel by wrestling with and overthrowing the temptations to which Israel had succumbed, 'lusting for bread' and 'tempting God.' His second forty-day fast, as Deuteronomy tells us in so many words, was undertaken in direct atonement for devil-worship or apostasy from the true God. For, while Moses communed with heaven on the mountain top, the people, losing faith and patience, set up the worship of the Golden

Calf. Therefore it was (says Moses in Deuteronomy 9.18, 25) that he repeated the fast which had accompanied his first receiving of the tables of the Law from God's hand. His intercession was accepted, and Israel continued as God's people.

Moses, then, vanquished in the Spirit the sins to which Israel had fallen in the flesh, lust for bread, tempting of God, and apostasy from God to Satan. These were the first three of the great rebellions of which Israel proved guilty in their forty years' wandering between Egypt and the Promised Land; it is natural to view them as typical of all the rest. So St Matthew might fairly tell himself (as we can see he did) that Moses in his forty days up the mountain vanquished on Israel's behalf the sins which blackened their forty years' privation in the wilderness: for example, their lusting for bread, their tempting of God, and their apostasy from his worship.

The story of Israel's sins and Moses's fasts is told in Exodus according to plain historical order. The subject-matter is gone over again in Deuteronomy, not as systematic history, but by way of illustration to a sermon. Moses is himself the preacher: he is making a last exhortation to his people before his death. It is in Deuteronomy, as we have just said, that Moses's fasting is directly stated to be the atonement of his people's sin; and since this point is of special interest to St Matthew, it is not surprising that he should have started from the text which contains it, in developing his parallel between Moses and Christ. Having picked up his theme from Deuteronomy, he goes on with Deuteronomy. Jesus's three repulses of the tempter are phrased in the very language of Deuteronomic quotations: 'Man shall not live by bread alone, but by every word that issues from the mouth of God' – 'Thou shalt not put the Lord thy God to the test' – 'The Lord thy God shalt thou worship, and him shalt thou serve.'

To a Jewish Christian, like St Matthew, the Bible is as real as the everyday world. Its several parts and features are all in position; and there are familiar paths leading from one to another. St Matthew's subject – the forty days' fast – lands him in Deuteronomy 9, as we have seen. He is no sooner there, than he feels the pull of the one supremely great Deuteronomic text: 'Hear, O Israel: the Lord thy God is ONE Lord; and thou shalt love the Lord thy God with all thy heart ...' The text lies three chapters behind him, in Deuteronomy 6.4. He works his way back to it like a man picking his way across a stream on stepping-stones – from 9.9 (the forty days and forty nights) to 8.3 (Not by bread alone) and so back to 6.16 (Thou shalt not tempt the Lord) from which it is a short step to 6.13 (The Lord ... shalt thou serve) which can be easily combined with 6.4 to yield the joint quotation, 'Him shalt thou serve ALONE' (for he is *One* Lord, and thou shalt love him with *all* thy heart). We see, then, how Satan attacks the New Moses in his fast, and, by successive temptations, forces him back from point to point of the doctrine, until he reaches the supreme principle of the Holy Law, from which all the rest springs: undivided loyalty to God. That brings the episode to an end: Satan can carry the case to no higher court than this; when he comes up against 'the Lord ALONE' he is finished.

I do not doubt that St Matthew saw his way back through Deuteronomy by the steps which are so visible in his story; I do not know, nor can any one know, that he was the first to make that mental journey. The Christian is free to believe that the mind of Jesus had been that way before; 'This' he may have said to his disciples 'is the path along which the Tempter drove me' – making a thoroughly Jewish and scriptural interpretation of his experience. He may or may not have done so – our safest course is to keep firm hold of St Matthew. We can look over his shoulder as he writes, and see how he moves from one idea to another. We cannot claim to be so favourably placed for reading the thought of Jesus, speaking (if he did so speak) to his disciples on an unrecorded occasion.

But we still want not only to know what St Matthew does, we want to understand what he means. Jesus defeats the temptations which defeated Israel under Moses. What sort of temptations were these taken to be? Were they very advanced temptations, or very commonplace temptations? Were they temptations thrown up by very special circumstances, or quite typical of common life? The question we have to ask is not, of course, what things were actually like for Moses and his contemporaries in the second millennium before Christ. The question is, how the story was viewed in St Matthew's time. He tells his readers or hearers that Jesus broke the wilderness temptations. What would the statement convey to them? How had they been taught to view these temptations?

The answer is plain enough. The temptations of the Exodus were treated as typical human temptations; when Christ is shown to undergo them, he is shown to be 'tempted at all points like as we are.' Not that these temptations are typical of human nature outside the scope of God's covenant. Men without religion encounter moral difficulties, but they are not tempted to 'try God out' or to desert God for Satan. How could they be? Such temptations are the temptations of God's people.

In the tenth chapter of his first epistle to Corinth, St Paul wishes to illustrate the principle that spiritual privilege will not save us; we must discipline our lives. All the Israelites who came out of Egypt, he writes, were marked by the tokens of God's favour, yet most of them never saw the Promised Land. They succumbed to the wilderness-temptations, and met with summary justice. St Paul's scripture-sermon rolls ready made from his mouth; we recognize it as the Christian version of a Jewish commonplace. Said the Rabbi to his heathen convert, 'My son, if thou comest to serve the Lord, prepare thy soul for temptation (Ecclus. 2.1). The Lord has passed thee through the water of his baptism, as he passed our fathers through the Red Sea. He hath washed off the Egypt of thy heathendom, he hath set a barrier between thee and the house of thy former bondage. He has made thee to taste the sweet manna of his law, and refreshed thee with waters of life, struck out of the flinty rock; he has spread over thee the cloud and fire of his glory. His fatherly care hath strewn thee that thou art a son indeed, as it is written in the answer of the Lord to Pharaoh, "Israel is my son, my firstborn." And again it is written in the prophet, "I have called my son out of Egypt." But think not that because of these things thou shalt be spared temptation. Fear therefore, and pray that thou fall not as our fathers fell' – and so the Rabbi proceeded with the catalogue of temptations.

St Paul shows himself to be a Christian rabbi by relating the miraculous blessings of the Exodus to Christ and to his sacraments. The Jewish convert was baptized with water, the Christian with water and the Spirit. So, while the Red Sea remains the symbol of baptismal water, let the Glory-Cloud symbolize the Holy Ghost. The Christian descends into the water; the Spirit, like the cloud, descends upon him. (Any one who has walked through mountain-cloud will see the sense of saying that Israel was 'dipped,' or baptized, in the cloud as well as in the sea.) The heavenly manna and the miraculous waterspring will stand for Christ's other sacrament, the bread and the wine of life.

So St Paul writes as follows: 'Our fathers were all under the Cloud, and all passed through the Sea; they all received their Moses-baptism in cloud and in sea. All ate the same divine food and drank the same divine drink – for they drank from a divine rock which everywhere met them, and that rock was Christ. Nevertheless God was displeased with most of them, for they perished in the wilderness. These things were examples to us, not to hanker after evil as did they. And do not be idolaters, like some of them, as it is written "The people sat down to eat and to drink, and rose up to play." Let us not commit fornication, either, as did some of them, and fell in one day three and twenty thousand. Nor let us put the Lord to the test, as some of them did and were killed by the serpents; nor yet murmur as some of them murmured, and were killed by the destroying angel. These things happened to them by way of example, and were recorded for a warning to us, upon whom the last days have come. Let him therefore who thinks that he stands take heed lest he fall.'

St Paul had no difficulty in applying Israel's temptations to his hearers' circumstances. Nothing could be more painfully relevant, as a glance at 1 Corinthians will show. The newly baptized found themselves hankering after the tainted fleshpots of a heathendom which they had renounced. It was hard not to compromise with the idolatrous customs of their gentile neighbours, harder still to maintain the sexual standards of their new faith. St Paul is able to remind them that their situation is absolutely typical; the model was set from the very beginning of Covenant-Religion by the experiences of the Exodus.

It is only in 1 Corinthians 10 that the apostle makes Israel in the wilderness his example of the need to chasten all-too-human desires. His usual appeal is to the *example* of Christ. Christ overcame every natural impulse when he submitted his flesh to the torment of the cross. Though it is not exactly the example of Christ St Paul pleads; it is the grace of Christ. The Christ who crucified his own flesh crucified ours in his. The appeal is, that we should let him have his way with us, and so raise us with himself to newness of life.

Christ and the 'fathers' in the wilderness are to St Paul's mind such different sorts of examples, it would surprise us if he were to bring them into direct connection with one another. We nowhere find him saying in fact that Jesus vanquished those very temptations which had vanquished the 'fathers'. The Cross was the comprehensive victory over the 'flesh' and all its temptations; when you had said that, you had said all there was to say.

The follower of St Paul who wrote the Epistle to the Hebrews took the step which his master had not taken. This writer's arguments from ancient scripture are notoriously complicated: to bring out the train of his thought which interests us, we will give a one-sided sketch of his theme, leaving aside what does not concern us. The passage we shall summarize is 2.18—5.8. Because of what Christ endured under temptation (says this author) he is able to succour those that are tempted. He stood faithful to the God who made him our High Priest – faithful as was Moses, but in a higher capacity. In union with him we are required to hold the beginning of our faith firm until the end; unlike the followers of Moses who (in spite of the glorious beginning they also had made) succumbed to the wilderness-temptations, and forfeited their promised 'rest'. Moses's successor, the Old Testament Jesus (that is, Joshua the Son of Nun) brought the second generation into the land of Canaan; but it was a makeshift business, a poor substitute for the blessed state the people would have inherited, if they had not broken the Covenant. The fullness of the promise (says this author) has now been renewed by a new Jesus, the Son of God. The Son of Nun opened the road into Canaan, the Son of God has opened the way into Heaven. Like the Jewish High Priest on Atonement Day, he has penetrated into the Holy of Holies on his people's behalf. So there is our High Priest – a Priest not untouched with the feeling of our infirmities, but tempted in all things as we are, only without sin. God said to him 'Thou art my Son, this day have I fathered thee.' Yet Son though he was, he learnt obedience through the trials he underwent, and became the author of everlasting salvation to all who obey him.

The author to the Hebrews undoubtedly sees the faithful endurance of Christ as the antidote of guilt incurred in the wilderness (and ever since) by the People of the Covenant. There is no reason, indeed, to suppose that he has in mind anything like St Matthew's story of Christ's own wilderness temptations; the steadfastness he speaks of is the endurance of the Passion, and of the persecutions or privations which led up to it. But in another respect he provides a startling parallel to St Matthew's narrative; and that is in his relating of Christ's temptations to his Sonship. The Father 'said unto him, Thou art my Son, this day have I fathered thee ... Who in the days of his flesh, having offered up prayers and supplications with strong crying and tears unto him that was able to save him from death, and having been heard because of his godly fear, Son though he was, yet learned obedience through the things he suffered' (Heb. 5.5–8). 'Thou art my Son' is quoted from the Psalm which is also echoed by the Father's voice in Jesus's baptism as St Matthew describes it; and the moral of the first two rebuffs to Satan which directly follow in his Gospel is that though he is a Son, Jesus refuses to exert special privileges or exempt himself from suffering. 'If thou art the Son of God, command that these stones be bread ... If thou art the Son of God, cast thyself down, for it is written, he shall give his angels charge of thee ...' No: though he is the Son of God – indeed, because he is the Son of God – Jesus will spare himself neither the pain of hunger nor the pain of faith; he will, by enduring these things, learn obedience to his Father's will.

A study of 1 Corinthians 10 and Hebrews 2—5 side by side is bound to make us aware of the salient fact – St Matthew's story of the Baptism and Temptation is one story, not two. Jesus is presented as the model of Christian initiation. Like the fathers in the wilderness, like the Christian convert from paganism, he was baptized in water and in Spirit, and straightway called upon to face temptation. He was assured of sonship to God, and yet schooled in obedience by the trials he suffered.

St Mark

Published in 1960 in Said or Sung *(American title:* A Faith of Our Own*) – the only collection of Farrer's sermons to be selected and arranged by Farrer himself – and reprinted in* The Essential Sermons. *A sermon delivered in the Chapel of Trinity College Oxford while he was still the Chaplain. Farrer devoted considerable amounts of his academic energy into studying the Gospels, especially Mark and Matthew. This sermon expresses his deep love for the earliest evangelist, and contains the memorable summary: 'Shall we reduce St Mark's Gospel to three lines?*

God gives you everything.
Give everything to God.
You can't.'

In the heavenly state I daresay the satisfaction of earthly curiosity will not seem important. But looking at it from the earthly side, I can feel a lively interest in the hope of some day seeing St Mark and discovering who he is. For I know him, and I do not know him; rather as you might know a telephone voice you never met, a voice who often talked with you but who never talked about himself; the competent secretary of some important person with whom your business often lay. What colour are his eyes? You do not know. Where does he live? You do not know. Is he single, married, a father, childless; what are his hobbies and tastes? No information on any of these points; and yet he has a characteristic way of handling his employer's affairs, which makes him a familiar person to you. You may say you know the way he thinks. It is in some such fashion that the careful students of his gospel may reckon to know St Mark.

We know him, but how little we know about him! He may be the John Mark concerning whom the Acts of the Apostles inform us. But then again he may be some other Mark. He may have written at Rome a few years after St Peter and St Paul died, at a time when Jerusalem was under siege, and Nero had just been murdered, when the world was in confusion and no one knew what would happen next. That would be in AD 68, some forty years after the crucifixion, and as likely a year, perhaps, as any for St Mark to compose the first of all gospels. But no one can prove beyond a doubt that he did not write three years earlier or fifteen years later and, it may be, not at Rome at all.

Happily for us, the certainty of the Christian faith does not depend on the answering of these questions one way or another; and I think it is worth insisting a little on the point. For people are often and mistakenly inclined to reason as follows: Christ is set before us as a historical figure; the documents about his history are the Gospels; the authorship date, character and sources of the Gospels are open to dispute; and so nothing about the historical Christ can be indisputable, or better than a matter of pious belief. Such reasoning is entirely false, for the simple cause that our primary witness to a historical Christ is not any of the Evangelists, but St Paul. And with St Paul the case is quite different: he is himself a historical character of flesh and blood; his great letters are genuine beyond doubt, and can even be accurately dated.

It may help us to appreciate the force of the evidence if we apply the time-scale of the twentieth century to the first century of our era. Here you are in the late '50s, are you not? You are, let us suppose, the congregation at Corinth. The man who taught you your Christian faith, St Paul, is a man of the age of your present College Chaplain though in other respects dissimilar. He is sometimes here, sometimes away touring the Mediterranean, but not for reasons of health. Last term, so to speak, he sent you a letter taking you severely to task for giving his deputy, a man called Stephanas, a terrible time. Some of you were maintaining preposterous opinions; among others, that there is no resurrection; in refutation of which, the Apostle's letter reminds you about the bare facts of the gospel he has always preached. They concern Jesus of Nazareth, a man born with the century, about five years older than St Paul himself, and many years younger (of course) than many hale and hearty persons still living, than our own senior fellows, for example. This Jesus died in the early '30s – as it would be in our century, at the dead middle between the two wars. He was buried, he rose again and conversed with many people, St Paul being the last. His familiar companions are still mostly alive, and well known to St Paul. Paul does not see eye to eye with them about the law of Moses, but about the facts of Christ's wonderful life, death and resurrection there is no disagreement among the Apostles.

It is through St Paul, then, that our faith is rooted in history; and a firm root it is. And so it is not necessary, even if it were honourable, to press the evidence about the authorship, date or sources of the Gospels further than it will go. Here are men, the Evangelists, built like St Paul and like ourselves upon the common faith, the apostolic witness, writing anyhow early in the history of our religion, when there were memories of Christ still to be gathered, and when the Spirit of the same Christ was still most active in the special work of revelation. The Christ of hearsay was interpreted for them by the Christ in the heart. And so under the double control of memory and inspiration, the Gospels were composed. To cold historians they have not the same evidential value as St Paul's words; but to those of us who have already believed the Apostles and become Christians, the Gospels carry conviction; for the Christ we believe in speaks to us as a real person from the gospel pages. To borrow St John's language, the shepherd calls, and the sheep know his voice.

And yet, as I began by saying, alongside the voice of Christ there is the voice of his interpreter, of each evangelist: among whom, to speak for myself, I dearly and specially love St Mark. This is St Mark's day. What then, in the few minutes I still have, can I tell you about the mind of this glorious saint? We must stick to the broadest lines, the principal stages which he brings out in the development of his story.

In the first part of his gospel healings predominate. And if we did not know what was still to come, we might say, What sort of a religion is this? It is a medicine, apparently, for securing health and sanity. But if so, it enters into competition with every other medicine. If science can do more for men than faith and miracle, science is the better medicine, the better psychiatry, and supernatural grace may retire from the field.

But we have no sooner formulated our objection than the scene changes. He who had healed the paralysed foot and restored the withered hand, he who had opened the eyes of the blind begins to say,

'If your hand is your undoing, cut it off and cast it from you. Off with the offending foot, out with the covetous eye; make sure of everlasting life, however the pursuit of it may maim and limit you in this present world.' He who had raised the dead before, now calls for martyrs; 'Take up your cross,' he says, 'and go with me to die.'

Ah, we say, this may be terrible, but this is religion; Christ, like Churchill, is calling for heroes. It is not, after all, 'What can we get out of God?' That was only a beginning, a religion for children. Now it is, 'What can we do for God?' This is the religion of men. Let us turn the page, and read the story of their finest hour. We turn it, and what do we read?

'Amen, I say to thee, before the cock crows twice thou shalt thrice deny me ... He came and found them sleeping ... They all forsook him and fled ... Peter began to curse and to swear, I know not the man ... And' (the very last words of St Mark's authentic text) 'they went out quickly and ran from the tomb, gripped by an ecstasy of terror, and said nothing to any one; for they were afraid.'

Shall we reduce St Mark's Gospel to three lines?

God gives you everything.
Give everything to God.
You can't.

True, there is a fourth line; Christ will make you able, for he has risen from the dead. But this is almost overshadowed in St Mark's Gospel by the emphasis on self-distrust. St Mark seems even more afraid that his readers will trust themselves than that they will distrust Christ's risen power.

Well, perhaps the Mark of the gospel was the John Mark of Acts, after all. And perhaps all this emphasis on desertion, running away, the failure of good intentions has something to do with that most painful text in the Book of Acts: 'Barnabas wished to take John called Mark with them; but Paul thought it not well to take with them him who had turned back from them in Pamphylia, and not gone with them to the work.' If the Evangelist is that Mark who had once turned back, and of whom St Paul had thought the worse for his turning back, then he had evidently learned from his turning back what God wished him to learn from it: that it is not in us to follow Christ, it is Christ's gift.

Happy is the man who learns from his own failures. He certainly won't learn from any one else's. Here I am on a safe ground, for you are all failures, are you not? when it comes to serving God. So there is no fear of my missing my target in any of you, and especially, perhaps, just at the end of a vacation. Vacations tend to be spiritual disappointments. It is humiliating how, when you get back into your families, childish faults of temper reassert themselves which you hoped you had outgrown; humiliating how, as soon as you lose the encouraging company of your Christian friends here, your religion languishes. You have not prayed nor worked nor controlled yourself as you hoped to do. God has given you much; you have not given anything worth mentioning to God. Well, St Mark (if he is indeed the same man) went back from the work in Pamphylia, and in Gethsemane none of the disciples behaved with credit. It is by these desolating experiences that God teaches us to trust him, not ourselves. The more emptied out you are, the more hope there is of your learning to be a Christian. Now is the very moment – there will never be a better – for you to put your trust in the God who makes something from nothing, who raises the dead.

Mary, Scripture and Tradition

Published in 1963 in a collection entitled The Blessed Virgin Mary: Essays by Anglican Writers, *and reprinted in* Interpretation and Belief. *This essay is much more scholarly and academic than the previous selections (even 'Images and Inspiration' from* The Glass of Vision*). Despite its more challenging nature, it was deliberately chosen to bridge the first two sections of the reader – 'Scripture' and 'Tradition' – for despite the common and convenient distinction, one cannot rigidly separate the two. Indeed, the sharp divide between Scripture and tradition characteristic of much Protestant thought is explicitly denied by Roman Catholic theology, and in practice denied by much Anglican theology as well. Here, as an Anglican theologian who sees himself as both Catholic* and *Reformed, Farrer considers what we can say about 'Mary's history and our knowledge of her history'. In particular, he provides an extended discussion of the historical and theological basis for belief in the Virgin Birth. After the first two paragraphs, we have cut out almost half of the paper, which simply summarizes the relevant biblical passages.*

The intention of this essay will be critical rather than purely theological. I do not propose, for the most part, to argue from accepted notions or beliefs, as is done when, presuming a faith in the incarnation of the Son of God, we ask what such a faith implies, as to the part played by a human parent in the coming-about of such a mystery. I propose instead to ask what evidence we have about Mary and how the ecclesiastical interpretations of that evidence can (when and if they can) be justified.

When we think of Mary, or of any saint departed this life, we are thinking of an actual citizen of Paradise. So we may be tempted to speculate about the structure of the heavenly kingdom, and of her place in it. The society of heaven is centred on the Heavenly Man, Jesus, in whom, and as who, the godhead is personally present. Surely his mother's seat must be next to his throne. Perhaps, if the King of Heaven has a mother. By an *a priori* speculation on the heavenly kingdom one would not know that he had; or that if he had, she was more specially related to him than his human father. Her heavenly place must be a deduction from what we know of her earthly place in relation to Jesus. So we come down to Mary's history and our knowledge of her history. Apart from that basis of fact we have nothing to build upon. . . .

We have summarized the evidence. What are we to say of it? The best-attested fact about Mary is that she remained outside the action of Christ's mission; and that she made common cause with his family in trying to bring him back home, if only for rest and refreshment. St Luke's statement that she was in the Church after the resurrection is almost equally well-founded, in view of independent evidence about the early adherence of the family (1 Cor. 15.7; 9.5; Gal. 2.9). In judging the bearing of these facts we have to remember the dependent position of a Jewish woman at that time. Jesus has left home: Mary remains one of the family, and very likely is their housekeeper.

The virginal conception rests on the testimony of St Matthew and St Luke, perhaps of St John. It is obvious from what we have written that a critic uninfluenced by motives of faith is free to conclude that the belief grew out of doctrinal considerations, of which the seeds can be found already in St Paul. The Church, that is, judged Christ to have been virginally conceived because they thought he must have been, not because they had evidence that he was. The late appearance of the story – say eighty years after the alleged event – will be cited as negative evidence; and though, on the orthodox hypothesis, explanations for the lateness of the written testimony can be found, they cannot give the hypothesis itself the support which early evidence could give. The evidence for any active or spiritual participation of Mary in the acceptance of her virginal motherhood lies in St Luke alone. A critic who will go no further, but only so far as to allow a simple genuine tradition of Mary's virginity, variously overlaid by St Matthew and St Luke with typological decoration, will have no *historical* ground whatever for the Catholic valuation of Mary's sanctity.

The most believing of us cannot fail to mark a notable difference between the evidence for the virginal conception of Christ, and the evidence for his resurrection. Whatever attempt we make to find coherent sense in the events following crucifixion and issuing in the emergence of the Church, we shall admit that something strange and powerful happened to the disciples to make them proclaim Christ risen from the dead. Because we share their faith and are touched by their inspiration we accept their account of the fundamental nature of their experiences. But if we did not, we should still give some account of it, though it was no more than to say that they suffered vivid hallucinations; or that they took a man who had recovered his injuries for a man who had conquered his death; or that they mistook one man for another. Whereas in the case of the virginal conception, there will, on the infidel hypothesis, be nothing that requires explanation of any kind. How did Mary come to conceive? St Matthew is at pains to explain to us why St Joseph had not taken her to wife. All the infidel need do is dispense with St Matthew's explanations.

How different, again, in the two cases is the time interval between fact and testimony to fact! St Paul, the preacher of the resurrection, is converted to a Church already proclaiming it within some three years of the event. St Matthew's infancy narrative may be eighty years after the nativity. It is perfectly easy to explain the late appearance of familiarity with the facts of Christ's birth if we first make the hypothesis that the facts were as our evangelists report them. But such an explanation merely removes a difficulty; it does nothing to establish the hypothesis.

Well, but the Church received the Gospels of St Matthew and St Luke with all acceptance; and before any creed was formulated, the virginal conception had the virtual status of a credal belief. The fact on which our faith reposes is not the fact of Christ's history alone, it is the double fact of that history taken together with the existence of the Spirit-filled Church, which proclaimed that history and lived by its fruits. And the Church accepted the virginal conception as a harmonious part of the sacred story; once it had been set forth it could not be thought away; it belonged so absolutely in its place. Inspired authority established the belief; Ignatius and Irenaeus make it a kernel of orthodoxy.

There is much matter for reflection here. What limits shall we set to the Church's function of inspired teaching? She is inspired to proclaim facts, and to interpret facts; but not to create facts: nothing can create a fact but its occurrence. A fact created by a subsequent declaration about it is false by definition. (True facts of a sort can be created by declaration – for example, you declare me your deputy and I am. But this sort of fact-creation has obviously no bearing on the case.)

It is too simple, however, to say that facts are first acknowledged, then interpreted. The whole of philosophical wisdom is opposed to so black-and-white a distinction. Facts, in their objective existence, are just occurrences; and occurrences occur, whatever we think or do not think. But no fact enters into human reckoning without receiving some initial interpretation from us, however immediate, however instinctive. And in cases where occurrence of the fact is open to doubt, our belief or disbelief will be conditioned by our ability or our willingness to interpret. You tell me that, passing a certain field in the dark, you saw an elephant at some distance. I can interpret the presence of the elephant if *I know* that a circus-menagerie is camping there: I may be *willing so* to interpret the elephant's presence by supposing something of the sort out of deference to your accuracy of observation, though I have no such knowledge. If I have no such knowledge and no such willingness, I shall suppose you to have been mistaken. There was no elephant.

Now the Christian mind approaches historical evidence with what it takes to be a certain knowledge, and also with a certain willingness; and both are relevant to the interpretation of that evidence. What we take to be our knowledge is of God's dealings with mankind, whether in ancient Israel or in modern Christendom. This gives us a basis for interpreting events as divine interpositions and for judging in which direction such interpositions point. And faith is a willingness to trust God's (seeming) actions in the Christian dispensation and to take them for what they seem to be. Those who lack the knowledge of religious instruction, or the willingness of faith, will disbelieve the account of a divine interposition suddenly thrown at them without context. So no one can fail to see that interpretation not only values facts once acknowledged; it also contributes to making them acknowledged as facts. All this is mere commonplace; but when we come to theology, or rather, to sacred history, we touch upon a subtler point. The fact of sacred history receives not one interpretation but two interpretations on two different levels. Physically speaking, Mary conceives unaided, as happens often in the females of certain lower species; perhaps we should add that in her case the event is psychologically conditioned; a vision convinces her of her power so to conceive before she does. Theologically speaking, her conception is a special act of God, whereby the divine Son makes a beginning of incarnate existence. The subtle question is how the physical and the theological interpretations of the event are, or ought to be, related. We may state three possible positions.

First, it may be held that no physical fact can be established except through a physical, or at least a natural, interpretation. That is to say, I can only accept the virginal conception of Christ if I have physical, or psychophysical knowledge encouraging me to interpret the literary evidence as historical fact; or at least a willingness to stretch whatever physical analogy there is to cover such a case. On this view theology can only come in afterwards when the physical question has been settled on its merits. Only then is theology free to consider how the physical fact is related to the will and act of God.

Second, it may be held that theological interpretation will suffice alone in the entire absence of physical interpretation. Suppose, that is, that we can offer no natural interpretation whatever of Mary's conceiving; we may be content to be ignorant so long as it seems in the line of God's saving purposes that she should conceive without a male partner. The context, that is, which makes the physical event credible need not be a physical context at all, but the context of God's dealings with his people.

A third position would be that of compromise between the first two. Theological interpretation will not suffice, there must be some degree of natural interpretation. Nevertheless, the two can act together in making the alleged physical fact acceptable. This will mean in practice that the physical interpretation fails to decide us for belief; the theological interpretation turns the scale.

If we look at these three positions, we shall perhaps be likely to agree that they reduce to two; for there is no practical difference between the second and the third. Every physical event must receive *some* degree of natural interpretation, must be fitted into the continuous context of natural happenings, or it simply would not have the value to us of a physical event at all. We shall at least suppose that conception and embryonic growth proceed in the production of the Christ-child as they do in that of other children. Even for the unique beginning of the process St Luke suggests natural analogies. John Baptist's conception suggests that Christ's is something like the case of a child produced by old parents, through a surprising spurt of vitality, when they seemed to have lost the power. Here at least is analogy for conception taking place outside the scope of the usual rules. Again, the attribution of the effect to the action of the Holy Spirit, and its connection with Mary's vision, tacitly invokes the analogy of people acquiring or revealing physical powers they did not appear to possess, under the influence of 'inspiration' – which, on its psychological side, is perceptible as strong religious emotion or conviction. Nevertheless, it is evident that the decisive interpretative context for St Luke, and that which makes the event credible to him, is the context of God's ways with Israel, his continued action in Christ, and his action through the Spirit in the Church.

We are left, then, with two positions to consider. According to the first, no physical event can be accepted as credible except by a stern application of physical or at least natural criteria: theological or supernatural interpretation cannot be applied except to an independently established natural belief. According to the second, we may accept as Christians what as mere naturalists we might reject.

The way to argue for the first position is to show what a floodgate to superstition will be opened if we once depart from it. The way to argue for the second is to point out that an interpretation of Christianity in terms of the first is totally unreal. The whole supernatural story of the gospel never was believed on natural evidence: it was accepted by men who, catching the apostolic preacher's attitude, believed that God had come to them and had shaped natural facts in such fashion as his merciful purpose required. And the way for the upholders of the second position to meet the 'flood-gates' argument is to point out that there is such a thing as Christian common sense, and that it operates in perfectly describable ways. The Christian mind may have a normal defence-mechanism against the supernatural, such as not to give way except under overwhelming pressures.

Without going further into the argument, we may venture to conclude that any Christianity other than the most radical and iconoclastic modernism must be committed to the second position. If, then, it is the function of the Paraclete in the apostolic Church to interpret the facts of the gospel by however theological or supernatural an interpretation, it is on that very account his function to make credible and accepted the gospel facts themselves, even the physical facts. And the extreme case of a fact made credible in this way is the fact of Christ's conception, for not only is the fact physically improbable, the evidence for it lies in testimonies both late and (though capable of harmonization) not *prima facie* harmonious.

Nevertheless, the post-apostolic Church accepted the testimony and put the fact in the Creed – Conceived by Holy Ghost, born of Mary in her virginity. If we say that the Church, or her hierarchy, was *inspired* to acknowledge the virginity of Mary, by using that word we do not excuse ourselves from logical considerations. What the Paraclete inspires is an activity of feeling, thinking, or judging; he sustains it, and sends it divinely right. The inspired process of mind, being itself human, should be either visible or inferable, and its divine rightness should be appreciable, anyhow after the event. What sort of right-judging, then, did the inspired Church do? Surely, in this case, it was not so much that she judged the testimony to rest on sound historical evidences, as that she judged the fact testified to be absolutely fitting, and therefore presumed the soundness of the testimony. That is, the Church accepted on other grounds the resurrection, eternal kingdom, and divine sonship of Jesus; and when told by the first and third evangelists that he came into the world by virginal conception, she said 'Yes, that is how he came into the world; how else?' It was thus that the general credit due to these evangelists' histories was readily extended to cover their infancy narratives. Such men would not write carelessly about so important a point; and there was no reason to think they had done so, for the testimony they bore was worthy of God and of his Christ.

'It was fitting, and so it was the fact.' Put like that, the formula awakens the deepest misgivings. Surely the human mind, assisted or unassisted by the Spirit of God, does not validly infer from theological fittingness to fact of history. What God does is not what we expect: it is paradoxical, surprising to us; only after the event are we inspired to see that it was divinely best. If we trust our inspirations about what God must have done, we shall err with Peter, when he judged that God *could not have* destined his Son to suffer. So long as Peter confined himself to putting a value on what God had visibly done, in Jesus's ministry and mighty works, his inspiration took him right. This was the Christ; flesh and blood had not revealed it to him, but the Father in Heaven. He began to speculate and he was lost.

The objection is just. But in fact the formula is ambiguous. 'It is fitting, and so it was the fact' may be acceptable or unacceptable, according to the sort of thing that 'It' stands for. 'It' may be 'our conjecture' or it may be 'these men's professedly historical account'. If the first, then the formula is unacceptable. If the second, it is acceptable. For it is commonly through someone's testimony that we are informed of those paradoxically right acts of God, which we see to be fitting once we have digested our surprise. (St Matthew insists on the paradox, or scandal, of the virgin birth itself. It involved a domestic disgrace and it meant that the destined Son of David had not a drop of David's blood.)

Thus, though a pure historian might judge the literary testimony for Christ's virginal conception to be weak or indecisive, it is essential that there should be such testimony, and that it should be at least open to us to view it as resting on a real tradition. Christ was first known in his manhood, and preached as risen and ascended; the Gospel-story took form from the known facts, and found its beginning in the prophesying of John Baptist. The Palestinian church (we can suppose if we wish) became presently acquainted also with family traditions about Jesus's wonderful birth, but even then it was some while before the set form of Gospel-story was stretched to include them. Were it, on the other hand, impossible to see by what genuine channels our evangelists could have received their story, were the silence of St Mark and St Paul decisive, then we should be in the greatest difficulty about admitting that the post-apostolic Church was truly inspired to make the virginal conception into a credal belief. As it is, there is a *datum* for the Spirit to interpret; and in confirming the belief he leads us to give a favourable account of the transmission of the tradition to our evangelists.

We have said that revelation is effected by the concordant testimony of Gospel fact and inspired Church; and where, as in the case before us, belief must lean so heavily on the side of the Paraclete, our sense of dependence on the Church must be proportionately greater. I myself, let me hope, enter into the credal faith and appreciate the divine rightness and heavenly meaning of the virginal birth. Yet I would not trust my judgement unaided in such a matter. I should scarcely come to the decision of positive belief but for the massive consent of the primitive Church and of so many subsequent Catholic ages, confirmed by authoritative declarations, themselves in turn confirmed by Catholic consent.

Having defined the position we wish to commend, we may look briefly at tenets which lie to the left and to the right of it. On the one hand we have the man who, however willing to accept the Church's interpretative authority, cannot persuade himself that the historical evidence really amounts to anything at all, and concludes that, as there is nothing there for the Church to interpret, there is no fact for him to believe. On the other hand we have the position of the Roman Church, which, on the face of it at least, appears to claim for authoritative interpretation the power to establish facts which are vouched for by no historical testimony at all.

To take the former case first. We confine ourselves to the man who is in other respects orthodox and whose disbelief in Christ's virginal birth is simply forced on him by what he judges to be the inadmissability of the historical evidence. (His is the interesting case. Who does not know that there are negative heretics in all degrees, maintaining the name of Christian and, indeed, true lovers of Christ?) His orthodoxy, then, will incline him to accept the inspired guidance of the ancient and universal Church in a matter of credal belief. The Church was inspired to think rightly and Christianly about the evidence before her, so far as the common science of the time enabled her to understand it. What inspiration did not do was to equip her with an art of historical criticism and a science of natural fact, which have been the lesson to mankind of more recent centuries. And so, in matter of fact, she erred. What value, then, can be attached to that inspiration which enabled her to theologize correctly over evidence which our orthodox modernist judges to have been unsound?

He will observe how the Fathers reasoned. The conception of Christ by the Virgin was taken as evidence of a double truth. Christ was both divine son and a real member of the human race. Our orthodox modernist agrees; and he accepts the infancy narratives as symbolical stories, or myths, enshrining and protecting these truths for an age which, perhaps, could not have grasped them otherwise. For himself, he is able to believe that the eternally begotten Son of God took flesh of man from two human parents, not from one only.

Shall we say that the man is fundamentally orthodox in intention if he can say *Decuisset, si factum esset*, 'It would have been fitting, had it been the fact', and really heretical if he says *Nec factum est, nec factum decuisset*, 'It neither happened in fact, nor was it fitting it should'? No, we can scarcely distinguish in such terms as these. For it cannot be orthodox to say that it would have been fitting for God to have done otherwise than he did; there cannot have been a better way for him to enter into our condition than that which he chose (whatever it was). Indeed we may be sure that our orthodox modernist will feel that a completely natural fashion of birth most perfectly secures and expresses the entirety of Christ's manhood; a virginal birth would, in the long run, set him too much apart from us. In the short run, however, he may allow that it was otherwise. It would not have been fitting for Christ to have been virginally conceived, but it was fitting that the primitive Church should have projected her understanding of his divine humanity in mythic terms, the only terms, perhaps, in which she could have grasped the fundamental truth of his Person. By contrast it will be fundamentally heretical to say that the Church was misguided to formulate the credal belief, because, *in the terms of that day*, it was theologically misleading, and indeed more so than a denial of the virginal conception would have been.

One cannot but sympathize with the modernist *malgré lui*, whom plain honesty of mind, and historical conscience, cuts off from fullness of communion with the Church's credal faith. He loses the dearest of saints from his calendar. For, apart from the drama of Christ's conception, birth, and childhood, there is nothing to give any features to the mother of Christ.

We will turn now to the opposite case. Romanists appear to us to accept traditions about Mary, supported at certain points by an ecclesiastical authority claimed as infallible, but for which no historical testimony in the ordinary sense can be found. On the face of it, the acceptance of such traditions requires some justification and it may be of interest barely to list several positions that might be taken.

First, it might be said that, in so far as the approved mariological traditions state facts about Mary's historical existence, they must have obtained credence on historical evidence after all. There really was an oral tradition extending in unbroken and unperverted continuity from apostolic times to the Dark Ages, though it was only in the Dark Ages that these matters came to light. The subsequent massive acceptance of the traditions in the Church, confirmed by the seal of papal authority, is sufficient to assure the Catholic believer that the chain of historical testimony, though now perfectly invisible, was sound in every link.

What this amounts to is the extension of the argument from the history of the thing believed to the evidence for the belief. Not only must it have happened, there must also have been a chain of testimony to tell us that it did. The principle of argument is surely vicious; but that is not the worst of it. The allegation about the chain of testimony is liable to collide with historical probability at any point. We may have to admit that the vocal part of Christendom at any given period was not only silent as to the alleged belief but talked as though they believed otherwise.

A second position possible is to admit that there is no distinct testimony to matter-of-fact other than that contained in Scripture itself or in other genuinely historical sources, and to claim that the substance of the tradition you defend is reasonably educible from the known historical evidence. All, in fact, that the Church has been inspired to do is to draw out or interpret the sense. (We say that the *substance* of the traditions is educible from the evidence. Of course we shall have to admit the currency of pious legends embodying truth in tales.)

This line of defence is sound in itself if only it will stretch to cover the case. Its applicability is likely to depend very much on the view you take of biblical inspiration. Was St Luke guided to record inerrantly the very words Gabriel spoke, as it were out of the mouth of God? And was St Jerome guided to give a Latin translation valid in itself? '*Ave, plena gratia!*' It has been divinely said, then, that Mary has fullness of grace; and so the whole theology of grace as worked out from Augustine to Aquinas may be brought to bear, and we may boldly describe Mary's existence from the moment of her conception as one from which no grace was withheld, which God and the Schoolmen know how to give. But if we feel obliged to fall back on St Luke's Greek, we find a charming play on words. Puns cannot be translated: 'Good day to you, since God's so good to you!' gives the general effect. The suggestion is that a newly granted favour from heaven makes her day, or, to stick to the Greek, gives her reason to be glad. What the angel brings is news. So Mary is dumbfounded and wonders what the news is.

But perhaps Gabriel did not speak in Greek either;[1] and perhaps the most we have the right to expect of St Luke is that he should express in good old biblical style and image what St James said Mary had said about an overwhelming experience. Tacitly yielding to such modern considerations as these, the Catholic theologian will no longer rely on possessing a divine utterance which virtually informs him that Mary was conceived immaculate. Her having been so conceived must be made to depend on what is presupposed in her playing the part that she does. But no sooner is this said than the logic of the case is altered. The eduction of implications from (guaranteed) statements is one thing; the inference to antecedents from the occurrence of events, is another. And the possibility of doing it with any confidence is in direct proportion to the commonplaceness of the event. 'Kettles never boil, unless they have been heated.' – 'A man never writes a poem of outstanding merit, unless he has ...' Well, unless he has *what?* And the composition of poetical masterpieces is itself a commonplace event compared with that of experiencing and accepting a call to become virgin mother of the Son of God.

If God has not (implicitly) told us that Mary was conceived immaculate, then it seems that we are involved in the presumption of inferring from one unique divine act another unique divine act. 'It was fitting that the God who did thus should also have done thus, and so no doubt he did.' If such reasoning is vicious, it will not have been divinely supported or inspired; and if Catholics in the mass have thought thus, it reveals a common infirmity of the human mind. The difficulty is not met by pointing out that such events as the immaculate conception and the assumption (anyhow in the most refined and theologized version of that mystery) are by their nature invisible happenings and therefore no parts of the history for which historical testimony is either demanded or forthcoming. For it does not lessen the presumption of inferring what God must have done, that there is not merely no evidence that he did it, but no possibility even that there should be any. It is not a less impertinence to tell a man what he says to himself in solitude than to give him an unevidenced account of what he must have said in the market-place. God's invisible acts are only known if he reveals them in perceptible effects.

1. In Semitic speech he would need a pun: 'Peace, daughter of peace!' would do it.

I incline to judge that the best defence for the believer in the papal dogmas is a counterattack against the absoluteness of the canon we have just laid down. It is presumption to argue 'It was fitting, and so it was the fact' of the ways of God. Nevertheless, no one can think of the continuous action of God through a whole train of events without filling in a few gaps in the evidence. We cannot argue, 'This is the *proper* thing for God to have done, so he did it.' But we cannot help supposing that the path of God's will from one revealed action to another, when the two are in series, was continuous; nor can we withhold ourselves from conceiving the bridge, or transition, between the two. And the Church, we might hold, has been supported and directed by the divine Spirit in thinking such transitions.

The defence may be allowed in general. It might apply to the transition between the death on the cross and the resurrection. 'He descended into hades'; the transition was through the state of being dead, Christ touched the bottom of our condition. The fact was not visible; the Church learned to think it. If the transition from God's dealing with old Israel to the incarnation of the Word could be charted with the same sort of reason as passing through the immaculate conception, I might believe that the Church had been guided to think so. And, presumably, if I were a willing subject of the Pope, I should take it on his authority that such a charting of the divine path was reasonably and Christianly drawn.

However that may be, devotion to Mary does not need such extraordinary justifications. If she is loved, it is because she is; she has her place in the Body of Christ and it is a place no other creature can share. Christ is worshipped for what he uniquely is in each of his sainted members; the relation of Mary to Jesus is an endless subject of fruitful contemplation, and her will is a handle to take hold of the will of God. Her glory is that she is the virgin mother of God; what more can be added to it?

Mary appears in Scripture as a glorified figure only in the vision of the Apocalypse (Rev. 12), and the reference of even this passage to Mary has been disputed – mistakenly, indeed. How could St John write of a new Eve who bears the Messiah to crush the old serpent without even thinking of Mary? Still, the figure is not primarily the figure of Mary nor, indeed, of a *new* Eve. It is the figure of Eve, that is, of woman, attaining the fulfilment of the promise implicit in the curse laid upon her in Eden. In one sense of the promise and the curse, woman (let us say, Eve) has always been bringing forth her children in sorrow, and they have always been at odds with the serpent. But in another sense, her travail is fruitless until she brings forth the man-child who bruises the serpent's head; and this she does in the person of the ecclesia of God, and more narrowly, in the person of Mary. Even this account is simpler than St John's picture; for what he sees is not just the literal birth of the earthly Christ at Bethlehem, but the birth of the heavenly Man who now reigns and will come to judge. The event of the heavenly Man's birth is in fact earthly, for he is threatened by the serpent and needs to be caught up into the throne by his ascension before the failure of the serpent's lying-in-wait becomes evident. Yet since it is the birth of the heavenly Man rather than the incarnation of the Son of God that St John sees, it has all the dignity of a heavenly birth, and the mother becomes a heavenly figure.

What sort of glorification of Mary is involved in this picture? The ecclesia of God is glorified, or celestialized, by association with the heavenly Man she is privileged to bring forth; and this she does in Mary. It is through the person of Mary that she becomes the Mother of Christ. But only in the moment of the birth. When St John goes on to recount the Woman's further history, her flight from the serpent and the persecution of 'the rest of her seed' by the serpent's seed (Antichrist), we have no right to suppose that he is thinking of Mary, or making her the mother of Christians, or the mystical substance of the Church. For the figure of the vision is Eve, not Mary; she does her childbearing at Bethlehem in her Mary-phase, she travails in the sorrow of Christ's disciples (says St John's Gospel, 16.20–2) over his 'birth' from the Easter sepulchre into the light of heaven; she bears her other children, the brethren of Messiah, in her role of Ecclesia.

Mary, then, according to this vision is not seen as the foundation-member, or archetype, or universal matrix of the Church. The relation is exactly opposite: the Church comes first, that is, the people of God under the womanly guise of mother to the children of God. Mary is glorified by being taken up into this function in a unique way; she is the embodiment of the Community in the physical bearing of *the* Child of God, the fruit of all Eve's travail.

Part Two
Tradition

Infallibility and Historical Revelation

Published in 1968, the year of Farrer's death, in a collection entitled Infallibility in the Church: An Anglican–Catholic Dialogue, *and reprinted in* Interpretation and Belief. *A companion essay to the previous one on 'Mary, Scripture, and Tradition', it also bridges Scripture and tradition, although with a broader topic. Here again Farrer engages as an Anglican scholar with Catholic dogma, exploring 'the relation of ecclesiastical infallibility, however conceived, to the historical revelation'. In dealing with the possibility of an infallible Church, Farrer says that it his 'special concern, as a reformed Christian, to emphasize the necessity of a constant overhaul of dogmatic development by the standard of Christian origins; and "Christian origins" can only mean in practice the* evidences we have *for Christian origins; and they come down pretty nearly to the New Testament writings, and the primitive sacramental usages'. This means that doctrinal claims must 'submit to scholarship or historianship; and the scholar or historian is fallible; his work is endlessly corrigible, or subject to revision'. Since 'a fallible historian and an infallible dogmatist make strange bedfellows', Farrer denies true infallibility to the Church just as he earlier denied it to the Bible. As he puts it, 'Our faith is that God is infallible, the Church is not; she is* indefectible.'

The subject I propose to discuss is a relation – the relation of ecclesiastical infallibility, however conceived, to the historical revelation. On the one side of the relation I broaden the theme; on the other side I narrow it. I broaden it on the side of infallibility, for I do not confine it to the papal office or to any organ of the Catholic Church. For the purposes of my discussion you can place infallibility where you like; anywhere, that is, in the living Ecclesia. On the other side I narrow the theme, for there are many matters which might be thought to concern or to require infallible decision; but I propose to consider no other matters beside those which constitute historical revelation. Whatever else an infallible voice may be called upon to define, the content of the revelation historically given through the saving incarnation must by all agreement find a place.

My concern is with the effective hold upon the Church of the once-for-all enacted events which are the foundation of faith. In expressing this concern, I do not wish to assert any particular doctrine of the balance between Scripture and tradition or of the balance between primitive datum and subsequent development. I mean to take common ground – ground common, anyhow, to all confessions which even claim credal orthodoxy; for I take it all agree that the Church is bound by historic title-deeds in some manner. And what I want to discuss is the part that can or should be played by infallible living authority in making the control of the Church's title-deeds upon her faith and her practice effective.

To talk of title-deeds is admittedly to talk metaphor. There are no title-deeds. If we mistake the metaphor for literal fact, we allow ourselves an all-too-tempting simplification of the issues. Title-deeds are legal instruments, and as such carry with them an implicit reference to a legal authority which will determine their interpretation and enforce their provisions. Indeed, apart from their reference to such an authority they would be of no force or validity. They ought to be so written and so phrased that their intention is unambiguous and that all sound lawyers must agree as to their practical bearing. But no document can be so drawn as to provide against every contingency, and some documents are not so well drawn as they should have been. Never mind; though the document admits of contrary interpretations the magistrate is empowered to interpret it. If the necessary law is not in the document, the magistrate makes the law required; in the last resort, the court of law is a law-factory. The decision of a first court may indeed be upset by a court of appeal, but ultimately, law is what ultimate authority determines. And there is no scandal or paradox in that; for though law has regard and should have regard to what is factually true and to what is morally just, law as such is neither ideal justice nor factual truth; it is the standing will of public power, and will is what it wills to be.

There is no need to enlarge at the present time on the harm that has been done by the abuse of juridical analogies in theology; and if I now proceed to draw out the fallacious parallel, it is not with the suggestion that any of my hearers would wish to support it. The parallel is this: the Church has her title-deeds in the New Testament, in primitive tradition, in whatever else you like to name: title-deeds drawn not by man, but by the Spirit of the Living God. Shall we then accuse Almighty Wisdom of folly – of instituting statutes without reference to a visible authority whose decision will make them effectively binding? Heaven forbid! Did not Christ in fact confer upon the apostolic college, under the headship of Peter, the power to bind and to loose?

I said that the legal parallel was fallacious; and so it is, but not wholly so. Christ's language about binding and loosing was drawn from the vocabulary of what we may not too misleadingly call the canon law of the Jews, and his use of such language implies that law and legal decision would have a part in the new Ecclesia. In the sphere of legal discipline it was indeed necessary that there should be an effective authority; and, with the divine assistance, Peter and his colleagues were to make law on earth which would have the sanction of heaven. For their law would be the will of the body through which Christ worked here below; and it would be heaven's will it should be obeyed. Here we have, if you like, a divinely authenticated law-factory; and the claim, if astounding, is still acceptable.

It is when we turn from binding laws to saving facts that the legal comparison becomes so very questionable. A law-factory may be all very well; but a fact-factory is another thing entirely. And the core of dogmatic faith is concerned with facts, with what God did in human flesh almost two millennia ago. Now it is the nature of facts to show themselves to a candid, patient, and relevant investigation. Facts are not determined by authority. Authority can make law to be law; authority cannot make facts to be facts. Facts show themselves by evidence, they are not established by authority.

Note that it is when we begin to talk about authoritative pronouncements upon matters of dogmatic fact that the notion of infallibility really comes in. If Peter and his colleagues make law in applying the Lord's precepts, or in spiritualizing Moses, their law is the law of Christ's Church, the best (if you will) that God's Spirit can make with human instruments there and then, and, as such, to be obeyed as the will of God himself. But to call Peter *infallible* in this connection is to misplace an epithet. Infallibility is a habit in inerrancy, a conformity to some objective standard. If Peter makes good law, it is good, not inerrant, not correct. To make it seem so you would need to import the notion of a perfect conformity of Peter's decision with a foreordaining will of God, conceived as a creative blueprint, or Platonic idea, which Peter faithfully copies. But you will observe that this is precisely the reverse of what Christ promises to Peter. He does not promise him infallible correctness in reproducing on earth the eternal decrees of heaven. He promises him that the decisions he makes below will be sanctioned from above. Doubtless the divine will always anticipates us, just as the divine grace always prevents us* but there is no occasion here to think of any other precedent will than the will of God for what he will do in Peter, Peter being such as he is. If Peter makes as good law as he can make there and then he is doing the will of God.

But whereas there is no need to think of legal decisions as faithfully representing paragraphs in a pre-existent *codex juris divini* laid up in heaven, there is every need to think of pronouncements upon gospel verities as representing (or should I say, expressing) histories pre-enacted upon earth. In this province, there is no good definition which is not correct, nor any perfect definition which is not absolutely so. It is no use having good ideas about Mary's conception or about her assumption if she was not in fact thus conceived nor thus taken up. Peter can loose the rule of circumcision and bind the rule of kosher butchery upon the faithful without being either correct or incorrect; it is enough he should be wise. But wisdom will not suffice for Peter's umpteenth successor to be justified in dogmatizing the immaculate conception; it is necessary that Mary should have been conceived immaculate. And if any living authority is to be infallible in deciding that she was, that authority will need a *charisma* of a very particular kind: either a *charisma* for perfectly appreciating historical evidences, or a *charisma* for miraculously knowing historical fact over the heads of the evidences, or, indeed, in default of any.

Of the alternative views of the *charisma* I have just suggested, we shall in fact be bound to vote for the second or more extreme; the former and more modest simply will not do the job. A perfect wisdom

* Farrer means this in its early sense of 'precedes'.

or enlightenment in judging evidence will merely enable one to judge on the evidence then available and according to the techniques and topics then in force for the interpretation of that evidence. If the evidence changes and the modes of interpretation change, we may hold that a decision which was perfectly correct within scholastic terms of reference is, to the best of our present belief, factually false. For example, it was fair enough to argue that *Ave plena gratia* was a divine assertion that Mary had the plenitude of grace; and you could then go on to work out what that amounted to, with an infallible propriety of judgement. But the angel did not (we now remark) speak in Latin, nor even in Greek. What he is probably meant by St Luke to have said is '*Shalom bath-shalom*,' 'Peace, daughter of peace,' that is, 'Blessing on you who are blessed indeed'; which, since the Greeks said in greeting '*Chaire*,' 'rejoice', not 'Peace' (on you), presented St Luke with a translator's problem, very neatly solved by the pun χαῖρε κεχαριτωμένη as we might say with a similar assonance but a different sense, 'Hail, thou that art hallowed.' If St Jerome had seen his way into St Luke's Semitic background, and wished to preserve the word-play, he might very well have written '*Salve, quam salvam vult deus*,' but he chose to write '*Ave plena gratia*'. Now suppose that an interpreter of infallible wisdom was drawing dogmatic conclusions from that text in an age when it was taken for granted that authorized translations were inspired comments on the sense of the original. It would then be wise, or subjectively justified on his part to draw conclusions about Mary's plenitude of grace. But if in so doing he was to be not only subjectively justified, but objectively correct, in drawing these conclusions he would need to be guided by an inspiration which by-passes the evidence and guarantees by miracle the conformity of his judgement with objective fact about Mary's state in grace. And so no *charisma* of infallibility will serve but one which has this purely miraculous character. The infallible interpreter does not perform a supernaturalized human act, where Grace elevates the working of wisdom. He is enlightened with regard to a fact for which he has no justifying evidence by a direct fulguration of deity.

But I am digressing. Returning into the main stream of my argument I may sum up what I principally wish to say at this point. It is that infallibility looks like being a hybrid notion, arising out of a confusion between the two functions of making law and of interpreting evidence for fact. A true law-maker is neither fallible nor infallible, but simply sovereign. An interpreter of fact is neither sovereign nor infallible, but (at the best) illuminating. On the side of law, statutes or title-deeds are made effective by a sovereign authority applying them; on the side of fact, historical reality achieves its impact upon us by a complete openness, or exposure of our minds to all the evidences, and a complete integrity in the weighing of them. Well, if that is my case, may not I just as well close it at this point? Have not I said my say? Ah, but whatever you may have been thinking of me, I do really know that the matter is not as simple as that. Allowing that infallibility is a hybrid notion, the confusion would never have arisen if the lines were as hard and clear as I have drawn them. I have talked as though the divine events of the saving incarnation were just like any common or garden historical events; and as though their binding control over our present belief were of the same nature as the binding control of any other secular histories on our opinion of them. And that is, of course simply absurd.

So now let me start making the subject if not as difficult as it is, at any rate far more difficult than I have yet allowed it to be. How do the saving facts of the incarnation differ from common facts of history? First, no doubt, by having as it were one foot in time and one foot in eternity, so that the saving acts of Christ are present with us now in a way in which the virtuous acts of Aristides are not. Nevertheless, our redemption has a place in past history and is historically known; we are not free to rewrite the Gospels from the impressions we form of Christ's bearing upon us today. It is what we are constantly tempted to do, but in so far as we yield to the temptation, we escape from the control of history and cease to be subject to an historical revelation. And it is precisely this historical control that I am concerned to discuss.

Second, the saving events are seen as such only if they are accepted as the acts of God, and the acts of God are not appreciated as such by a mere flat historical judgement, as are the acts of Caesar or Napoleon. They are spiritually discerned. The point is sometimes put in the form that saving history consists of facts plus faith; but that way of talking is most dangerously misleading and I would almost say downright apostatical. Saving history consists of fact and fact alone, for God fully and really entered the created sphere and acted under the conditions of created existence; and so his acts, however purely divine, were historically factual. It is not the facts but our apprehension of them that bifurcates; the human in Christ is historically known, the divine is spiritually discerned. The discernment is not something subsequent to the facts, for Christ saw the supernatural character and efficacy of his own action, and indeed acted out of that discernment; the discernment and the action were together from the start. Christ knew what he did humanly and meant what he did divinely; both the knowledge of the action and the discernment of the intention passed into the Apostolic Church. The saving facts were proclaimed as a gospel, that is, not as a mere narrative of human facts but as a declaration of God's redeeming acts, and in so far as they were thus proclaimed, they challenged the hearers to undergo an awakening in themselves of the same discernment as that which informed the proclamation.

Now it is obvious from painful facts of history that the discernment of the divine action in the redeeming facts is not a matter of a simple sensitivity for spiritual things, like the fineness of ear which enables those who have it to hear the cry of bats. We do not either simply appreciate the divine in the facts or else simply fail to appreciate it: we interpret it, and we may do so inadequately or erroneously; and no mere historical expertise or scholarly soundness in settling the human facts will assure a correct reading of the divine meaning. It is had by faith, and faith is the possession of the Church. Jesus Christ was the supreme interpreter of himself; his apostles continued the interpretative work, determining truth of doctrine for their contemporaries with an authority not to be gainsaid; and since Christ by his own promise is with and indeed in the apostolic ministry, must not the Church always possess an infallible organ of interpretation – infallible not, of course, with regard to every trifle, but in determining the limits of tolerable doctrine, and in dogmatizing those things necessary to salvation?

Can we not, then, divide the field amicably between the fallible historian and the infallible dogmatist? The historian establishes his facts; the dogmatic authority regulates the interpretation, and why not infallibly? What rival authority is to challenge him? Very pretty: but it will not do. For to begin with there is the absurdity here so often complained of in Aristotle's conception of science. Science is a rigorous deduction from premisses; but the premisses of the Aristotelian physics are established by the merest guess-work; they are said to be evident, but they are not; so that we have rigorous reasoning from speculative grounds; and however rigorous the reasoning, the conclusions it produces can be no more solid or certain than the grounds from which it proceeds. And so it must also be, if we have an infallible dogmatizing of the interpretation to be placed on the facts established by a fallible history. One who with infallible correctness establishes the theological sense of human facts only probably inferred, cannot give us an infallible guidance concerning the saving acts of God. But this is not the whole of the trouble; there is worse to follow. We were working with a simple division of the field between the historian and the dogmatic authority; the historian was not to concern himself with theological interpretation, nor the dogmatic authority with history. So far we have shown that the dogmatic authority must concern itself with history; for it must build on an historical foundation. We will now proceed to show the reverse – that the historian must concern himself with theological interpretation. This is so because the dogmatic authority is bound not only to interpret historically accredited facts; it is bound also to interpret in some sort of continuity with the interpretation made by Christ and his apostles, the interpretation which formed the faith of the primitive Church. There is no need for me to go into the difficult question as to what constitutes an acceptable continuity of dogma, or when doctrinal developments can be considered legitimate. Whatever views we take on those agonizingly difficult issues, it remains that the dogmatic authority must claim to be in genuine line with the apostles' theology; and such a claim involves a judgement as to what the apostles' theology was. And here once more historical scholarship butts in; for it is an historical question, not merely what humanly happened in Christ, but what the apostles understood to have happened divinely in him. The question, what theological interpretation of events the apostles held, is an historical question, a matter of reading evidence, of interpreting the literal sense of texts. We cannot accept the bare allegation of the living Church that what it propounds was implicitly or seminally contained in the faith of apostolic times; we have got to see whether it appears on historical grounds to have been so contained or not; and historical judgements are fallible.

It is my special concern, as a reformed Christian, to emphasize the necessity of a constant overhaul of dogmatic development by the standard of Christian origins; and 'Christian origins' can only mean in practice the *evidences we have* for Christian origins; and they come down pretty nearly to the New Testament writings, and the primitive sacramental usages. It is clear enough that the contemporary Catholic Church in communion with the Pope is most eager to embrace whatever is sound in the reformation in principle; to prune the somewhat luxuriant growth of Catholic practice and opinion with the pruning-hooks of primitivity. What I have to point out is that to admit primitivity as a judge or as a control is to submit to scholarship or historianship; and the scholar or historian is fallible; his work is endlessly corrigible, or subject to revision. Now a fallible historian and an infallible dogmatist make strange bedfellows, anyhow in the case where the infallible dogmatist accepts from the fallible historian data upon which he infallibly dogmatizes.

I realize, of course, that my main contention in this whole argument wears superficially the face of paradox. For what am I saying? That Christian developments must be anchored to Christian origins, and that the anchor-chains will only be strong if the links composing them are weak – the links of infallible authority would be less effective in binding us to our origins than would the most fallible procedures of historical science. But if there is a paradox here, it is a paradox which the modern world is happy to swallow every day for breakfast, lunch, and dinner. Until some time in the early eighteenth century it was commonly supposed that the truth of nature could not be effectively binding on our minds unless it informed us through infallible reasonings derived from incontestable axioms. We have now most thoroughly repented of any such belief. By admitting the purely provisional and wholly corrigible character of our physical investigations we have learnt how to expose ourselves to the truth. It is a matter of choosing between appropriate procedures admitted fallible and pretended infallible procedures proved inappropriate. It does not help for an instrument to be infallible if it is the wrong instrument for the job. A foot-rule is, within certain terms of reference, a virtually infallible instrument; but that does not make it any more useful for the purpose of measuring intellectual capacity.

Now it must seem to the rest of us that the papal communion is today engaged in making a somewhat delayed catch-up and is moving out of an Aristotelian into – what shall we say – an Einsteinian world. Indeed, the Italians have a word for it. At the same time the strongly traditionalist stance of the Church prevents her from ever unambiguously burying her dead; and so instead of putting a tombstone over infallibility we are to rally round and give its moribund image a shot in the arm, and a suit of new clothes; so that, like Ahab smitten to death at the battle of Ramoth-Gilead, it may be stayed up in its chariot until the going down of the sun, lest the troops of God's Israel should scatter on the mountains as sheep having no shepherd. Whether I should describe the predicament as comic or tragic, I am at a loss to decide; but anyhow it is a predicament that must awaken our liveliest sympathy, or concern. We must see that the Latin theologian is simply not in a position to write infallibility off; he is obliged to save the name even if he virtually drops the thing; he must go through the motions of what used to be called *coloratio* or 'putting a complexion upon', the inconvenient item – as it might be upon some unwelcome sentence of a formidable authority. In the thirteenth century *coloratio* belonged to science; now it has changed its sphere and found a place in politics; and perhaps the Church may still be called infallible, as the Crown is still called sovereign in England, or as dictatorship is called democracy in East Germany. And perhaps if we are to put ecumenism first, then instead of carping at infallibility we ought to join in the game of giving it a false beard and whiskers, while merely making sure that it hasn't got any teeth.

But that is not the note on which I wish to conclude. For while 'infallibility' appears to me a misnomer, the last thing I want to do is to depreciate the Church's authority or to underestimate the gravity of her obligation to give dogmatic guidance. And one of the most manifest advantages to us of a reassembly of our confessions under the papal aegis would be the strengthening of such guidance so far as it affects ourselves. So now I want to make some sort of amends for my polemics and to correct the onesidedness of my previous remarks. . . .

I have not changed my mind, unless it is a change to become firmly settled in a position once held tentatively. The intervening years have served only to disgust me with the inconclusiveness and the irresponsibility of supposedly scientific New Testament scholarship or supposedly neutral historical investigation of Christian origins. Great systems of organized and co-operative folly take the field and establish themselves as the academic orthodoxy of the day. To the detached observer, the theological or philosophical bias animating much of this work is obvious; sometimes the *parti pris* is unconscious, sometimes it is openly professed. There is no such thing as a neutral or purely scientific study of Christian origins, whether we are concerned to establish the history of events or to interpret the primitive theology of them. If I am to see myself as taking a hand in historical scholarship, I should hope to approach the evidence in the faith of the Church, and by the beaten path of Catholic conviction. But the Catholic historian, however Catholic, is as much an historian as any other. He has Catholic expectations, he cannot force facts. Nor can he neglect to use any of the instruments, techniques, or logical models which the art of history or of hermeneutic has developed in his day. My *a priori* expectations may be as Catholic as you like, but they will not allow me to make such deductions from *Ave plena gratia* as a scholastic theologian might make; not will they allow me to postulate a continuous invisible tradition of Mary's assumption running through the primitive Church like water through a lead pipe and leaving no trace on the visible history. A Catholic historian will be as obedient to facts as any historian – indeed, in so far as he is the ideal historian he will be ideally obedient. It still follows, therefore, that Catholic dogmatic thought about the saving facts is corrigible, not incorrigible; for history, including Catholic history, is corrigible; and what is corrigible cannot be called infallible, or only by emptying out the sense of infallible to an absolute vacuity.

I have been discussing the relation of the infallibility idea to the control of the Saving History upon the Church's faith; that is all. It has been no part of my endeavour to do justice to what is most vital in the infallibility idea. But with whatever irrelevance, I should like to say something about it, in a sort of footnote, before I conclude. Infallibility is an expression of the faith that God will effectively guide his Church in the way of truth and of salvation. For how can he be said to do so, unless there is in the Church an ultimate and substantial *charisma* of truth? Through toil and tribulation, and tumult of her war – through an unending tension and debate between schools of thought within the Church – between the Church and her critics, between theological faculties and pastoral authority – it must be our faith that God guides the Church into truth, that the Catholic mind settles ever more and more firmly on essentials; and it is the function of supreme ecclesiastical authority to express the Catholic mind as faithfully as possible from time to time as circumstances may demand or topics become urgent. Where, then, does infallibility reside? I reply, nowhere. Infallibility has the status of what Emmanuel Kant called a regulative, but non-constitutive idea. I apologize for the jargon. He meant an ideally perfect model to inspire our study of an elusive subject matter. For example, we may usefully approach the investigation of physical nature as being the creature of a wise artificer. It will lead us never to despair of finding in nature more and more of the rational order we look for. It will not justify us in spotting the particular intentions of God, nor in forcing the facts to any preconceived pattern of what a God would do with them. So, then, with infallibility. God, we are to say, is an infallible guide and the guidance takes effect in the history of the Church, through God knows what confusions and backslidings and refusals of co-operation. By holding such a faith we are led to look for God's guidance with all seriousness, to respect the decisions of the Church, and to do our own dogmatic thinking in the humble but serious belief that it is an item in the great divine process. But infallibility is not to be spotted, pinned down, identified with an ecclesiastical organ, or demanded on a given occasion. Infallibility is not an oracle you can consult.

When I talk to enlightened Latin theologians I form the impression that their working belief is what I have just attempted to sketch. It is an article of faith that the Church must be ultimately infallible and that God will at need move her to defend essential truth. But they are almost morbidly shy of tying infallibility down. The Pope is the mouthpiece of infallibility but it is terribly unwise to specify either the occasions on which he has infallibly spoken or the degree of precision that is to be given to the verbal form of his utterances *qua* infallible. An unsympathetic empiricist would say that such theologians want both to have their cake and eat it – they want the consoling assurance of infallible guidance and they want their freedom from all concretely incorrigible dogmatizations. I prefer to put it differently, and more sympathetically, since I hope I share the faith which I suppose the idea *de facto* to express. So I prefer to call infallibility a regulative idea, in the Kantian sense. Only, since most of us are not Kantians, I prefer still more to call infallibility by another name, which enables us to bring it right down to earth. Our faith is that God is infallible, the Church is not; she is *indefectible*.

And that, I suppose, is my *irenicon*. I will have infallibility, if it is indefectibility cast into the guise of a Kantian idea. But I shall need to be assured that the utterances which dogmatized the immaculate conception and the corporeal assumption need not be held incorrigible. It is this sort of thing that frightens me so much; in those two decrees we have the alarming appearance of an infallible fact-factory going full blast.

On Praying the Creed

Published in 1958 as the first chapter of Lord I Believe: Suggestions for Turning the Creed into Prayer. *This short book on the Apostles' Creed is one of Farrer's very best, and perfectly expresses his personal union of doctrinal and spiritual theology. So, whereas the previous essay was a critical and historical investigation of Christian doctrine, this is a prayerful one. Here, rather than the criteria of objective facts and evidence established by scholarship, Farrer insists on subjective involvement, commitment and prayer. Here, his rule is: 'No dogma deserves its place unless it is prayable, and no Christian deserves his dogmas who does not pray them.'*

Prayer and dogma are inseparable. They alone can explain each other. Either without the other is meaningless and dead. If he hears a dogma of faith discussed as a cool speculation, about which theories can be held and arguments propounded, the Christian cannot escape disquiet. 'What are these people doing?' he will ask. 'Do not they know what they are discussing? How can they make it an open question what the country is like, which they enter when they pray?'

To put the matter the other way round, suppose that our believing friends express bewilderment over the use and function of prayer. Shall we not ask them what they imagine their belief to be about? They may say it gives them a true description of the world in which they are called upon to act. Certainly; but not, surely, an obvious description, nor a description which, once learnt, continues steadily to illuminate the realities of life. I believe in God the Father Almighty, maker of heaven and earth; and yet I may run this pen over the paper all morning without thought for that infusion of the divine likeness into flesh, which makes intelligence act in my fingers, and my fingers drive the pen. I believe in Jesus Christ, born, suffering, risen; yet I may leave the desk for the table, and find in my fellow diners the objects of my rivalry or the sources of my amusement, but never see the Christ in their hearts, or acknowledge in mine the Christ who goes out to meet them.

Our creed shows us the truth of things, but when shall we attend to the truth it shows? The life of the world is a strong conspiracy not of silence only but of blindness concerning the side of things which faith reveals. We were born into the conspiracy and reared in it, it is our second nature, and the Christianity into which we are baptized makes little headway against it during the most part of our waking hours. But if we go into our room and shut the door, by main force stop the wheel of worldly care from turning in our head, and simply recollect; without either vision or love barely recall the creed, and re-describe a corner of our world in the light of it; then we have done something towards using and possessing a truth which Jesus died to tell, and rose to be.

We have done something, but the truth of Christ is living truth, and will do more. Truth will do much for us unknown to us, clearing our eyes and purging our heart, when we seem to be observing the merest custom of prayer. But often truth will shine and strike us: 'What have I been thinking? What have I been missing? How could I be such a fool, to forget Jesus in my friends, and to see them as so many claimants, rivals, bores, obstacles, instruments? Such a fool (but it was worse than folly) as to turn steadily from the will of God, which alone is my bread and sunlight and breathable air, and fill my hours with self-seeking?' Then we are broken-hearted and then we rejoice, broken-hearted at what we have refused to see, but rejoicing more, because we see it; and we go on in our prayer to express some rudiments of love for our neighbour and our God, and devise some way for giving that love effect.

Prayer is the active use or exercise of faith; and the creed defines the contours of that world on which faith trains her eyes. These statements are, or ought to be, platitudes. No dogma deserves its place unless it is prayable, and no Christian deserves his dogmas who does not pray them. But if so, what are we to say to that high doctrine of the saints, which tells us when we pray to aim at utter simplicity, stilling first our imagination, then thought, and adhering by naked will to a God we forbear to conceive? How strange this sounds! The saints who teach the doctrine are Christian saints, and they tell us, as any Christian must, that our salvation hangs on the revelation Christ achieved, and of which the shape is given us in the creed. They wish us treasure the dogmas which our teachers laboured so hard to bring home to us; they wish us to be no less patient ourselves in handing them on to others. Can it then really be the intention of the saints that we should hold our treasures as a miser holds his wealth, and make no use of them? The sublime doctrines of our faith cannot affect our lives except through prayer, and yet, if we are to take the maxims of the saints at their face value, must not we make it our whole endeavour to forget the doctrines when we pray?

The paradox is not really so sharp as it sounds. The high instruction of the saints is not for beginners. It is addressed to those who have done the necessary work of preparation, and made the creed their own through much reflection on it. An analogy may help those of my readers who have had the experience to which it refers. Those who fall in love may seem to themselves, especially after the event, to have been simply swept away by the beauty they have seen. And it may sometimes be so, indeed most probably so if bodily beauty alone has captured the heart. But if we have loved the person, or the soul, we have loved what cannot be seen, either with the eyes or with any other organ of sense. Our vision of the person is a knowledge of their thoughts and ways, acquired piecemeal from their conduct and brought together into a single view. And this bringing together is something that we do, it does not happen of itself. If we remember carefully we may recall a time of intense mental activity, when we were comparing the actions and opinions, the habits and expressions of our friend, and trying to make them fit. We thought we knew the person more vividly than we had ever known any one, and then found ourselves suddenly baffled; a stranger stood before us, and we began all over again.

There was such a time, but it came to an end at last, and we knew our friend, not as God knows his creature, but as well as one creature hopes to know another. To bring our friend before us we no longer needed to make explorations in the field of memory. We had only to say the name 'John' or 'Mary', or whatever it might be, to find ourselves at a point of mental vision like the convergence of the avenues in an old-fashioned park. As though the very word 'Mary' or 'John' were a statue or a pillar marking the place where all our vistas crossed; we could rest upon it and enjoy our mental paradise in peace. We had no need to explore the avenues to their ends, we could see down them from the place where we were, and recognize what we saw, for we had often been there to look. Even to shift our eyes too curiously from one line of vision to another would have disturbed our intimacy with the spirit of the garden; it was better to let the scene flow in upon us, and not to know what our eyes were at; to dwell with quiet affection on the beloved name and let the fragrance of the person gather round it.

Now to apply the comparison to the thing: there was a time when the lover of God, like the lover of Mary or of John, was putting together his knowledge of God, gathered piecemeal from reflection on the ways and works of God, as they are delineated in the creed and recognized in life. But again, there was a time, not so soon reached but reached at last, when the knowledge of God gathered round the Name of God; and though it remained often profitable to explore one by one his glorious works, and necessary often to wrestle in particular with the interpretation of his ways, yet it was good, and indeed best of all, to be quiet at the place from which sprang all the paths of light and name the Name of God, giving up the soul entirely to that unity of all perfection for which the Name had come to stand.

The saint is happy to be able to do this, and can do it, because he formerly explored and meditated the compass of the creed. There he marked out the widely spread circumference of God's revealing action, from which he has since moved in to find the centre. We, perhaps, are still plotting the circle of our faith, or have not even properly begun. If so, let us not leave off at the call of a false mysticism which mistakes the end for the beginning, moves inward from the tracings of thought and imagination before anything has been either imagined or thought, and dwells in a centre which is as yet the centre of nothing.

Comparisons of human things with divine, the more vivid they are, the more they mislead us; and the analogy we draw between the love of God and the love of our fellow-man fails at a capital point. Although the idea of a person whom we love speaks in a name, and lives in our heart, it speaks with no voice and lives with no life of its own. Like the image in our eyes when we see, the idea in our mind moves and acts by reflection only of the person it mirrors. For the friend whom we love is outside us and cannot, except by a poetic fiction, be said to inhabit our mind, even when our thoughts are full of nothing else. If I speak to the idea in my heart, I speak to a puppet who cannot answer me, except through a trick of ventriloquism on my own part. If the answers are such as the real person would give, that is because I know the person and judge rightly of what I know. It is true that the images of our friends grow and change powerfully in our minds apart from any influence from without; but then it is our minds that grow and alter, and the images of our friends only in so far as they have become incorporated with our minds. We mark our hearts with beloved names as boys mark trees with them; the names grow and change their shape with the growth of the tree.

In so far as we owe the image or idea of God to our Christian upbringing, it is, like the images of our friends, scored on our minds from without, and grows as our minds grow. But God is what our friends are not – he is the ground of our being, and principle of our growth; so that the way in which his idea develops in us becomes his own concern, for our whole growth is his concern. It is possible, then, for him to live and act in our idea of him as no friend can do, and our faith trusts him to do precisely this – to become in us an active, living truth. So, when we speak to him under the form of our idea of him, we do not address a puppet of our own, nor do we ventriloquize the puppet's answers. No; if there are any puppets in the case it is we, with all our ideas, who are the puppets – puppets in the hand of God; and our prayer is this, that God, fashioning our thought and especially our thought of God, would make his handiwork speak with his voice. And this he will do, if he so pleases, not by a conjuror's pretence but out of our own throats. What the ventriloquist feigns the Creator performs. He who has moulded man from clay breathes into his nostrils the Holy Ghost and man becomes a living soul, especially in that part of him which is his thought of God. When I pray, let my heart ask God to speak through my heart, that my prayer, continued by his inspiration, may become the answer to itself.

Though God be in me, yet without the creed to guide me I should know neither how to call upon God, nor on what God to call. God may be the very sap of my growth and substance of my action; but the tree has grown so crooked and is so deformed and cankered in its parts, that I should be at a loss to distinguish the divine power among the misuses of the power given. Were I to worship God as the principle of my life, I should merely worship myself under another name, with all my good and evil. So I take refuge in that image of God which we have described as branded from outside upon the bark. Here is a token I can trust, for he branded it there himself; he branded it on the stock of man when he stretched out his hands and feet and shed his precious blood. The pattern of the brand was traced on me by those who gave the creed to me; God will deepen it and burn it into me, as I submit my thoughts to him in meditation.

I may pray for God to act in me by shaping his idea in me, but he, the living God in me, is not the idea but the power who shapes it. When I speak to God I fix my eyes on my idea of God and do not, in practice, distinguish it from him. Yet I cannot always shut out the truth – no idea of God is God; and there is a gulf, a break, a leap of the mind as, turning from the visible God to the invisible, it rejects the image it contemplates. 'O God' we may say 'I have been tracing your image. It was given and imprinted by you, but you it was not. You are the free omnipotence who make all images and are confined in none of them, nor will I limit you by any. Be yourself in your own way through my heart and in my heart; why should I be concerned to figure how you work or what you are? I throw myself back into the claypit from which you took me, to be fashioned again. I surrender my spirit to the God who gave it; quicken me with such life as it pleases you to breathe.'

What is divine about the mystical saints is what God does with them when they have discreated themselves thus and put themselves back into God. Of that divine action in the saints there are several stages and degrees, which they have employed all their subtlety in trying to describe. They have also left us their accounts of the states and conditions of the soul which lay it most open to God, and the methods and courses of life by which such states are to be approached. Such is the high doctrine of mystical prayer, something far beyond us, and about which nothing will be said in this book. It is enough for us to consider two points which we have already touched, two renunciations which are made in more ordinary prayer,

First, we renounce the detailed consideration of God, all running to and fro of the mind over his nature or his ways, and let our knowledge gather quietly round his Name, content to dwell upon it or to make simple acts of affection towards it. Second, we reject everything that has gathered there, however unobtrusively and tranquilly it is present to us, and appeal from the picture to the Painter, asking to be paint under his brush rather than eyes before his finished portrait.

These two renunciations are not peculiar to the saints, or to souls advanced in prayer, but are profitable to everyone who meditates. The question is, When should they be made? Those who are at work on fundamentals, praying the dogmas of the creed and the mysteries of the gospel, should always hope to make the first renunciation before they rise from their knees, loving in the unity of his Name the God whom they have considered in the variety of his ways. Those who have done some of the preparatory work may often begin, and not end, with this renunciation, putting consideration aside and directly invoking a God who is sufficiently present to them by his Name alone. The truths which gather round the Name swarm unbidden from the caverns of their memories, they are awakened by the words of a book or the voice of a preacher. There is no need to go forth and collect them; the soul may go on quietly to bless the Name of God.

As to the second renunciation, it is often not necessary that we should set ourselves to make it, but only as we may be moved. But when we seem to be hearing our own voice, or are distressed by the artificiality of the thoughts we build or the sentiments we express, then at all events the second renunciation is a blessed refuge, and a means of turning the unprofitableness of our prayer to positive advantage. 'O God, all that I tell you about yourself is empty and false, but what does it matter? You are no set of words, you are the living God. I do not grasp you, but you grasp me and will not let me go. You are here, or rather, you are that place where I am when I say that I am here. I am with you and you are yourself, and for what else should I care? I cannot think of you, but you can think in me, or keep silence in me; above all, you can love in me.'

Renunciations are meaningless when there is nothing to renounce. Before we renounce the use of intellect and imagination we must use them well, we must meditate the creed. And those who have in some fashion mapped the country of their faith will not find that they have taken their bearings once and for all, or that they can, without further looking about, move single-mindedly towards the Centre. They must return often to their starting point and work in afresh from the circumference. For no spiritual truth, however fundamental, is once and for all acquired like gold locked in a safe. We think it is there – 'That certainty is mine for good,' we say. But when we look for it, either it has vanished or it is no longer gold. It has turned as dull and soft as lead, and must be transmuted back to gold by the alchemy of living meditation.

The chapters which follow handle certain essential doctrines not in the actual form of prayer but in the attitude of one who means to pray, and so perhaps my readers will be ready to use the prayers appended to them. Written prayers must, of course, be said and not read, said slowly and with full intention; and if, having said them once, we seem not to have said what is in them, we can say them over again, and as often as they continue to serve us. And one way of making what we have called the 'first renunciation' is to continue saying a very simple formula over and over, until it becomes a mere support for the mind in loving God; as when St Francis (by his own confession) spent the night saying 'Deus meus et omnia,' 'My God and my all.'

Very God and Very Man

A paper first published posthumously in Interpretation and Belief. *Its exact date of composition and the occasion of its original delivery are uncertain, but Charles Conti says that it was written on the reverse side of* The Crown of the Year *manuscript, a book which was published in 1952. We have omitted the first half and so begin in the middle of Farrer's argument. The subject of the essay is the incarnation of Christ. Farrer says that 'To talk about "divine nature" and "human nature" as though God's nature were one of the ways of being alongside the human way is sheer paganism,' and he instead proposes the formula of Christ's incarnation as 'Infinite God living the existence of one of his creatures, through self-limitation to a particular created destiny.' Much of the essay is an extended whimsical dialogue between a 'phenomenally stupid' missionary priest trying to explain the incarnation to a 'phenomenally intelligent' African boy. This conversation leads up to introducing the British philosopher Gilbert Ryle's distinction between 'knowing how' and 'knowing that', which Farrer finds useful in thinking about Christ's self-consciousness. According to Farrer, Jesus knew* how *to be the Son of God, even if he could not fully know in his earthly life* that *he was the Son of God.*

. . . God's creative will takes effect in every creature's becoming of its own sort; every creature is, so to speak, handed a limited charter of privileges and a limited set of rules to which it has to work: that's what makes it the creature it is, and in being that creature it can be no other. But God himself, the creator, is not subject to any such limitation or particularity of sphere or of kind: he is the sheer creative energy from which all such limitations proceed. To talk about 'divine nature' and 'human nature' as though God's nature were one of the ways of being alongside the human way is sheer paganism.

Thus 'very God and very man' is not the botching together of two ways of being, the divine way and the human way. No: it says something more like this. The infinite energy who creates the human Jesus fortifies and redoubles his creative act in living, or being, that man by personal identification. And God, infinite God, no more ceases to be God by thus being Jesus than he ceases to be God by making Jesus. But neither, on its side, is the humanity of Jesus forced, altered, or overborne. For God's incarnation consists precisely in being the man Jesus and not in being anything else. God, becoming incarnate, does not first become a non-human angelic form and then go and force that form on Jesus. Jesus is the form his incarnation takes, and Jesus is a man.

What, then, is the formula? 'Infinite God living the existence of one of his creatures, through self-limitation to a particular created destiny'? There, perhaps, is an acceptable set of words, but does it mean anything?

Suppose I had never heard of Jesus Christ; suppose, for example, I were a little African boy being instructed by a missionary who was so stupid as to begin with the abstract doctrine of incarnation and only afterwards go on to historical fact. Suppose, then, that the missionary says to me, 'Infinite God living the existence of one of his creatures, through self-limitation to a particular created destiny. Now, my boy, what sort of a person would you expect this incarnation of Godhead to be?' We will suppose that the boy is as phenomenally intelligent as the missionary is phenomenally stupid, and furthermore that he has been fortified with all sorts of philosophical techniques and cautions – in fact, he is a surprisingly mature, sophisticated and learned child, except in the one particular of Jewish history on which his mind is a perfect blank. What, then, will the boy reply? 'Father,' he says, 'I do not think it will be a baboon or a crocodile, I think it will be a man. It will be a good man, a wise man; a man full of the power of Spirit. But not like you, Father. You are full of the power of the Spirit: you get him by going into the prayer hut and asking. He will not do that. Who would he pray to? He is God. He will not pray to himself. He will say to the others, Come and pray to me. I give you what is good for you. I tell you all the answers.'

'Oh dear', says the missionary to himself, 'this instruction isn't going at all as I intended. This was the point when I was going to whip the Gospel out of my cassock-pocket and say "Exactly! Here is the man. Go away and read about him." But as it is, that would never do. He will say: "That is not God. He prays to his Father in Heaven; and says: 'One only is God. Keep his commandments and thou shalt live.' He says: 'of that day and that hour none knows, not the angels in heaven, nor the Son, but the Father alone.'"'

'I have muffed it again', says the stupid missionary to himself. 'I know what it is: I left out the piece about the Trinity – or anyhow, about the Binity; the doctrine of the third person will keep for another day.'

So the missionary clears his throat, and starts again like this: 'My child, I have put you on the wrong track. It is not just Godhead that becomes incarnate, it is Godhead in the special form or person of Sonship. Divine Son becomes incarnate: and since Divine Son draws his whole person and being from the divine fatherhood anyhow, quite apart from his incarnation, when he becomes incarnate he does not cease to do so. He goes into the prayer hut, he goes out into the hills, he talks with his Father, he draws the Spirit of the Father into him, he opens himself to receive the power and the will. But, you will say, what is this about Divine Son? Are there two Gods? My child, I know you are clever when you want to be. Now concentrate, and I will tell you. My child, what do we know about God? What but that he is the cause of all? An infinite energy of making, giving, self-outpouring; a bounty that has no limit; a life that ceaselessly mirrors himself in the faces of living things. The golden bounty splashes down, the creatures catch it in a million little cups, and still it overflows. The living spirit is mirrored in a million faces: in yours, my child, and mine, and doubly so when we go into the prayer hut and look back into the divine countenance and throw back his own light upon himself and the beam dances between us full of angels. But how little, cracked, and dusty a mirror in you or me to give God back the light of his countenance; and how confused and splintered a reflection does he receive from all the variety of creatures taken together? Is there nowhere a face to look into his eyes with equal eyes, nowhere a bowl to catch and treasure and contain the whole overflow of infinite bounty? My child, do you believe God is almighty? Do you believe that there lacks anything to his perfection, or his joy? Then tell me: does he or does he not, from all eternity and always, give himself a son?'

'Now what can we say of this Son? He is utterly receptive, wholly derived; in fact, a Son. But he is also infinite: all that his Father is, for his Father has withheld from him none of what he is himself, and he has the capacity to receive all that the Father gives. But these are not two Gods operating independently or even forming an amicable and voluntary alliance. They are the two persons of one divine life which could not exist at all otherwise than in them. For the Father, the source of Godhead, is an overflowing bounty; a giver, a cause, and he is all this in being the Father of this Son continually.'

'Yes,' says the boy, 'I suppose so. But have you not taken away from us the love of God? If this is the Son in whom he is content, why will he trouble with us? He does not need us. He ... Oh, excuse me, Father ...' The boy broke off to recapture a little furry animal which had jumped out of his pocket. It was soon comfortable between his hands and he looked at it with manifest benevolence.

'What's that?' said the missionary.

The boy laughed. 'He's my little friend.'

'Rather a small friend,' said the missionary. 'Haven't you any bigger ones?'

'Yes, you know: the boy Azarias. Why d'you ask?'

'Never mind,' said that tiresome and didactic priest, obviously improving the occasion. 'Now concentrate: think. If we had just had animals, no fellow men, each of us alone in a patch of forest, would we ever have called the animals our friends, or made friends of them?'

'No,' said the boy, 'I think not. No other man, no friendship: no talk, no give and take, no anything.'

'Still,' said the priest, 'now you have got Azarias and the others, you make a little friend of the squirrel.'

'Yes,' says the boy, 'I put the friendship on him, I talk to him, I pretend he understands.'

'But is it all pretending? Does he understand nothing?'

The boy laughed again. 'He's a very clever squirrel. He understands about ten different things. And I think he really likes me a bit.'

'Well then,' said the missionary, 'and what about God? God is not just a fairly loving person. He is just love, that's what the book says.

Now do you think he could be the love he is if he had only us? Do you not think that the Love the Father is loves his son, and then his love overflows on to little creatures like us, so that, as you said about you and your squirrel, he puts the friendship on us and treats us as though we were his Son? And not content with that, he sends his Son into the world to associate us with that Son, and make us resemble him, and, as far as possible, parts of that Son, so that his love for us might be part of his love for his Son. That association is called the mystical body of Christ.'

The missionary's hand returned to his cassock-pocket and he brought out his Gospel-book with an air of chastened triumph. 'There,' he said, 'go and read how the Divine Son came into the world, in which he still remains.'

I must apologize for this nineteenth-century missionary idyll, which is hardly, I fear, to the taste of the present day, but the thing ran away with me and I have no time to rewrite. Oh, how awful! I see that there is going to be another scene of it.

A day or two later the missionary came upon the boy sitting with his nose in the book and a frown of intense concentration. 'How are you getting on with it?' he asked.

'Very nice,' said the boy. 'This man, he does the work, he speaks the words of the Son of God. But he doesn't know who he is himself, he has to find out. He is thirty years old and he still doesn't know. He comes to a man called John who is baptizing the people to make them clean and ready for someone called Messiah, someone very great, to come. Jesus is baptized too, and then bang! the sky splits, down comes the dove, down comes the voice, You are that Messiah, you are my beloved Son. He goes away into the bush to think. The bad spirit comes to him and bothers him plenty, "*If* you really are the Son of God" he keeps saying to Jesus in his mind. And even to the very end he never says just like you told me, "I am the Son of God who is God too." It is a funny thing if Divine Son has to find out that he is Divine Son and never quite manages it. He comes as a man: – all right; that is, he hides himself from the others. But does he hide himself from himself? I mean like this. Divine Son is divine Son because of his thought, not because of his hands, feet, lungs, heart, for those are just like anyone's. But if divine Son doesn't think he is divine Son, how can he be divine Son because of his thought?'

'My boy,' said the missionary, 'did you ever see a picture of President Eisenhower?'

'Yes, plenty ... with a grin from ear to ear.'

'Yes, I know: they teach them to do that in America. But did you ever see a picture without a grin?'

'Yes, once. Him taking the oath.'

'Good. Well, there is a man rather like that in my native country: he is not top man in politics like Eisenhower, he's top man at thinking. He's called Gilbert Ryle. And he says ...'

At this moment there was a blood-curdling roar. In jumped a lion, and ate the missionary. The boy ran screaming out, and was eaten by a leopard. So now we have got rid of these tiresome characters and can proceed in our own way.

I want to apply Ryle's famous distinction between *knowing how* and *knowing that* to the mystery of the incarnate consciousness. The little African rightly said that the divine Son could not be in Jesus otherwise than as mind; and rightly, too, that mind must be expressed in knowing, or what is it? But the little African, like so many victims of Ryle's criticism, assumes that 'knowing' means *knowing that,* knowing clear factual truths; for example, in this case, that the thinker is very God of very God, begotten not made, consubstantial with the Father, and mediator of the whole creative process. But such a supposition not only conflicts (as the little African objects) with the evidence in the Gospels, it conflicts no less with the very possibility of genuine incarnation. Christ is very God, indeed, but also very man; and an omniscient being who knows all the answers before he thinks and all the future before he acts is not a man at all, he has escaped the human predicament. And (not to speak of omniscience in general, but to restrict ourselves to the single point of self-knowledge) how can a person who knows his unique metaphysical status with more than Aristotelian exactitude be a largely self-taught Galilean village boy whose store of ideas derived from the Synagogue? How, moreover, can he be tempted at all times like as we are, or fight a lifelong battle of faith, and suffer seeming dereliction on the cross?

On the other hand, he *knows how* to be Son of God in the several situations of his gradually unfolding destiny, and in the way appropriate to each. He is tempted to depart from that knowledge, but he resists the temptation. And that suffices for the incarnation to be real.

For 'being the Son of God' is the exercise of a sort of life; and in order to exercise it he must know how to exercise that life: it is a question of practical knowledge. A theoretical knowledge about the nature of the life he lives is unnecessary, it suffices that he should live it. 'I would rather know how to repent than know the definition of repentance' is an ancient saying; and it was enough for Jesus to exercise the personal existence of the Second Person in the Trinity: he might leave to schoolmen the definition of the Trinity, especially in view of the fact that it cannot be verbally defined. There is indeed, something shocking and absurd about the thought of the divine person talking divinity, as Alexander Pope says in criticising the bathos of Milton's heavenly scenes: 'And God the Father turns a school-divine.'

God is that life which schoolmen falter to express, and which an eternity of exploration will not exhaust; but it will be ever new to those deemed worthy of that blessedness.

And God the Son on earth is a fullness of holy life within the limit of mortality; it is for him to be, and for theologians endlessly and never sufficiently, to define.

But *knowing how* commonly involves elements of *knowing that;* for example, knowing how to set a broken leg involves knowing what is the form and function of the bones and muscles you are handling. And knowing how to be Divine Son in earthly flesh doubtless involved knowledge of the realities with which the existence of that Son is concerned and especially a practical and contemplative and, shall we say, a mystical, knowledge of the Father. If it is true that the saint knows God, it is true that Jesus knew his Father, and in a surpassing degree, so that God was absolutely and continually real to him and he drew his whole life and action with simplicity of heart out of that blessed fountain. To *be* the Son was to *know* the Father, not for the Son to know himself. What is the profit of real knowledge? How happy we should be if we could forget ourselves, especially when we pray.

I will, in closing, confide to you, for what it is worth, a speculation, which is, as I see it, a probable consequence of the 'knowing-how' view of the consciousness of the Son of God. It is this. His knowledge of his unique Sonship will be largely negative. It will be the sad and progressive discovery that other men have not the Sonship he has – they are not all pure incarnations of divine Sonship; indeed none of them is that. For, as the divine Child grows, he lives a life filially divine, because, after all, that is the way for him to live and be; he seizes all that his religious training, or the works of nature, offer him wherewith to think the thought and conceive the image of his Father and God and lives in perfect faith. How does he know that other children, other men, are not so? He discovers it in living. Sin is not an occasional breakdown, but a state; irreligion not an occasional distraction but a dominant attitude; wilfulness not a flourish of play but the set-direction of existence. The experiment was not complete until his countrymen had crucified him and his disciples ran from him.

There are many questions concerning the powers and acts of God incarnate besides the question of his knowledge on which alone I have touched. But I must bring this desultory paper to an end and, since desultory it has been, I will conclude with a summary of the points I have made.

1. Why we should say 'very God and very man' of Christ is not a matter of mere historical inquiry because Christians do not pretend to know about the divine Christ by mere history but through testimony, faith, and life. So what we are asking is whether the formula properly describes the reality with which Christians believe themselves to have to do.

2. The combination of God and Man in Christ is not the combination of two determinate sorts of being, the divine and the human, either compatible with one another or incompatible. It is the act of the Infinite Godhead finitizing his personal action in a unique way, and so that he is purely divine in being purely human.

3. We cannot understand the incarnation without the Trinity. What becomes incarnate is not just the Godhead but the divine Sonship in the Godhead. That is what is translated into human terms, for that is what we are adopted into by association: the sonship is spread to embrace us.

4. The incarnation is not just an accepting of the formal conditions of humanity in general, it is the becoming an actual particular man in the limitation of his circumstances and his knowledge. The divine infallibility of Christ's knowledge as Son of God is concerned with knowing how to play his divine part rather than with knowing that his part was, in a metaphysical sense, divine.

5. It is an apparent corollary of this that his sense of his uniqueness would be arrived at negatively by the discovery that other men lacked

what he was. It was, indeed, a function of his divine compassion for us sinners.

There: that is all I have said. I have really done no more than define and explain a few of the things which the Christian Church teaches and believes. I have proved nothing.

A Grasp of the Hand

A Christian sermon preached in Christ Church Cathedral, Oxford, published in 1960 in Said or Sung, *and reprinted in* The Essential Sermons. *Here Farrer further develops, in sermon form, some implications of the previous essay's position that the earthly Jesus was not omniscient. But he also considers in more detail the nature of power, both human and divine. Farrer beautifully portrays the incarnation of infinite power and knowledge into infantile weakness and ignorance: 'The maker of the world is born a begging child; he begs for milk, and does not know that it is milk for which he begs.'*

It may easily happen to any of us, and especially in the wintry part of the year, to learn suddenly that an old friend has fallen ill. We go to visit him; we find him already unconscious, nothing left of his life but the breathing; and he makes an awkward job of that. Unable to talk to him, we take him by the hand. But his hand is a surprise; it is lively, fresh and warm, and he returns our grasp with all the vigour of old kindness.

No doubt it would be difficult to justify in cool reason the way a thing like this can turn our heart over. We imagine that our friend, buried deep under accumulating layers of unconsciousness, has stretched a hand to us. But a doctor would tell us that our friend has done nothing; the soul, the mind was not involved, the action was reflex or automatic. A lifetime of ready response to our greetings has got him the habit of returning our pressures; the habit is in the hand, and continues to act after the mind is gone.

That is what reason would surely say, but our heart is not convinced. The mysterious unity of personal life through sleep on into waking, through death into resurrection, fascinates us. Sleep – there now, sleep is a parallel. For he might take my hand or murmur to me in his sleep; and who can resist the impression that kind words spoken by sleeping lips come from the heart? Here again reason tells us that since the sleeper has no control over what he says, he cannot fairly be credited with meaning to say it; but instinct turns the argument upside down. He did not mean to say it, no, he just said it, and how much better that was!

The expression of his kindness to us came from him because he could not hold it back, like water overflowing from a spring. What do I care for the things people mean to say? Every one in full command of his wits, the master of his hands and tongue, is up to some game; and if the game is virtue, so much the worse. Are you kind to me on principle? Is it to fill in a picture you draw of yourself as a Christian soul? Is it in execution of a plan of yours labelled 'friendship with me'? then take your kindness somewhere else, I do not care for it. Whereas, here is a sleeper who will mutter my name, here is a man unconscious yet ready to grasp my hand, yes, and here is my little child; I give him my finger and he clings to it. So Jesus clung to Mary's at Bethlehem long ago; and maybe the shepherds put their fingers into his little palms.

The moral of this strange argument is the suspicion of power; a suspicion, alas, all too well founded. God, printing on mankind the image of his own likeness, gave us some faint resemblance of that making, that self-determining power, by which he creates the world. It is this that is heavenly in us, and it is this that is satanic. Satan abused angelic power to be his own god, and we have abused our godlike power to play our own game; and our abuse of power is nowhere more seen than in our insufferable virtue, or more felt than in our synthetic kindness. Speech and thought are the beginnings of power; for even where there is no power to act, there is the power to lie, to fabricate, to invent, to deceive ourselves, to make up a story and to live in it. By this, true religion and false religion are most sharply tested. For true religion crumbles the structure of selfish invention; false religion gives to the world we make, the world God disowns, a firmness and elaboration which no irreligious thinking could ever give to it. We love the exercise of power in ourselves, it is the citadel of our being, our darling sin. We hate it in our neighbours, and in order to escape from it, we take a pathetic refuge in meaninglessness; in the seeming affection of infants, or even of brutes, uncorrupted by thought. We value slips of the tongue above sensible speech, and the muttering of sleepers above the words of wakeful men.

If the mere rudiment of power, the simple possession of conscious thought awakens suspicion, what shall we say of power full blown? The ingratitude of poor men to their rich benefactors is notorious, but it is also very natural. They feel themselves to be pawns in someone else's game of virtue, they do not feel themselves to be loved, and they are probably right. And as for political power, who credits the public smiles of public men? They are no worse men than we, indeed; no less capable of kindness in their families. But their official capacity ties them to servicing the great machine of power. Whatever faces they may make, we know we are only numbers in their arithmetic. Somewhere there may be a statesman or a prince of more than human goodness, who carries his people in his heart, and prays for them as devotedly as he governs them. But he will not easily obtain the credit of his kindness; his possession of power may not corrupt his action, but it will poison our appreciation; he will do well if he earns the favour of being accounted the least bad among necessary evils.

The universal misuse of human power has the sad effect that power, however lovingly used, is hated. To confer benefits is surely more god-like than to ask them; yet our hearts go out more easily to begging children than they do to generous masters. We have so mishandled the sceptre of God which we have usurped, we have played providence so tyrannically to one another, that we are made incapable of loving the government of God himself or feeling the caress of an almighty kindness. Are not his making hands always upon us, do we draw a single breath but by his mercy, has not he given us one another and the world to delight us, and kindled our eyes with a divine intelligence? Yet all his dear and infinite kindness is lost behind the mask of power. Overwhelmed by omnipotence, we miss the heart of love. How can I matter to him? we say. It makes no sense; he has the world, and even that he does not need. It is folly even to imagine him like myself, to credit him with eyes into which I could ever look, a heart that could ever beat for my sorrows or joys, a hand he could hold out to me. For even if the childish picture be allowed, that hand must be cupped to hold the universe, and I am a speck of dust on the star-dust of the world.

Yet Mary holds her finger out, and a divine hand closes on it. The maker of the world is born a begging child; he begs for milk, and does not know that it is milk for which he begs. We will not lift our hands to pull the love of God down to us, but he lifts his hands to pull human compassion down upon his cradle. So the weakness of God proves stronger than men, and the folly of God proves wiser than men. Love is the strongest instrument of omnipotence, for accomplishing those tasks he cares most dearly to perform; and this is how he brings his love to bear on human pride; by weakness not by strength, by need and not by bounty.

A child considered in its actual wordless state may seem no better than a kitten; but we do not view it as the animal it is, we see in it the germ of a boy, and beyond the boy, of a man. Yet not perhaps of the man that on sad calculation it will probably become; our knowledge of our fallen state betrays itself in this, that we instinctively clothe the child with an unfallen candour. We see in its simplicity, its freedom from craft or guile, its confiding physical warmth, the promise of a manhood in which power, as it grows, will remain the servant of affection. So Mary saw the infant at her breast, but with how much better reason! As he grew in stature, he grew in grace, and unfolded the exercise of a power which was love in action. He could still beg, he kept that about him to endear him; as he had pressed Mary for milk, he asked the Samaritaness for water; and there was still the day when he would be asking soldiers for vinegar. But far more, he could give; and so pure was his heart, so single in its union with the fatherly love, that he did not need to rein in his power, or measure the force of his beneficent actions. When he vindicated the humble and rebuked the proud it was without restraint; so when he drove away the demon, and so when, unsparing of his vital spirit, he healed the sick. His love was like a fire; and so he seemed, as he was, more than man. His disciples feared him, and when in visionary trance on the mountain he blazed with light, it seemed the visible outbreak of what he invisibly was. For all his humbleness, his tradesman's hands, his common dress, his Galilean speech, he unfolded weakness into power when he spread the child into the man, and there were more in those days struck with awe and admiration than touched with any kindness. For even when power is the development of love, it may amaze us more than it warms us. But God's wisdom was not to be baffled, it took refuge once more in a folly; his power had its way by sinking back into weakness. The cross closed the scene which the manger had opened, the powerlessness of infancy was crowned by the powerlessness of defeat, and the unconscious agony of birth by a conscious agony of dying.

For God will be loved, whatever it may cost; and when he had expanded the flower of glory in his human life, he crushed it into a handful of bruised petals, for fear that power and wonder might stand between his kindness and our affections.

We must love God, it is our maker's command, and in such love our salvation lies. We must love God; yet what has love to do with 'must'? Love is free, duty cannot drive it. Yet we must love God, there is no resisting such love if we once see his face and feel the touches of his hands. The power of God perplexes us, but his weakness is still all about us; this is still the engine with which he moves our minds. By the birth in which he is born to-day, the son of God makes all mankind his own. Men's virtues indeed seldom illustrate his action more than they darken it, but all men's weakness speaks for his humiliation. Christ is every sufferer, every child; whatever hand pulls at us is the hand which clutched at Mary, and would have clutched at the friends standing round his cross, if it had not been nailed. If we would but see from how many eyes the weakness of God looks into our own, we would have no time to ask, Where is the God of Love?

According to his own express words Christ left two sorts of deputies in the world, two sorts of human substitutes for himself, beside that one divine invisible deputy, the Holy Ghost, who is the soul of all the love we have. But these are deputies of flesh and blood; the deputies of his power and the deputies of his weakness. The deputies of his power are his apostolic ministers, to whom he says, 'He that receiveth you receiveth me, and he that receiveth me receiveth him that sent me.' They speak his word, they pronounce his pardon, they give his body and his blood. The deputies of his weakness are the little and the needy; and of these equally he says, 'He that receiveth one such child in my name, receiveth me.' Neither sort of deputies represent Christ by virtue of their merits. The infirmity of the ministers always hinders the word, and yet faith can hear through all their folly the voice of Jesus. And the weak, the little, are not always amiable. Are we not all both little and weak, but mostly on the side of our faults and vices?

Yet faith can see the passion of Christ in all; and faith is the gift of that greater and better deputy, the Holy Ghost who will not fail us, the love of God being shed abroad in our hearts by the Spirit whom Jesus was born to bring us.

By his inspiration, then, we will receive Christ in both sorts of his human deputies; but more endearing, more revealing, more present to us at all times, are the deputies of his weakness. These are the deputies through whom his infant hands receive our Christmas gifts, and his gratitude, unlike ours, is undying. For when the nations shall stand in flocks before the everlasting Shepherd, thus shall he say to those whom he guides towards his right hand: 'Come ye blessed of my Father, inherit the kingdom prepared for you from the foundation of the world; for I was an hungered and ye gave me meat, I was thirsty and ye gave me drink, I was a stranger and ye took me in, naked and ye clothed me, sick and ye visited me, I was in prison and ye came unto me.' And when they deny that they ever did him such services, he will answer, 'Inasmuch as ye did it unto the least of these my brethren, ye did it unto me.' In these then is very God to be found, and everlasting life; and we can turn our backs on idols.

As to what the eternal Judge will say to those on his left hand, this is not the time to think; for to-day is a day of gladness, a day to ring all the bells in earth and heaven, because the love of God is born into the world, so strongly armed with weakness that it must prevail. Love is nowhere more truly omnipotent than in the manger; in the speechless child we adore the Word who made the worlds, the Son of the everlasting God, the express image of uncreated glory; to whom now, therefore, with the Father and the Holy Ghost, in three Persons one love, one light, one God, be ascribed, as is most justly due, all might, dominion, majesty and power, henceforth and for ever.

The Body of Christ

Published in 1952 as the concluding essay of The Crown of the Year: Weekly Paragraphs for the Holy Sacrament. *Christ's incarnation continues in the Holy Eucharist, individual Christians and the collective Church. 'Jesus, conceived by the Holy Ghost in the womb of Mary, established in the world a body joined uniquely to the life of God, and our bodies are to be united with his body in one extended body, the mystical Church. Our state of redemption, like our existence, like his incarnate existence, is to begin with the body.' Through baptism and bread we find 'a web of bodily relations binding our bodies together'. A brilliant meditation on the bodily nature of our salvation, as* au courant *as contemporary postmodern reflections.*

The Catholic Church has made much (an historian might incline to think) of a few figurative gestures and words used by Christ when he supped last with his disciples. They weigh light against the whole body of his deeds and sayings, even in his short recorded ministry; yet how great a part of the Church's existence have they shaped and filled! But a man's words and actions are not to be reckoned by bulk, and even though you consider Christ solely as man, you must expect the most pressing occasion to draw from him the most significant act. For he was not, clearly, one of those men, whether inhibited, clumsy, or ironic, whose expressions are habitually disproportioned to their occasions. Here he had his last free and familiar converse with his disciples; it was the most intimate ceremony of domestic piety in the Jewish year, and death stood over his head. Not all that he said in all his life before will be of more concern to us than what that moment drew from him.

If, on the other hand, you consider Christ in his Godhead also, then you will perceive a perfect concord between the dynamism of his human act, and the wisdom of eternal providence. What was pressed from the heart of manhood by supreme occasion was ordained by everlasting God to flow when it would speak most movingly to the world. Everything that went before was so disposed as to prepare for this moment, and to give meaning to it when it came. Then, if ever, things were said and done of which the significance was inexhaustible. St Paul, beginning to put them before us, sets them in their proper key: 'The Lord Jesus', he says, 'on the night in which he was betrayed'. 'Lord' for the Godhead, 'Jesus' for the man, and his betrayal-night for the occasion.

He blessed the bread, he broke it, and he said 'This is my body'. His words have the sound of a sentence identifying a thing. 'That' says a woman, bringing her batch out of the oven, 'is the bread for today', identifying the pieces she has made most suitable to be eaten hot, and appointing them to their use. She begins with what is superficially evident, the 'that' of colour and shape which meets the eye, or of mass which resists the fingers. She goes on to give a more thorough account of 'that': 'That is my bread for today – I made just so much suitable to be eaten hot, and that is it.' The woman speaks the way round that she does, because she is beginning from the children to whom she speaks, and from the impressions in their senses. It would be possible, though not in such a case at all natural, for her to speak the other way about, beginning from those special pieces of bread. '*The bread I made for today* stands on that part of the table and is recognisable by such and such signs.' If she did speak so, her words might seem more purely objective, having less to do with the observer, and more to do with the thing. Whether it is observed or not, such-and-such bread occupies a certain place, has a certain shape, and so on. Jesus says, '*This* is my body', beginning from the senses of his hearers, from what they can see his fingers to be touching. He is not, indeed, like the woman, identifying now what he made previously; he makes it to be his body by his word. But the words having been spoken, the bread is what the words make it, and our faith, desiring to speak of the things as they are in themselves, can turn the sentence the other way about, and say, '*Christ's body* is there, showing itself in what we observe his fingers to be breaking.'

Christ is speaking of physical things, body and bread. Now when anything physical is said to be *there,* it is understood to be actively inserting itself into its environment. The woman's bread presses upon the table, puts a steam into our nostrils and throws back rays of the light against our eyes. But the mysterious body of which Christ speaks does not insert itself into its environment by activities like these. Nothing expressing Christ's body radiates from between his fingers, what radiates from there expresses bread. The body which is Christ himself as he sits at the table inserts itself into its environment after the manner of a body, the body which he holds and calls his body does not. How then does it show itself to be his body?

We reply that Christ's sacramental body inserts itself into an environment which is indeed physical, being made up of our bodies; but that the manner of insertion is different. Let us consider it.

Our bodies are to extend the body of Christ, his body is to annexe our bodies to itself – our bodies, not our bare souls. Body is the foundation, we start from body. My thoughts and actions lift themselves out of my body, play around it, alter and pass; my body remains. By virtue of my body I am founded in time and place, through it I am inserted in my environment. Jesus, conceived by the Holy Ghost in the womb of Mary, established in the world a body joined uniquely to the life of God, and our bodies are to be united with his body in one extended body, the mystical Church. Our state of redemption, like our existence, like his incarnate existence, is to begin with the body.

The existence of each Christian in this world is a bodily fact. Can we say that the incorporation of Christians together in one mystical body is likewise a bodily fact? We could not say so, if the links between the several members were mental only. But they are not merely mental, Christ will not have them to be so. He will have us all grafted into his body by baptism. Here is a physical fact: each of us has either been baptised, or he has not; the baptismal water has either flowed upon us, or it has not. Again, he will have us all to take the actual bread, actually blessed and consecrated by the one apostolic priesthood. Here is bodily fact once more, a fact constantly repeated, through which Christ renews, actualizes and reveals his mystical body on earth.

Here, then, is a web of bodily relations binding our bodies together. But it is a web created by the insertion of the sacraments into the context of our bodily existence, not a web already there. When the woman puts her bread upon the table, the physical context, the environment of the bread, is already bound together by a web of physical interactions. The table is upheld by the floor and pressed upon by the air, light streams in through the window, strikes the surface and rebounds. The insertion of the bread into this system of interchange merely disturbs and complicates it somewhat by introducing an additional factor into it; it does not give rise to any different order of relations altogether. Whereas the sacramental body of Christ creates the whole texture of mystical body by turning men into communicants. The words 'This is my body' are creative words; and as they consecrate the Host, so they constitute the mystical body.

It is not, of course, to be thought that the mystical body is non-existent on any given morning, until the day's eucharist is celebrated and gives it existence. By far the most part of the mystical body is in paradise, bound to Christ not by sacramental but by social bonds, through actual co-presence with him. And even on earth those who come to any eucharist have communicated before, or having been baptised, they have been given a sacramental relation towards the eucharist, bathed as it were by divine hands and dressed and brought to the door of the banqueting hall. The sacramental body of Christ does not communicate existence to the mystical body as a seal does to an impress, which until it is stamped has no being, and once stamped has no more need of the seal. If the effect of Christ's body upon us were of such a sort, there would be no need of eucharist, baptism would suffice. For baptism, or rather the second and more positive part of it, the spiritual gift, was anciently called 'the seal', as being the stamp upon us of divine possession. The stamp, once given, is not repeated, but the possession is an infinite glory, the fullness of him who fulfils all in all, and of that fulfilling there can be no end. The grace of baptism is both asserted and extended in every eucharist. For the body of Christ is in the mystical body as the constant source of its life, from which it cannot be separated, any more than our world of light and warmth is separable from the sun. Without the luminary there would be no light, but the luminary being there light constantly flows from it. Christ's body is in heaven with the blessed but continually inserts itself among us sacramentally in many eucharists and in many tabernacles, to keep us bodily in being as a mystical body of Christ. But why introduce the figure of light, when the bread speaks for itself? Christ bestows himself as bread, and we are sustained as a mystical body, so long as we do not starve ourselves of this bread.

But again, the figure of light has its own advantages, for a body is fed with what is less excellent than itself; food is a fuel, a mere material; the principles both of structure and of action come wholly from the recipient. Whereas, feeding on Christ's body, we draw our Christendom from him, as a thing illuminated draws its splendour from the sun. We receive what we become; our heavenly embodiment is the overflow of his heavenly body made sacramentally present to us.

'Christ's natural body', to borrow the language of our rubric, 'is in heaven', there his resurrection-being is simply itself, both for him who wears it and for the blessed saints who know him in it. 'Christ's natural body' in an earlier, a fleshly state was likewise present with his disciples at the table. But at the same time he held his body, sacramentally, between his hands; his body, not in the simple 'truth' of its bodiliness, but in the special character of a gift made up for bestowal upon them. He held his body in his hands, neither as what it was in him, nor as what it was to be in them, but on the hinge of change between the two, and as it were suspended in the act of turning over from the one embodiment into the other. He held his body in his hands, as what he was giving away; 'Take it', he said, 'and eat it'.

The sacramental body must be thus seen as what is being given, as Christ's body given to constitute the bond and substance of his mystical body, the Church. For otherwise we cannot understand the divergent phrasing of the word about the cup as St Paul records it. 'This is my body', said Jesus, but not (according to him) 'This is my blood'. 'This cup', he said 'is the *new covenant* in my blood.' What Christ bestows is indeed the new covenant, the principle and life of the mystical body. But for that very reason what he bestows is his blood, his blood being the cause, substance and bond of the new covenant. And St Paul himself would have seen no material difference between the words he records and the words as they came back into the mind of St Mark, 'This is my new-covenant blood'.

What we lay on the altar and consecrate is the substance of our Christendom, what we are through Christ lies there. But it is what we are through Christ, because it is what Christ is. We reverence it first in him and offer it to the eternal Father, before we receive it to ourselves to assimilate, or rather, that we may be assimilated to it.

It is the mercy of Christ to begin my salvation with my body. This me, the mere opaque bodily fact, the me which is there before my will, and whether I will or no, and which I can only remove by self-destruction, by the insane pretence to dispose of what is not mine either to create or to destroy; this me, in which is founded all my power to use or to misuse, and which is also the instrument of all my usings and misusings, or else of my neglect, left to rust, and not used at all; Christ takes this me, and annexes it to himself by bodily bonds, without waiting for the sanctification of its acts and uses. He takes it, and presents it as part of himself that it may be sanctified. Meanwhile he acknowledges it for his, his body and blood, so long as I have faith, and repent my deadly sins.

My salvation begins from my body as a line begins from a point. The point, the strictly mathematical point, having no magnitude, is nothing but the beginning of the line. Unless the line is drawn out beyond the point, the point can have no being. And the salvation of my body cannot be, unless the sanctification of its use makes at least some beginning. Christ annexes no body to his body, without quickening its life through the Holy Ghost. The Holy Ghost is the principle of life and of resurrection. He is the breath of God breathed into the nostrils of a new mankind, that man may be living soul. And the recipient of the resurrecting breath is the body of Jesus Christ. By eating the flesh and drinking the blood of the Son of Man we are incorporated in the recipient of resurrection; our bodies lie with Christ in the Easter sepulchre, to receive with him the inbreathing of the everlasting Spirit, the life of divine charity.

But the condition of resurrection is sacrifice. Christ was crucified that he might rise, and he brought his crucifixion into the institution of the sacrament, breaking the bread that he named his body, and adding 'which is on your behalf'. He gave a further signification of his death by consecrating blood as distinct from body, and speaking of it as efficacious in the way the blood of a slaughtered victim was. Christ consecrated no body but what he sacrificed, he blessed no bread that he did not break. We were in that body, that bread; in sacrificing himself he sacrificed us.

Apart from sacrifice the body of Christ could not overflow its own boundaries and annexe us to itself, it could not extend into a mystical body. There are many bodies in the world, containing each within itself its principle of organisation. And when bodies in the secondary sense, corporate societies arise, their principle of union is founded in the bodily natures of their constituent parts. So a family coheres by the ties of blood, and a nation through the common physical and psychological needs of people dwelling in neighbourhood and subjecting themselves to a system of administration. But the body of Christ is a society whose organising principle is not founded in the special nature of its bodily parts, but in the will of God. And so it is simply by the sacrifice of the members' bodies to God that its unity consists. Either it is nothing, or it is a divine society; a new creation of the divine will, not the by-product nor even the sublimation of human concerns and interests. The members are one by oblation to God and selfless love for one another in him.

The sacrifice of Christ is present on the altar in the same way as the body of Christ is present; that is, in being set amongst us and united with us. As 'the truth of Christ's body' requires it to be 'in heaven', so the 'truth' of Christ's death requires it to have been on Calvary. Both sacrifice and body, the one heavenly body and the sacrifice once for all offered, extend themselves to embrace us in the sacrament. Divine generosity makes us bodily members of Christ's body from the beginning of our redemption, that we may live out our membership spiritually in the Holy Ghost. And Divine generosity makes us from the beginning bodily parts of Christ's acceptable offering. He sacrifices us in himself, but only that, through the power of the same Spirit, we may make our self-sacrifice effective, or rather, allow Christ to work out his sacrifice in us and work us into his sacrifice.

This, then, is requisite beyond all else in those who come to the altar, an adherence to the will of Christ which gives them away, as parts of himself, both to God and to their fellows. That will must be found in the particularity of sincere resolutions for daily living, and the resolutions must be honoured, and all unfaithfulness made matter of repentance. The worship of Christians is the sacrifice of Christ. The eucharist is the focus of it but the field of it is their common life together. Of that, perhaps, it is still more important to write, but it is not what we are writing of here.

I hope it is unnecessary to say that my intention has been to describe the sacramental unity of Christ's body as he constituted it and as it should be accepted by us, not at all to deny all membership in Christ to those who believe and practise otherwise. Christ established the body by his sacraments, and Christ has extended the grace of the body to sincere disciples reared in error, or scandalised and turned back from the sacraments by our sins.

Trinity XXI

Published in 1952 in The Crown of the Year: Weekly Paragraphs for the Holy Sacrament. *As a college chaplain celebrating early morning Eucharists, Farrer set himself the discipline of preaching a homily no longer than the lectionary Gospel text, while the congregation remained standing. Here is one such 'Farrergraph', preached on the Twenty-first Sunday after Trinity. It contains Farrer's memorable summary of the Eucharist: 'This sacrament is not a special part of our religion, it is just our religion, sacramentally enacted.'*

This sacrament is not a special part of our religion, it is just our religion, sacramentally enacted. It is whatever Christ is, and Christ is everything to Christian people. In particular, he is the supreme bond between us. Everyone of you communicating is bound to his neighbour by this, that the same Christ who lives in one, lives in the other. You care for your fellow Christian as you would care for Christ, and that in you which does the caring is also Christ. Christ in each cares for Christ in all when we communicate together. The same bond unites us with the saints in paradise, who make up by far the greater part of Christ's people, and with our departed friends who may not yet be in paradise, but for whom we care, and for whom we pray.

Sin and Redemption

Published in 1964 as the fourth chapter of Saving Belief: A Discussion of Essentials. *Originally delivered as a series of lectures to Oxford undergraduates, this is the closest Farrer came to writing a systematic theology. As the title indicates, in this chapter he considers both sin and redemption, but we have chosen to focus only on his treatment of the latter. The state from which 'God's grace redeems us ... is one of actual infringement of God's will'. Therefore, 'Between God and sinners there is a real battle of wills', and so our redemption consists in having our sinful will reconciled to God. Farrer writes, 'What, then, did God do for his people's redemption? He came among them, bringing his kingdom, and he let events take their human course. He set the divine life in the human neighbourhood. Men discovered it in struggling with it and were captured by it in crucifying it. What could be simpler? And what more divine?' In the course of his discussion Farrer is forced to deal with the popular theory – often called the satisfaction theory or substitutionary atonement – which says that our redemption consists in Christ's paying a debt we owe to God. Farrer finds great power in this theory considered as a parable, but not considered as good theology. He agrees that 'the blood-shedding of Jesus was the price of our forgiveness', but the price was not paid to settle a debt with God. Rather, it was paid 'to convince us that if we ever thought God did, or would, withhold forgiveness, we were wrong'.*

. . . Let us leave the question, how far the state of man apart from Grace is felt as sin, and turn to consider a little more thoroughly what the state is, from which God's grace redeems us. It is one of actual infringement of God's will. The analogy which inevitably presents itself is an offender's infringement of statute-law. But the analogy is more misleading than helpful; the will of God is so utterly different from the law of the land. The law is a set of rules which exist merely by being enacted and recorded. They are not embodied in any live action, unless either we are at pains to obey them, or our disobedience of them is avenged by public justice. The will of God cannot be anything like this; for the will of God is God himself in action, and God is always in action. If I go against the will of God, I do not simply go against a rule which God has revealed for my guidance; I go against what Omnipotence is doing with me, would I but let him. It is indeed the supreme paradox of our condition, that an Almighty Power respects our freewill; but his respecting of it does not mean that he sits back and watches it. He works upon free creatures through all the infinite operations of his providence.

When Scripture speaks of a state of war, a mutual hostility between God and man, it is giving expression to this fact. Modern humanitarianism recoils in horror, protesting that the enmity is on man's side only. The protest is justified, if the purpose is to deny that God is subject to negative passions, or actuated by destructive intentions; the danger it carries is of denying activity on God's part, as well as malice. Between God and sinners there is a real battle of wills. The fighting is let up from time to time on the human side, for sinners have to sleep. It is never let up on the divine side, for God neither sleeps nor slumbers. The divine antagonist may fight like a strong, compassionate man struggling to master an armed lunatic; he fights all the same, until we surrender.

Setting aside conflicts with the divine will on the part of men who know nothing of it, we may distinguish two degrees of conflict between that will and ours. The sharp degree of conflict is where we will *not* to do the will of God as known to us. The weak degree is where we will to do his will in general, but oppose it in particular through ignorance or error. The most tragic conflict of all is where men will to do the will of God in general, or so they think; but their conception of his whole will, and not of certain particulars only, is so false that they are more damagingly in conflict with his purposes than lazy, rebellious or ungodly men might be. Such, perhaps, was the conflict of the divine will with those who procured the crucifixion of Christ.

Only less serious than the mistake of denying any battle of God against us is the mistake of supposing that the battle was called off from the divine side when Christ came into the world, and that some different, conciliatory sort of divine action took its place. On the contrary; the incarnation of the Son of God was the crisis of the campaign and the supremely typical act of the divine strategy. God's battle against us is aimed at two objectives: the mitigation of the harm we might do ourselves or others, and the bringing of us into reconciliation with God. In a literal and earthly war, we may desire both to break the enemy's destructiveness and to recover his goodwill, but the two purposes will be pursued through different trains of action; let us say with guns on the field, and with propaganda over the air. Whereas the battle of the divine will with ours is a battle against our enmity; and when it breaks our opposition it secures our reconciliation.

And how is it done? It has become customary with theologians to let themselves off a plain answer. They will say that the reconciliation effected by Christ's death is an unspeakable mystery, for which a whole series of different parables was offered by scriptural writers and afterwards by the Church; that none of them is adequate, and several of them seem contradictory; we must see what each of them will tell us, and we must leave it at that. I cannot agree. Everything that God does has an abyss of mystery in it, because it has God in it. But in the saving action of the Incarnation God came all lengths to meet us, and dealt humanly with human creatures. If ever he made his ways plain, it was there. The variety of parables express the love that went into the redemption, or the blessings that flow from it. They are not needed to state the thing that was done.

What, then, did God do for his people's redemption? He came among them, bringing his kingdom, and he let events take their human course. He set the divine life in human neighbourhood. Men discovered it in struggling with it and were captured by it in crucifying it. What could be simpler? And what more divine?

In the very brief statement I have just made, I have done what I said was needless, and brought in a parable. That kingship is a parable is evident. God is not king to the world, he is God to it. The parable has nevertheless a proper place in the literal statement, for it was from such a parable that Christ's work began. It was no parable, indeed, to those who first heard him. They hoped that as the Persians, the Greeks and the Romans had in turn held the kingdom or empire of the world, so the people of God should hold it. The hope was crucified on Calvary, it rose transfigured from the Easter Sepulchre.

When we are doing theology, not just history or Bible-exposition, we make it our aim to see truth not as it was provisionally stated, but as it is ultimately revealed to be. God is not king, but God; if, in a parable, he made men partakers of his kingdom, he will, in a more literal form of statement, make them associate with his Godhead. This is not to say that even God's own grace effaces the distinction between what it is to be God, and what it is to be his creature. He alone is eternal, having existence of himself, and in his own right; we exist, and only can exist, by his good pleasure. Even so, we are privileged above irrational creatures, and have that in us which allows of association with the divine. . . .

We cannot think God's thoughts or love God's loves, in God. But how if he descends to think his thoughts and love his loves in man, and under the human form, through statement, comparison, decision, through word, image, feeling – all the familiar mechanisms of the created instrument? This will be the way to associate us with the Divine activity. The scriptural parable will have its fulfilment: we shall be made sharers in the divine kingship, through union of mind and will with the sovereignty that wields the world. For that sovereignty is of its nature communicable. Before the sovereign thought or love is extended outside the Godhead, it is already extended within it; so God constitutes in blessed Trinity the society of his own life. There is divine sonship by nature, before there is or can be sonship by adoption. There is an equal friendship or association of the Father and the Son, into which the Son may bring us by living as man, and by making us the disciples and partners of his life.

We have been digging a little with the tools of theology behind the parabolic façade, 'divine kingdom'. For, we said, the form in which our salvation was first proclaimed, was of God bringing his kingdom among men. How, then, did he do this? He sent forth the divine life in the person of his Son to live as man; and he began calling men into association with him. Not only did he proclaim that this was the 'kingdom', he showed both by word and deed the living will and action of the 'king'. It was in resisting the action and the claim of divine sovereignty, and in maintaining their own, that Caiaphas and Pilate crucified Christ. They crucified him, and by doing so they gave him the occasion of decisive victory: a victory over fear, error, pride, malice – all the human negatives, all the barriers set up by man against God.

If the reader is already a Christian, and kindly disposed to the line of exposition I have taken, he will perhaps be willing to agree that whatever else may be true or false concerning the Christian faith in salvation, what I have stated is at least true. But, he may say, if such is the basic truth of Christ's atoning action, how are we to fit in with it a very different account of the matter; an account for which scriptural authority can be claimed, but which is more neatly summarized in Mrs Alexander's line, 'There was no other good enough to pay the price of sin'? Is it true, or is it not, that the sins of men already committed run them into debt with some intrinsic law of justice, the debt incurred being a punishment or forfeit of some kind? And is it true that the score having assumed infinite proportions can never be worked off, as another hymn-writer informs us:

Could my zeal no respite know,
Could my tears for ever flow,
All for sin would not atone?

And finally, is it true that the divine Son took our place, underwent our penalty, and cleared our score?

If you ask whether these propositions are true or not true, and require a Yes or No answer, you force me to vote for the negative: they are not true. But I shall vote with reluctance, because the parable of the hopeless debtor redeemed by Christ's infinite generosity is an excellent parable. It becomes a monstrosity only if it is proposed as a piece of solid theology. Taken as such it is monstrous enough. The theologian will be bound to ask what he is to make of a debt to a Supernatural Bank of Justice. The idea is utterly meaningless; and if we try to give it substance by personifying the Bank as God himself, we merely exchange nonsense for blasphemy. . . .

'To pay the price of sin.' And what is the price of sin? Not literally what it costs; say, what the prodigal paid the harlots. Christ did not pay for us to go on sinning. Then what price did he pay? What it costs to reconcile sinners with their creator's will. And what does it cost? Surely not the serving of a sentence in some supernatural Dartmoor, or forty lashes of the best. It costs the abandonment of a false attitude, it costs a struggle against despair of virtue, a sacrifice of the pride which attaches us to the defence of our conduct, all the amends we can make to persons we have wronged – what else? The catalogue could be greatly lengthened. Such are the costs of our reconciliation, and such costs as these are not remitted to us, even by the sacrifice of Christ. We have all these things to do, only that Christ's initiative sets us in motion. He took us, and associated us with his divine life, even while we struggled against him. He has wrought all our repenting in us.

But still, I think, you are not satisfied, or you ought not to be; there is still something in the parable of penal debt paid which our story has not covered. No Christian can deny or forgo the claim that the blood-shedding of Jesus was the price of our forgiveness. And without the theory, however mysterious, of a debt to the bank of Justice, what are we to make of that? If there is no score to be cleared before God can forgive, surely God forgives us in any case, and before he sends Christ to achieve our reconciliation. What has Christ's death to do with the matter? Only, it would seem, to convince us that if we ever thought God did, or would, withhold forgiveness, we were wrong.

What are we to say to this? Let us begin by recalling who and what God is. God is almighty, and all his action in our regard affects our very existence. It cannot be supposed that God makes mere gestures towards his creatures. What could you mean by saying that he forgives? Surely not that he scratches an entry or pronounces words of indulgence. He who has the power and does not act is convicted of insincerity if he expresses the intention. Since God does not bear grudges, he has no need to set them aside; what, then, can his forgiveness be, but his ceasing to battle against our wills, and taking us into his fellowship? We, thinking by human analogy, will naturally distinguish God's forgiving us from his reconciling us to himself. The forgiveness is what would be, in a man, the attitude; the reconciling what would be, in a man, the consequent action. But God has no attitudes which are not actions; the two things are one. And so if Christ's blood is the price of reconciliation, so it is of forgiveness. And still there is no need for the theory of the Bank of Justice.

But even so, you will not be satisfied – at least I hope not; for you ought not to be satisfied with less than the whole truth. And you will still wish to say, will you not, that God has forgiven all men through Christ, even those whom he has not yet brought into reconciliation with his holy will. Yes; but his forgiving all men through Christ, even the yet unreconciled, is nothing so formal or so ineffective as the deletion of a ledger entry on account of payment received from a third party. God's act of universal forgiveness is the whole train of action he sets working through Christ, through the Spirit, through the Church, through all-embracing providence, towards the reconciliation of the unreconciled, whether in this world, or in a world to come. And of this great process Christ's blood was, once more, the cost.

I hope now that I have shown two things: first, that the parable about the payment of our penal debt is not the sober nor the ultimate truth; and second, how admirable a parable it is. For it brings into relief several points of great concern, which in the plainness of the basic account might otherwise go unobserved. By the way, I have done a third thing, which I did not (I confess) set out to do. I have not only told my readers the theological truth, as I see it; I have also carried them through an exercise in the way theology is done, and how it works upon parabolic material.

In a theological enquiry, we look for theological formulations. But never let us mistake such formulations for God's revelation. That would be like mistaking a knowledge of Greek grammar for a knowledge of Greek literature. The study of the grammar has its own cool fascination, but it is not the same thing as the enjoyment of Homer or Aeschylus; and its main purpose is, to act as a rule by which to understand such authors correctly. So theology is a rule by which to understand that divine utterance which is also divine action, the revelation of God in Jesus Christ. We do not read the story of the cross to make theological deductions. We draw out our theology that we may rightly read the story of the cross.

The Burning-Glass

Preached in St Mary the Virgin, in Oxford, published in 1960 in Said or Sung, *and reprinted in* The Essential Sermons. *A poetic, provocative and nearly perfect sermon about God's grace, which Farrer compares to light focused through a 'burning [magnifying] glass'. This light is 'nothing but Jesus Christ, God and man, burning his way through the wall of the heart'. If the previous essay sounds a somewhat semi-Pelagian note, here Farrer shows a more Augustinian side: 'We come to throw ourselves on grace, but it is by grace that we throw ourselves on grace. Before we touch the cross, Christ has shouldered it; before we shape a prayer, Christ has prayed it.' The end result of grace is the 'crucified will' we see most clearly in the saints, but which even ordinary Christians should begin to know within themselves: 'Christ in us, feeding the deep root of the will; Christ, giving himself to be our self.'*

In the name of the Father, and of the Son, and of the Holy Ghost. That is how we are taught to begin our discourse, placing what we say under the protection of God, that we may speak on his behalf, not on our own. And if it is the general rule for preachers to clothe themselves with the holy name and lose themselves in the truth they preach, more particularly it applies when we preach on the grace of God. For no one of himself can preach the grace of God, he can only stand aside and let it shine; the dart of light comes out of the body of light, and the sharp point of the dart which touches and pierces us is called the grace of God.

Let us begin with the New Testament. Grace, on the lips of St Paul or St John, is often an equivalent almost for God himself. 'By grace were ye saved.' Well, but by what are we saved? By nothing but the act of God. Grace then is God, or the saving act of God. St John says that God is love; it is almost an accident that he nowhere affirms him to be grace. Grace is the love of God in its most lovely aspect. If we say that God is love, we establish the substance of him, we say that he is the pure act of inexhaustible self-giving. If we call God by the name of mercy, we show the face of his love turned upon misery and need. But if we call him grace, we manifest the generosity of his love. Grace is gratuitous, nothing merits or calls for it. Suppose I were to preach to you about giving things to God, and you were to reply, 'But who can give anything to bounty itself?' Bounty itself – a fair New Testament translation of your remark might be, 'How can I repay the grace of God?'

When the Church calls God love, or grace, or mercy, she is not subscribing to the vapid doctrine that all we mean by God is the presence of these qualities, wherever they happen to appear in the world. No, God is God, even though there were no world to reflect his goodness. We start from that. God is God, an infinite intensity of personal life. But when we ask what is the life of God, we say, 'An everlasting act of love.' And this love shines variously in different relations. Between the Persons of the Godhead it is good-pleasure and social delight. Towards the miserable it is mercy, and towards the undeserving, grace.

God's generosity is not, like ours, a principle on which he acts from time to time. He neither slumbers nor sleeps; he never wakes up into action, he acts always; his bountifulness is what he always bountifully does. Of the variety of that bounty I will not speak – creation, preservation, so many blessings of this life – but I will speak of the heart of bounty, Jesus dying on the cross for us men and for our salvation. Indeed when St Paul (to take him for our example) speaks of grace, it is of this that he speaks. Jesus dying is the place, and substance, and act of grace; and the colour of grace in it is its being free and unmerited. 'While we were yet sinners,' says this Apostle, 'Christ died for us ungodly.'

Now it is a general principle that the flavour of everything is brought out by contrast, sour by sweet and light by darkness. We are told to taste and see that the Lord is gracious, and our palate feels it most by contrast with some opposite. And so grace most shines in St Paul's pages when it is opposed to merit or desert. 'God being rich in mercy, for the great love that he bore us took us dead in our transgressions, and brought us to life with Christ. By grace are ye saved. He raised us up with him and set us in heavenly thrones with Christ Jesus, to display in future ages the abounding riches of his grace, and his loving-kindness to us in Jesus Christ. For by grace are ye saved through faith; it comes not of you, the gift is God's. It comes not of achievement, lest any should boast; for we are his handiwork, created in Christ Jesus for the achievement of a good, which God has prepared for us to walk in.'

By Jesus' dying and rising, that is by God's grace, not by our work, merit, achievement or desert. Such is St Paul's contrast, as though he were saying: The fire is kindled by no business of ours, no preparing or striking of matches on our part, but by sunlight falling through the burning-glass of faith. Now such a contrast focuses attention on that precise point where the sunlight does the work of the match, and lights the tinder. Such a contrast leaves it for others to measure the shaft of light reaching from the sun to us, and concentrates all attention upon the very end of the shaft, tapered to a point by the lens, and piercing the dry leaves with a needle of fire. So, in thinking of grace, the Church has come to turn from the fount of light which is God in God, and the shaft of light which is Jesus in his incarnation, to look at the very needle of light which pierces the heart. But though we may choose to attend to the burning-point, what draws to that point, and makes that point, is nothing but Jesus Christ, God and man, burning his way through the wall of the heart.

I think we have taken this parable far enough; for what we have to do is not to give external descriptions of God's grace, but to stand out of his way and let grace do its work. And grace will not do its work by our thinking about burning-glasses, but by our watching and hearing and eating and drinking Jesus Christ. Perhaps with all my burning-glasses and stuff, I am merely putting off the moment when I tell you what it is for a Christian, and so I suppose for me, to have the grace of God. The moment has come; and what am I to say? To speak as though we had anything seems presumptuous; yet we cannot be so ungrateful to God's mercy, as to deny that he has given us grace. It is useless to preach unless we can claim some taste of the things we describe; just enough taste of them to interpret what we hear from the saints, or see in them.

Once again, therefore, what is the grace of Christ? It is that Christ penetrates us, and that this penetration has real effects. It is our prejudice to think that all persons are separate units, and that we communicate only by signalling to one another across physical spaces by physical signs, whether gestures or words. Such is our prejudice. It is called common sense, but it simply is not true. In the world of the spirit our prayers invade and enliven one another; and what are our prayers? They are our souls in action. The saints support and carry us; their life is the life of the Church. But the saints themselves, and we, are supported and enlivened by Jesus Christ. For he, being God, is also man; he crosses from the divine side to ours, to share with us as we share with one another; to be the heart in that community of spiritual creatures which serves the Father Almighty.

So grace is Jesus Christ entering us, Jesus Christ under the skin, the sacrifice of Jesus and the resurrection of Jesus spreading and fulfilling themselves in us. As the well-known prayer expresses it, 'Soul of Christ hallow me, Body of Christ save me, Blood of Christ enflame me, Passion of Christ strengthen me.' And does the grace of Christ so abound, that he gives himself to those who thus pray? Yes, we have seen it in the saints, in those whose wills are crucified, who in praying such a prayer desire nothing so much as that it should come to pass. But the crucifixion of the will – how slow a thing it is, and for most of us in this life, before we have achieved it our powers begin to fail and our habits to form, we become old and difficult and foolish, we die, and we have not been saints. May God, while there is time, give us the crucifixion of the will; for here also the resources of his grace are still unexhausted. We come to throw ourselves on grace, but it is by grace that we throw ourselves on grace. Before we touch the cross, Christ has shouldered it; before we shape a prayer, Christ has prayed it. Let the prayer of Christ, let the sacrifice of Christ, placed in my baptism under the root of my heart, break upwards and displace the sunny rubbish of self-will, to become my prayer and my resolution.

The saints who have crucified their wills are the visible incarnations of grace. Grace triumphs in them during this mortal life; they love the love and will the will of God. And though we are not so, God gives us grace, even to us. We are incorporate in Jesus with all the saints, we eat and drink him in the sacrament. And are there no fruits? Certainly there are fruits. There is the fruit of continual repentance. Again and again our most uncrucified will is reunited with the cross; we are forgiven and accepted as living parts of Christ. Moreover by grace we receive many good desires, and the expulsion of many that are evil. We pray for those whom we dislike, and care for them; we pray to do the duties we detest, and delight in them. Such are the fruits of grace; and to such fruits ordinary Christians can testify.

I need hardly say that the effects of grace are put down by unbelievers to suggestion, individual or corporate. Nothing comes in from outside, they say; it is all something into which we think ourselves. In a sense, Christians do not disagree; nothing comes in from outside; it is just us, thinking ourselves into our best nature. It is just us; but what are we? That is the point, what are we? According to the unbelieving philosophy, we are complex single beings; but according to faith, we are complex double beings. At a level deeper than that which any science studies, Christ feeds with himself the springs of our action. Nothing comes in from outside; when we act from the resources of divine grace, all the action and all the thought is in us; but it is Christ in us, feeding the deep root of the will; Christ, giving himself to be our self.

For we must use figures and parables; but how they mislead! The parables of grace – and we have Christ's own authority for them – speak of the branch drawing sap from the vine, and the seed building the plant from the materials of soil and rain. But grace is no process of nature, no ray of light kindling into flame, no soil or water feeding a vegetable root; it is the sheer bounty of God. And so when we preach the grace of God, this is what we preach: 'We are ambassadors on Christ's behalf, as though God did beseech you by us; we implore you on Christ's behalf, Be reconciled to God. Him that knew no sin he made sin for us, that we might be righteousness of God in him. Working with him, we beseech you also not to receive the grace of God in vain. For, he says, in a favourable hour I have heard thee, in a day of salvation I have succoured thee. Behold now is that favourable hour, now is that day of salvation'; this is the day to receive what God most longs to bestow, Jesus Christ, everlasting joy and inexhaustible grace; thereby to serve and praise the one Almighty God, unity in three Persons, Father, Son and Holy Ghost, both now and ever.

Walking Sacraments

Preached on 22 December 1968 (just seven days before Farrer's death), at the First Mass of Edward Ryan. Originally published in A Celebration of Faith *– the first posthumous collection of Farrer's sermons – and reprinted in* The Essential Sermons. *A classic description of the ordained ministry, cited by both George Carey and Rowan Williams among many others. What is the priest's* raison d'être? *It is to 'set forth the mystery of love, the body and blood of Christ, in bread and wine'. And the one 'who bears the Sacrament is sacramental himself; he is, one might say, himself a walking sacrament'.*

The Gospel for today shows us John the Baptist under fire. People want to know what he claims to be. They are not content to take his message on its merits. If they rally round him, round whom or round what will they be rallying? Round a man called John, certainly, the son of a priest called Zacharias. Anyone could know that much. But what is this man John? According to Jewish rules he is a priest, because the son of a priest was a priest himself. But all a Jewish priest could do was take his turn at ceremonial duties in the Temple at Jerusalem. And here was John, calling people out from Jerusalem into the wilderness, to consecrate themselves in readiness for a great act of God, a divine event which would involve them all. What right had he to do it? In the past God had given them a King, who had a first claim on their loyalty, being the Lord's anointed; and though the Kingdom had fallen, God had promised to revive the dynasty of David. Was John the promised King of glory? He said he was not: nor was he the promised Prophet, the second Moses; nor yet the reborn Elijah, who must come before Messiah the King. What then? John must say something about himself. He must pin himself down to some fixed position in the great unfolding purposes of God. He must claim some function conferred on him by God's own hand. And so he does, but he makes the humblest, the least pretentious claim which will meet the case. I am, he says, simply that herald-voice which, in Israel's prophecy, proclaims the coming of the Lord. I run, shouting, before his advance, that all may be ready to receive him. But when he comes to his inn, and turns in to lodge, my work is done: I am not fit to kneel before him or ease his travel-worn feet by taking off his sandals. Nevertheless, for all his unpretendingness, John is the heaven-sent herald, he has a place in the scheme of things which obliges all believing men to rally round him and accept his ministry.

John was under fire, he was called on to explain himself: and so it is with the Christian priest today. People want to know what he is, and what he claims to be. Like John, he has a message to deliver, but that's not enough: you want to know why you should pay him any particular attention. Why listen to a clergyman giving you his views on life in general? A student of politics will be more topical, and a philosopher will be more profound. He would be wise, you might think, to stick to theology and Bible-learning. But though he has certainly had some special training there, he has no monopoly. There is nothing to stop a layman from being a more learned and a more penetrating theologian than the priest of his parish; nothing, certainly to prevent a layman from being a much more understanding helper of people in any sort of trouble or sorrow. So when the Christian priest is brought under fire, like John the Baptist, what is he to say of himself? What is he when we come down to essentials? What distinctive place does he hold in the mighty purposes of God?

The answer is before your eyes. Here is a new-made priest, and what does he do? He hastens to the altar: he sets forth the mystery of love, the body and blood of Christ, in bread and wine.

You know what is the special mercy of Christ to us in the Sacraments. It is, that he just puts himself there. He does not make it depend on anything special in us who receive, certainly not in anything special in the bread and the wine; nor in anything special about the priest either, except just that he is a priest. That's the essential point. Apples don't drop from the sky, they grow on apple trees. And sacraments don't hurtle down here and there like lightning from heaven: they grow on the great branching tree of the Apostles' ministry, the tree planted by

Christ when he called twelve men and made them his ambassadors; a tree which has grown and spread and thrown its arms out all through history, to fill the whole earth. Into which tree, by virtue of his ordination, every new priest is grafted.

So, then a priest is a living stem, bearing sacraments as its fruits: he gives you the body and blood of Christ: he gives you, if you faithfully confess before him, Christ's own absolution. And that's not all; the man who bears the Sacrament is sacramental himself; he is, one might almost say, himself a walking sacrament. He is the appointed flag for Christ's people to rally round: the centre of unity to which we hold in every place. Just exactly what a priest is, you can see best in the Holy Eucharist. In a great part of that holy action he is, of course, no more than the voice of the congregation. Some of the prayers we say with him, some we let him say for us: it makes little difference. Or again, in receiving the sacrament, the priest is in the same position as any other Christian, receiving the body and blood of Christ. But there is a moment when the priest steps into the place of Christ himself, to do what Christ did, to bless and to break, to present the mysterious sacrifice before God Almighty. It is much the same in absolution. If you have gone and made your own confession to the priest, you will understand what I say, when I tell you that Christ speaks in him the absolving words.

These moments, certainly, are exceptional in the activity of a priest; exceptional, but still not disconnected with his whole life or character. The man who is as Christ in the Sacrament is not just like anyone else ever: he bears the stamp. He is always, as I said before, a sort of walking sacrament, a token of Christ wherever he is: in him Christ sets up the standard of his kingdom and calls us to the colours.

It is just this fact that shows up the priesthood so terribly, and makes us, and them too, so painfully aware of their deficiencies. No one's calling or profession shows them up as a priest's does. And indeed, as I began by saying, there is nothing to prevent a priest from being a very ordinary man; most priests must always have been so. Being a priest does not make a man more helpful to his fellow-Christians in matters of wisdom or of kindness; what it does do is give his fellow Christians a right to his services. It might well be (to take another case) that the woman next door to you had greater gifts for teaching small children than the school-mistress: but that doesn't mean you can expect her to teach your little family for you. You've a *right* to the school-mistress's services; she's given herself over to be eaten alive by the children of the place. And so with the priest: go on, eat him alive, it's what he's for; you needn't feel shy of devouring his time, so long, of course, as it's to fulfil a need.

Or again, in matters strictly of religion. Anyone may be a better Christian than the priest, more holy of life, more deeply versed in prayer. But the priest has a special obligation to lead a devout life, to study divinity, to pray; and so to be fit to give some help to his fellow-Christians in these supremely important concerns. Other people may expound the faith, and speak or write in Christ's name, more wisely and more competently than the priest. They *may* do such things, and even do them better; the priest *must*: he must keep the congregation supplied with its staple diet: he must keep giving them some word from God.

I've been talking all this while (have I not?) about the priesthood as 'they', as though I wasn't one of them. But of course I am, and I've been thinking about my own office. And as I talk to you I hope that you will be listening to me as to a priest – that is, you won't just be pulling my (no doubt inadequate) remarks to pieces, but that you'll be listening for something from the voice of God, spoken over my shoulders; for God commends to you, surely, his new-made priest, for you to take him to your hearts; to receive from him the blessings with which he has been entrusted, and to make him your common friend.

There is inevitably something absurd about our priesthood, because what we stand for is so infinitely greater than our poor little selves. But there's the same absurdity, really, about being a Christian at all. None of us can be let off being Christ in our place and our station: we are all pigmies in giants' armour. We have to put up with it: it's the price (how small a price!) paid for the supreme mercy of God, that he does not wait for our dignity or our perfection, but just puts himself there in our midst; in this bread and this wine: in this priest: in this Christian man, woman, or child.

He who gave himself to us first as an infant, crying in a cot, he who was hung up naked on the wood, does not stand on his own dignity. If Jesus is willing to be in us, and to let us show him to the world, it's a small thing that we should endure being fools for Christ's sake, and be shown up by the part we have to play. We must put up with such humiliation of ourselves, or better still, forget ourselves altogether. For God is here: let us adore him.

On Being an Anglican

Preached in Pusey House Oxford in 1960, published posthumously in The End of Man. *This sermon, delivered in one of the academic centres of Anglo-Catholicism, is a rare, direct statement of Farrer's ecclesiastical loyalties as an Anglican. It was recently criticized by Jeremy Morris for its 'harsh and polemical tone' in regard to Roman Catholicism, particularly the papacy.* But it seems to us that Morris's criticism is rather unjust. First, he does not acknowledge Farrer's overarching critical aim in the sermon, which is not simply to challenge Roman Catholic claims but in fact* all *ecclesial pretensions to finality. Farrer criticizes Rome and defends Canterbury, but the sermon explicitly repudiates any Anglican triumphialism and maintains that all churches are incomplete and provisional. Thus, Farrer says, 'The Church of England is not* the *Church; there is only one Church, as there is only one Christ. The centre of the Church is neither Rome nor Canterbury; it is the heart of Heaven.' Second, Morris does not take sufficient account of Farrer's time and place as a Baptist convert to Anglo-Catholicism in pre-Vatican II Oxford. Third, even after Vatican II and even in the light of subsequent Anglican–Roman Catholic ecumenical documents such as* The Gift of Authority, *Farrer's reasons (if not his rhetoric) for remaining an Anglican are still widely shared. That is, he accepts the divine origin of the Church and its role in God's plan of salvation, but he rejects the Roman Catholic centralization of the Church, especially as that is expressed in the papacy. In other words, although his rhetoric may be dated, here Farrer treads the classic Anglican* via media *of seeking to be both truly Catholic and truly Reformed. He believed that, as such, the Church of England*

---

* See J. N. Morris, '"An Infallible Fact-Factory Going Full Blast": Austin Farrer, Marian Doctrine, and the Travails of Anglo-Catholicism', in R. N. Swanson (ed.), *The Church and Mary: Papers Read at the 2001 Summer Meeting and the 2002 Winter Meeting of the Ecclesiastical History Society, Studies in Church History* 39 (Woodbridge, Suffolk: The Boydell Press, 2004), pp. 358–67.

is a valid church, and one in which he, as a specific individual, must remain. But even such modest ecclesial convictions are misguided if they distract us from Christ: the purpose of the Church, like a telescope, is to 'eliminate itself and leave us face to face with the object of vision'.

You know those correspondences they have in *The Times*. A reader in East Sussex has heard the cuckoo. This stimulates a reader in Cheshire to raise a question about the reason for calling cuckoo-flowers cuckoo-flowers; and a Lancashire reader rejoins with an attack on the teaching of botany in schools. I can't remember where this month's correspondence started from – perhaps it began with the decline of bird-watching among the rural clergy, but anyhow they have got round to discussing the bankruptcy of the parochial system. And now, in comes a man with a grievance – 'My conviction', he says, 'that the parochial system is finished, and my loss of confidence in the official Church leadership, led me to renounce my Orders several years ago.'

My interest in the *Times* correspondence is seldom strong enough to compete with the attractions of toast and coffee, but I own that when I got as far as this my consumption slacked off. Here was an extraordinary man. There was nothing indeed surprising in a priest's becoming discouraged by the ineffectiveness of his parochial ministry, or by the spectacle of an equal lack of success in neighbouring parishes; nothing surprising in his finding it the last straw that the diocesan bosses should be content to run the show as it was and remain innocent of any concern for radical reorganization. What I found staggering was, that a man should allege these simple facts, and then, with an apparent confidence in general approval, go on to tell the world: 'So I renounced my Orders.' It would be about as consequent to say: 'He called me a Scotsman, so I shot him through the head'; and expect the judge and jury to dismiss you without a stain on your character.

Or would it? Perhaps it all depends on the point of view. Suppose our letter-writer regards the Church of England as a propaganda society founded by Henry VIII for inducing the subjects of the crown to attend public worship. He was himself a paid official of the society. But finding that the propaganda machine didn't work, and that the head executives were bankrupt of ideas for making it work, he very naturally resigned his job. It was the conscientious (as well as, perhaps, the prudent) thing to do.

Yes, I know. But the reason why I find the ex-parson's letter so staggering is that it implies his holding this view of the Church, and how could he? It is true that we use such phrases as 'the ministry of the Church of England', 'a C. of E. parson'. Such phrases have their use. But fundamentally we are just Christian priests, priests in the Church of God. Did not Christ establish sacraments, and an apostolic ministry, and a visible company of faithful men? And have we not to make the best we can of it, by the grace of God? Are there too many ministers to give the sacraments to the Christians we have? Or are the sacraments to cease because the ministers find the ecclesiastical organization antiquated and suppose their bishops to be unimaginative? A is a layman and B is a laywoman, C is a priest and D is a nun: each, in the vocation wherewith he is called, goes to make the body of Christ; and between them the whole multitude of Christians must do the best they can, by the grace of God. Suppose the organization is antiquated, the leadership weak; we shall not help to modernize the former or invigorate the latter, by deserting our stations.

Well, but polity is more than party; a man dissatisfied with the Socialist machine, the Socialist ideology, may become a Liberal instead. The Church of England is only one among many organized Christian groups. To call it '*the* Church' is just social arrogance. It is the Church by law established, whatever that may mean; but in practice it has lost the privileges and retained the inconveniences of legal status. If I judge some other machine more effective than the Anglican for christianizing England, should I not transfer my allegiance?

No, for the political parallel is misleading. The true end of political action is to promote the prosperity, contentment and decent life of the citizens. The possession of these blessings is quite independent of membership of any political party. But the work of the Church is to incorporate men and women in the life of Incarnate God, and the Church is itself the means and the form of such an incorporation. We do not have our worldly happiness in the Socialist party, but we have our membership of Christ in the Church. So in the Church we must abide.

But look, you will protest, there you go again: 'In the Church'. There are many Churches; what business have you to call the Church of England *the* Church? It is time we grasped the nettle of the question. The Church of England is not *the* Church; there is only one Church, as there is only one Christ. The centre of the Church is neither Rome nor Canterbury; it is the heart of Heaven. There is a company of saints who enjoy the society of Jesus Christ more intimately than his disciples ever did on earth. We, who only know him by faith and touch him only in sacraments, are no more than outposts and colonies of his sacred empire. The fatherland is above, and there the vast body of the citizens reside. How many in heaven, and on earth, how few!

And even these few, how scattered, how divided! The everlasting shepherd promised that his flock should be one fold: and so it will at last in the heavenly Jerusalem. But as for earthly unity, in the present state of our warfare, it is a promise which, like other divine promises, depends on human obedience for its full effect. God has promised us salvation, and pledged it to us with his sacred blood. Yet he has warned us that where many are called, few may be chosen. He has promised us unity, and made his death the bond; but our perversity has made schisms and heresies. The Church feels herself to be one, and groans to find herself divided, but there is no easy way to heal all her divisions.

Meanwhile, how can I, truly and with a good conscience, abide in the Church of God? Only by remaining in the Church of England. But why? Because the people there are visibly the most pious, or the missionary action visibly the most efficacious, the ceremonies the most dignified or the most congenial? No. It is not for me to admire or embrace, or even prefer, a sect called Anglicanism. What is it then? There are two overriding considerations. I dare not dissociate myself from the apostolic ministry, and the continuous sacramental life of the Church extending unbroken from the first days until now. That is the first point, and the second is this: I dare not profess belief in the great Papal error. Christ did not found a Papacy. No such institution appeared for several hundred years. Its infallibilist claim is a blasphemy, and never has been accepted by the oriental part of Christendom. Its authority has been employed to establish as dogmas of faith, propositions utterly lacking in historical foundation. Nor is this an old or faded scandal – the papal fact-factory has been going full blast in our own time, manufacturing sacred history after the event.

I cannot desert the apostolic ministry, I cannot submit to the Pope.

And I was not born a Greek or Slavic Christian. I was born in this English-speaking world, where God's merciful providence has preserved the form and substance of the Catholic Church, and freed it from papal usurpation. At first, the Church, liberated from the Pope, fell heavily under the hand of the king, but the bondage was not lasting. That royalism is an accident to our faith, is made evident by the healthy condition of the American Episcopal Church, where prayers are not offered for Queen Elizabeth. The Crown is no part of our religion. Not that this need prevent us from wishing most fervently that God may save our royal house, to be the happy and unquestioned centre of our loyal affection, or the source of humane and Christian influences in the state. While we worship a King above, our vision will be assisted by the shadow of a throne below, and the very criticism which strips the unrealities of regal state, may discover to us the true pattern of sovereignty in him who made us.

When reunion is discussed, it is a sentiment as inevitable as it is amiable on diplomatic lips, to say that all Churches have their peculiar riches; that we disvalue no one's treasures by prizing our own, but hope that everything of worth may find its place in the final synthesis. Such sentiments are wholesome, if they lead us to look for merits rather than defects in other denominations. But the effect is less wholesome if we are led by such talk to suppose that Anglicanism should be valued as a charming or quaint or rare or beautiful species of ecclesiastical plant. We have our saints, some fostered by the Anglican spirit, some in revolt against it. But saints belong to Christendom: our saints are not ours. And though various edifying traditions of piety, learning and social action have flourished among us, they might perhaps as well have flourished somewhere else. It will be a sad admission, if our tree has produced no flowers or fruits – an admission we are happily not obliged to make. But we are not Anglicans because of these; because of George Herbert, or Dr Donne, or Isaac Walton, or Bishop Ken, or John Wesley, or John Keble – because of Prayer-Book English, or Cathedral psalmody, or Cambridge theology, or Oxford piety. No, we are Anglicans because we can obey Christ in this Church, by abiding in the stock and root of his planting, and in the sacramental life. We may begin by making a fuss about the Church, as a clever boy may make a fuss about a telescope, admiring its mechanism of tubes and lenses, and fiddling with the gadgets. But the purpose of the telescope is to eliminate itself and leave us face to face with the object of vision. So long as you are aware of the telescope you do not see the planet. But look, suddenly the focus is perfect; there is the hard ball of silver light, there are the sloping vaporous rings, and there the clear points, the satellites. And where is the telescope? It is no more to us than the window-pane through which we look into our garden.

The Church mediates Christ: her sacraments make Christ present, her creed presents the lineaments of his face, her fellowship incorporates us in his body. To be a loyal churchman is hobbyism or prejudice, unless it is the way to be a loyal Christian. Christ is our calling, Christ our life; he whom the cross could not daunt nor the grave retain will make our dry bones live, and restore to the universal Church that peace and unity that are agreeable to his will, that we may be one in him, as he with the Father and the Holy Ghost is one life, one love, one God.

The Trinity in Whom We Live

Original version broadcast by the BBC as a meditation for Trinity Sunday on 8 June 1952, published in Theology, *Volume 56, in 1953, and then reprinted as the second chapter of* Lord I Believe. *A remarkable meditation on the Trinity as related to the ordinary life of Christians, written some three decades ahead of the current renaissance of Trinitarian theology. 'The Trinity is both the meaning and the setting of that love which the Father has actually bestowed upon us. ... The Trinity is revealed to Christians because they are taken into the Trinity, because the threefold love of God wraps them round, because it is in the Trinity they have their Christian being.' It concludes with an equally remarkable prayer which is both distinctively Farrerian and yet also reminiscent of ancient Celtic benedictions.*

The Trinity cannot be explored except from the centre. And what is the centre? It is the Love of God. The name of Love has been fearfully profaned, and yet no other name will do. If, for example, we were content to contemplate the *benevolence* of God, we should not open up the region in which the Trinity is revealed, but only if we go beyond benevolence into love. Benevolence may be no more than a general and diffused well-wishing; love requires that a person should be infinitely prized. A headmaster might be sincerely benevolent, and not love a single one of his pupils; and that, perhaps, would be an ideal state of affairs. A father who was benevolent to his family and loved none of his children would not have done so well. The welfare state is a moral possibility if its officials are predominantly benevolent, but we do not expect them to love us.

In mentioning the welfare state we have hit upon a point of some religious importance, for the influence of political organization on religious feeling has been at all times profound. When we had absolute monarchy we had a theology of divine sovereignty; now we have welfare politics our religion is divine benevolence. It is instinctive in us to think of God's power as taking over where human power leaves off, as caring for the intimate distresses which no public officer relieves, controlling dangers no police can master, and, where the state hospital is defeated at last, raising the dead. But God's kingdom is not paternal government. Paternal government is only a bastard sort of fatherliness, and God is a true father so far as loving his children goes.

And that is easily said. It is easy to tell ourselves a tale about God's love for us, another thing to receive his love and reciprocate it, as it was Moses' privilege to do, when God is said to have spoken with him as a man speaks with his friend, face to face and without disguises. A man's face lights up the face of his friend, and Moses' face shone, reflecting that countenance which is the Light of the world. Moses was remembered by Israel not as a man who spoke of divine love edifyingly, but as a man to whom divine love spoke effectively, so that he answered that love, reflecting it back upon God in prayer, and outwards in devotion to mankind.

Why talk about Moses, who has been stylized into a myth by remote tradition, and not about Christian saints, whose histories are more exactly recorded? We would indeed talk about the saints if we were citing evidence, but at present we are doing no such thing. We are forming a picture to fix our minds on, and the pictorial qualities of the ancient figure are striking enough. And for the same reason let us, while we are about it, recall another antique personage. If God is said to have spoken with Moses as a man speaks to his friend, he is said to have honoured Abraham with the actual title: 'Abraham, my friend,' says the divine voice; his friend because he was admitted to his confidence. 'Shall I hide from Abraham,' said the Lord God, 'the thing that I do, seeing that I know him?' So Abraham was lifted into the counsels of God; and we read in the touching simplicity of the ancient story how, in the guise of a traveller unknown, God came upon Abraham sitting by his tent door in the cool of the day. Abraham, showing all hospitable kindness, entertained not only angels, but his Creator unawares, and had such discourses at his table as are to form the everlasting bliss of heaven.

What Genesis sets forth in the vividness of the picture is to be enjoyed by every Christian in the reality of spirit. God makes every one of us his friend, he sets us at his table, he shares his thought with us, he shows us his kindness, he puts an infinite price upon our love. Many truths of religion will bear endless meditation, but this above all; we can recall it as often as we pray, that God holds our love for him incomparably more dear than we hold the love of those who are dearest to us. Nothing moves our penitence more than to recognize that we have withheld what God desires and ourselves despised what he prizes most; nothing calls out our adoration more than a love which, knowing us to the bottom, continues to care for us under all our self-obsession and frivolity. It would be a great thing if we could love any single person as we love ourselves, but we cannot love even ourselves as our Creator loves us.

Friendship involves some kind of an equality, or, if not an equality, then an equalization. To make a friend of a child I must both be a child to him and also treat him as a grown person. God both descends to us, dealing humanly with his human creatures, and also lifts us to himself. It is by conversing with us that he brings us into conversation. There would be no light to shine back from Moses' face into the eyes of God, had Moses not received the shining of those heavenly eyes upon his own; no intercessions for Sodom in the mouth of Abraham, but that God provoked him into speech by first showing him the counsels of his judgment; no confidence to pray in any Christian heart, were it not warmed by the promises of mercy in Christ Jesus. To pray is to give God back the mind of God, coloured with our own. But we must first be given the mind of God, thoughts and concerns from a level above mortality.

God equalizes us with himself in the sense that he makes us party to a friendship with himself, but the equalization equalizes sheer inequalities. A man may make a friend of a child, some say of a dog or of a horse, and such an affection may be stronger than friendship; but friendship it is not, in the strict sense of the word; at the most it is a special extension of friendship, and friendship would never have received a name if this were all the friendship that there was. By making a friend of a child we extend to him what belongs properly to our equal, and by making friends of us our Father and our God extends to us by a stretch incomparably wider what belongs uniquely to his co-equal Son. If God's love for us were all the love there was, then divine love would never have been. It is only because divine love has a natural object that it overflows to embrace an adopted object. We are the children of God by adoption, the eternal Son of God is Son by nature.

Human friendship, belonging to our equals, can be extended to children, but there is a special case of such extension to which the name 'extension' most properly applies. I mean when my friendship for children is part of, an extension of, my friendship for their parent, when my friendship for him or her embraces them. There is an even more special case when the friendship we are thinking of is between my wife and me (for surely married affection is friendship, though it is also more). Then the children are specially hers, and yet I have (as the common saying goes) given them to her. And so she comes before me as one who says, 'I and the children you have given me,' not wishing to be loved apart from the children. The Epistle to the Hebrews puts almost those very words into the mouth of Christ. Our Redeemer is as one who says: 'I and the children whom God has given me.' For the heavenly Father has given Christians to Christ, though not, of course, in the way in which a husband gives children to his wife; we are not speaking of a sexual relationship, however spiritualized. Nevertheless, Christ, like the woman we were thinking of, comes before the Father with us his children, as though unwilling to be loved by him, unless his love is extended to us. But what fear is there that it will not be so extended, considering that the Father has given us to his Son?

The love whereby our divine Father loves us is an actual part of the one love with which he loves his eternal Son, for God is one and his love is one piece. He could not be one unless his love were one, for he *is* love, says St John, and only if there is one love can there be one God. So all the gifts of the Father's love to Christ are in a manner extended to Christians. 'Thou art my beloved Son, in thee I am well pleased' is an oracle of love that speaks to sinners, because they are among the number of whom Christ says: 'I and the children whom God has given me.'

'To know Christ is to know the benefits we derive from him,' says an old theologian. What benefit do we chiefly derive from him? The heavenly sonship which overflows from him to us. And how do we know him from that benefit? We see that what we have in part and by adoption he has by nature and in fullness, the pure and simple sonship is his. We do not best understand the Divine Father and the Divine Son by drawing analogies from human sons and human fathers, but by a method more real and more direct – that is, from experiencing divine sonship extended to ourselves.

But, having grasped the similarity, we must go on to seize the difference: the Son of God differs infinitely from us, his sonship from ours. It is usual to say that, whereas God *made* us, he begot his Son, but that is little better than a textbook formula. It draws a distinction, it does nothing to explain it. For we were not made, as we understand making, nor was he begotten, as we understand begetting. He was not begotten, for he was begotten in no womb, and we were not made, for we were made of no material. Both the only begotten Son and we, the many spirits created, depend and derive wholly from the Father of all. The Eternal Son is utterly derived, utterly dependent, but he is the full expression of his Father's nature and being, and, therefore, not less in nature or glory than the Father who begets him. The Son also is Eternal God, for otherwise the Father's act of begetting would be imperfect, he would not beget what is best or worthiest of himself. The Son has nothing that he does not derive from the Father, but he derives from the Father all the Father has to give. Were he not equal with the Father, he would lack the capacity to receive all that the Father has the bounty to bestow. His love, like ours, is a response and a reciprocation; and no spirit lower than God can reciprocate all the love of God. He depends on the Father not for less than we do, but for infinitely more. Like us, he depends on the Father for all things. We receive from the Father all we are, he alone receives from the Father all the Father is.

We were thinking just now of Moses, and the shining of his face by reflection of divine radiance. But what a narrow glass is the up-turned face of Moses to reflect the glory of the Light that warms the world! Only the face of God reflects the face of God, there alone is converse in true equality, and eyes that answer eyes with a perfect intelligence. St Paul, interpreting for us the shining of Moses' face, says that the God who inflows as light on Moses is the Holy Ghost. The apostle's interpretation is true to our experience; if we answer divine love it is by divine inspiration. But how little is there in us for the divine Spirit to inspire! The Holy Ghost is measured in us by the narrowness of our vessel, to the Eternal Son he gives himself without measure. The Son does not measure the Spirit by limiting him, he perfectly expresses him by perfectly receiving him. Holy Ghost means the divine life communicated or bestowed. Holy Ghost has no being except in another; the first and proper being of the Holy Ghost is in the Eternal Son.

What! Does the Eternal Son himself need to be inspired? If he is to answer his Father's love, cannot he answer of himself? The objection is a transposition into highest heaven of the famous English opinion that dependence on God is a weakness, that it would be better to be self-reliant. But Christianity leaves no place for the arguments of pride, least of all in the perfection of the Godhead. The Son delights to receive everything from his Father, and to draw all that is good from the only source of good. To answer the Father's love without the Father's inspiration would not (even if it were possible) be a heightening of bliss, but quite the reverse, for to be filled with God is exactly what we desire, or should desire; so what would be the blessedness of cutting off the channel? And heaven differs from earth chiefly in this, that the blessed are more completely dependent on God's inspiration than we are.

So there are two acts of God the Father, neither conceivable without the other – to beget and to bestow: to beget the Son, to bestow on him the Holy Ghost. Both acts are perfect: what is begotten is God, and what is bestowed is equally God. The divine Persons do not lack perfection by needing one another, for what they require they eternally possess. The Father does not lack for the expression of his Fatherhood, he expresses it perpetually in his Son. The Son lacks nothing of the Father's inspiration, since he has the Holy Ghost. The Spirit is not imperfectly real through being the completion of another's life; he enjoys perfection in being perfectly bestowed on a perfect recipient by a perfect giver. Here are not three Gods; here is one Godhead which can be what it essentially is, a society of Love, only through distribution in three Persons.

In the pursuit of such high mysteries our thought is lost; and yet the Trinity is no mere conjecture about the heart of Heaven. The Trinity is both the meaning and the setting of that love which the Father has actually bestowed upon us. We need have nothing to do with the Trinity as a cool speculation about the necessary nature of the Godhead; it would be idiocy to place such confidence in theological reasonings as to evolve it by rational argument. The Trinity is revealed to Christians because they are taken into the Trinity, because the threefold love of God wraps them round, because it is in the Trinity they have their Christian being. Every time I worship or pray or make the least motion of the heart towards God, I stand with the divine Son in face of the divine Father, the mantle of his sonship spread around me, and the love of the Father overflowing from him to me in the grace of the Holy Ghost.

A Christian who talks like this does not talk comfortably. His being in the Trinity is his Christian existence; it is the unspeakable gift of God's mercy to him. But all the gifts of God judge us as fast as they save us. It is the depth of my condemnation that I so meanly use the infinite generosity of God. And yet God's gifts save us as fast as they judge us, or they would not be gifts; his mercy prevails.

God above me, Father from whom my being descends, on whom my existence hangs, to whom I turn up my face, to whom I stretch out my hands:

God beside me, God in a man like me, Jesus Christ in the world with me, whose hand lays hold of me, presenting me, with yourself, to God:

God within me, soul of my soul, root of my will, inexhaustible fountain, Holy Ghost:

Threefold Love, one in yourself, unite your forces in me, come together in the citadel of my conquered heart.

You have loved me with an everlasting love. Teach me to care.

Thinking the Trinity

Another Trinity Sunday sermon, delivered in the Chapel of Trinity College Oxford in 1961, first published in A Celebration of Faith *and reprinted in* The Essential Sermons. *Yet another angle on Farrer's Trinitarian reflections, which also contain some of his distinctive thought about providence and creation. Citing an anonymous Jewish philosopher, Farrer says that 'God made the world, but He did not just make it; He made it make itself; for only so could it be itself.' He further says that, in the end, 'we cannot think the Blessed Trinity. But ... we can live the Trinity by grace of the Trinity.'*

When we were in America – and it feels odd, I must say, being in America. They treat the academic visitor as a talking book; the text is something you published twenty years ago, but footnotes, they hope are going to spurt *viva voce* from your living person, wherever they stick a pin into you. Under this sort of treatment, you can see that it is difficult not to grow a trifle pompous. And so there we were in a corner of New York, holding an open forum (or was it a colloquium?) and laying down the law about the action of the divine providence in the balancing of goods and evils. Some discussion ensued; until a Jewish scholar, whose presence had been hitherto unnoticed, pricked our little bubble for us. Not that he broke in – he waited for a full pause in the conversation; and when he spoke, it was with much gentleness. He had one of those thoughtful Jewish faces that seem to be moulded by a sense of their people's suffering, but at the same time by a patient faith in the God of Israel. He found it surprising, he said, to hear Christian theologians speculate so confidently on the place of pain and disaster in the counsels of God – a mystery which, not unnaturally, had occupied the Jewish mind a good deal. He said that he would express his own sense of the matter in a Jewish form, by quoting a rabbi of older days.

The rabbi's pupils came one morning and sat before him. They asked him the providential reason of some natural evil that had befallen – let us say that it was a neighbour's premature death. 'My children,' said the rabbi, 'there are questions into which a man may enter, and there is no way back out of them. Again, there are questions a man may enter upon, and there is a way back. And it is the first part of wisdom, when any question is proposed, to decide of which sort it is. Now I tell you that the question, why God permits this or that natural evil, is among the questions allowing of no way back, nor of any answer. And why? I will tell you this also. The Holy One (Blessed be He!) filled all immensity before the world was, and there was no place where He was not; and so neither was there any place where a world could be; for he was all, and in all. What did He do? He drew back the skirts of His glory, to make a little space where He was not; and there He created the world. And so, where the world is, there He is not. And that is why we look in vain for His hand in the chances of nature. Nevertheless (Blessed be He!) He has visited us with His lovingkindness.'

So said our Jewish philosopher; and when he had spoken, we had little appetite for resuming our previous discussion. We wanted to ponder the words of his ancient sage. There seemed to be a deep sense in them, but not a sense that lay on the surface. Obviously it takes you nowhere, to speak of God's being present or absent, in any plain way, at one place or another. In one way, he is everywhere absent, for no place bodily contains him. In another way, he is everywhere present; since whatever exists manifests his present will that it should exist; and as the Psalmist says, 'If I go down into hell, thou art there also.' For hell would not be, if God's will for its existence were withdrawn from it.

What, then, had the rabbi meant, when he spoke of God's vacating a space to allow for a world? We asked our Jewish friend, and he said the meaning was this: God gave the world room to be itself. He would not so inhabit it as to make it the passive reflection of his own ideas; or like the machine which does no more than embody the design of its constructor, and perform the wishes of its manipulator. God made the world, but he did not just make it; he made it make itself; for only so could it be itself. He released a half chaos of brimless forces as alien from his own being as anything could well be; and they blinded away, not in the paths of a godlike wisdom, but according to the very limited principles of action implanted in each. Nevertheless (said the rabbi), the Holy One has visited us with his lovingkindness; by an invisible art, and by a secret attraction, he has brought out of a blind interplay of forces many organised intricacies and much sentient life.

What, then, is the moral of the fable? The world is not like God, though it reveals his power and his glory. Nature is infinitely wasteful, but God wastes nothing. She is unfeeling; he is compassionate. She is blind; he is wise. For at the beginning and bottom of nature, there is a withdrawal, we may almost say a self-banishment, of God. Nature is not divine; we cannot be nature-worshippers, except by projecting upon nature a gilded image of our dreams. God made the world in unlikeness to himself; we look there in vain for the lineaments of his face. He made man in his own similitude, and it is in the face of man that we must look for the countenance of God.

Or rather, not in the face of man, but in the faces of men, turned towards one another; the light of understanding that passes between their eyes, in a sense that sounds through the interchange of their speech, in mutual liking kindled from heart to heart. Man's mind, not his bodily frame, is the similitude of God; and mentality always was a social, not a solitary, thing. We learnt to talk, because they talked to us; and to like, because they smiled at us. Because we could first talk, we can now think; that is, we can talk silently to the images of the absent, or we can pretend to be our own twin, and talk to ourself.

I can talk to myself, but it is hard work. How easily (alas for my pupils!) does my speech flow when I talk to them; with what sorrow and reluctance did I drive myself when I was preparing this sermon, although it was for people who have given me as much reason to like them as any people alive, and although the subject is of all others most fascinating. Yet it was a labour to compose, simply because you were not there, but only the visionary ghost of you. I had to pretend you; it was the best I could do.

God does not have to pretend; that is where he differs from us. He speaks with himself; but the self with whom he speaks, and who takes the responsive part, is a dear and real person, the Son of his love. And what they exchange between them is no fragmentary expression of a passing thought, it is the whole mind and heart and substance of their godhead.

That is all Christians know about the life of God. We can weigh it, and turn it over, and phrase it a hundred ways; we can consider it in relation to a hundred things; can guard it against a hundred misconceptions. But it all comes down to this; this is all we know. And even then, as you will be quick to tell me, we cannot know it; it baffles understanding. We cannot think of different persons, unless they are identified with several lumps of flesh; still less can we conceive a thought so powerful, that it really constitutes the Other in the mind, instead of merely pretending him. And so we cannot think the Blessed Trinity. But then, it is not required of us to think the Trinity. We can do better; we can live the Trinity by grace of the Trinity.

As I have implied already, the life of the Trinity is represented in us after two different fashions: in society with one another, and in discourse with one's self. Each fashion of representation has its special merit. Our society with our friends mirrors the reality of the Trinity; it is real society and the persons involved in it are real persons. A man's discourse with himself better represents the oneness of the Trinity: the divine Persons are as close to one another as a man's own thought is to a man; yes, and closer than that. Sometimes Holy Scripture speaks of a divine Father and a divine Son; and that is to speak of a society between kindred beings. Sometimes, on the other hand, Scripture speaks of God and his Word; and that is to use the figure of a single mind and its uttered expression. And I think you will find there are no other ways Scripture does take beyond these two, in writing of that supreme mystery.

It follows that we live the Trinity, in some sense, just by being men; and it is no blasphemy to say that this dear Trinity of ours [Trinity College, Oxford], in all the companionship it engenders or indeed, of which it consists, is the offspring of the divine Spirit. More particularly in the special work of a college, where the younger learn from the elder, and the elder find happiness in the vitality of younger wits, you have an enactment of the Blessed Trinity; a Trinity in which there is a Father and a Son, and yet no disparity, but an equal delight of each in each. But then again, it is specially characteristic of a college, that our studies, with all accompanying sidelines of mental stimulation, drive us to exercise in a more than trivial way that high privilege of a rational being, to enter into converse with himself, and to beget upon his own thought a new achievement of understanding.

Any man then, who has the character to be either a thinker or a friend lives the Trinity in some fashion, whether he is a Christian or not. Has not God made us all in his own similitude? We can achieve nothing truly human which is not also in a manner divine. And we may wonder without end at the simple fact, that anything so godlike as common friendship, or as ordinary rational discourse, should be actualised in physical bodies. These things are the masterpieces of the Creator, and in these he delights.

And yet the Blessed Trinity has a higher delight in us, and we a more heavenly partaking in the life of the Trinity, by our being Christians. We may see how this is, if we recall that what the divine Persons love in one another is not something that just happens to be; it is the perfect truth of eternal godhead. The Father loves the Son for perfectly expressing this; the Son adores the Father as the fount and archetype of all that his own being expresses. So Christians, in so far as they are Christians, like in their friends not what merely happens to be in them, good or bad; they prize in one another with a special regard what is sincerely good; that is to say, what expresses the goodness and the beauty of God. They see the will of God in one another's lives; they love the Creator Himself in his handiwork.

Or again, to speak of that other looking-glass of the Trinity, the discourse a man has with himself. That *alter ego* in the mind with whom we converse need not be the mere complacent shadow of our own desires, the bosom flatterer who is our own worst enemy: nor even the mere logical judge, the inner critic who forbids our getting away with dishonest argument. The Christian may go further; he may draw into converse with him an imagined other self who speaks for the very will of God. He may square his account with eternal truth and sovereign majesty, so far as he can find them in his heart, or see them bear upon his present life. Then suddenly he is not talking with himself at all, or with any system of his own imagining. The other person of his inward colloquy takes on the very name and character of the Creator. The principle of an eternal law warms with the kindness of a Father's care, encouraging us to speak with him as sons. So a Person of the divine Trinity, the Father of Heaven, shows through one of the parties to our inner dialogue. But no sooner has this happened, than the other participant is similarly transformed. When we respond in filial duty to so heavenly a Father, our very self reveals the action, and expresses the person of his heavenly Son. Who does not know that when we genuinely pray, it is Christ who prays in us? And as for the bond of mutual liking which unites the two persons of our colloquy, it is no other than the inspiration of the Holy Spirit; for where the Father and the Son are, there is he.

What I have spoken of is no exalted mystical ecstasy; it is just praying, or even, without the form of prayer, any attending to the presence and will of our Creator. *Tota Trinitas illabitur menti,* the whole Trinity moves into the mind, says the great St Augustine, writing of this very thing. But we have better authority. 'We will come, and make our abode with him,' says the Christ of St John's Gospel. 'We' – that is, the Father and the Son, by the indwelling of the Holy Spirit. And with whom will they take up their abode? With the man who 'will keep my words', says Christ; who guards and honours by his obedience this treasure in the soul, this viceroy of Heaven in the heart, the revealed thought and will of the godhead; a word able to come alive and to address us from the lips of God, drawing us into that happy converse, which brings the Trinity to earth, and raises earthly life to Heaven: where to the Triune Sovereignty alone is, was and shall be ascribed, as is most justly due, all might, dominion, majesty and power, in all eternity.

Part Three
Reason

A Midwinter Daydream

First published in 1951 in University: A Journal of Inquiry, *Volume 1, reprinted as 'A Theologian's Point of View' in* The Socratic, *Volume 5, 1952, and then slightly abridged as 'Theology and Philosophy' in* Reflective Faith. *A wonderful dialogue first between personifications of Philosophy and Theology, and then between Theology and a student. Philosophy here speaks in the voice of the dominant logical positivism of Farrer's day, and Theology responds in the voice of both Farrer himself and Lionel Thornton (1884–1960), a fellow Anglican philosopher and a priest of the Community of the Resurrection. The dialogue addresses the tense relation between theology and philosophy in the middle of the twentieth century, the nature of analogical thinking, and God's self-limitation in the incarnation. To be truly human, Farrer says, Christ must have thought as a real human of a particular time and place. Therefore, the Jewish context of early Christianity is indispensable, and cannot be stripped away in favour of a 'purely rational' philosophical perspective.*

I had a dream. There were Theology and Philosophy clothed in both the moral and the academic dignity of female professors. Theology held several slips of paper in her hand, with a single sentence written upon each: 'God exists' on one, 'The world was created' on another. Philosophy displayed several baskets on a table, marked with tickets describing sentences of different logical kinds, 'Moral Commands', 'Empirical Statements', 'Truths of Definition', and so forth. 'Into which of my baskets, dear Theology,' she said, 'would you like to put your statements?'

Theology looked at the baskets and hesitated. 'Do I have to?' she replied. 'I mean, is it certain that the right basket for my statements is on your table at all? Of course if it were demonstrable that all the possible sorts of logic baskets were represented here ...'

'Dear me, no,' said Philosophy, 'we can't claim to be sure of that. But don't you find some of these baskets rather alluring? Here is a brand new one, delivered only this morning by Logical Baskets Limited (limited, you know, or virtually so, to Oxford and Cambridge). It is called "Expressions of Attitude to Life". Isn't that what you want? Now be reasonable.'

'No, I'm afraid not,' Theology replied. 'You see when I say, "God loves what He has made," I do not mean that John Christian takes up, or would be well advised to take up, a benevolent attitude to things in general or to his neighbour in particular; nor that he either does or should view them in the rosy light cast upon them by association with the creator-God image. No, I mean what I say; I mean that the actual creator is doing this actual loving.'

'Good God!' said Philosophy, 'you don't say so! Well, if that's how it is, Basket Four is what you require,' pointing to a basket labelled 'Statements about Other Persons'. 'And in that case,' she continued, beginning to talk exceedingly fast, 'your statements will of course be subject to the routine tests of empirical verificability and falsificab ...'

'Please, please, not again,' said Theology, raising her hands to her ears. 'We've had this so many times before. Haven't I told you that statements about God are not statements about a person among persons, but about that transcendent subject to whom our personal existence bears only a distant, though a real, analogy?'

'And so,' said Philosophy, 'I suppose you are let off any attempt at relating your statements to real life.'

'Dear me, no,' said Theology, 'I don't get off that. Almost all religious thinking relates statements about God with statements or directions concerned with common life. Lots of people know how to do such thinking, but to know what its logical nature may be is a different matter. Perhaps you and I might hold a joint class, to find out how such thinking goes. I fear it will have to be an Advanced Class for theological talk will turn out to be less simple in its logic, I suspect, than "It is sweet and commendable to die for our country" or "This garden is kept by a gardener whom no one has caught at work."'

'Ah, I dare say,' said Philosophy. 'But as it would be foolish to anticipate the findings of your Advanced Class, allow me to take up another point here. You were saying that you attach great importance to the literal sense of "God loves what he has made". But the next moment you were protesting that the divine person is only distantly analogous to human persons, and so, presumably, that his making is only distantly analogous to human making, and his loving to human loving. If so, you mayn't seem to be saying anything very literal, or very clear, when you say that God loves what he has made. Are such meagre dregs of meaning worth bothering about? You have conceded agnosticism already. Be an atheist and have done with it.'

Theology replied: 'It isn't only believers in an Unknown God who admit that their talk comes far short of expressing God or his doings. We should all be agnostics if our knowledge of God were our exploration of him; as though God sat there impassive as a rock-cut Buddha, and we tortoises vainly tried to scale his knees. We cannot aspire to talk about God in (as it were) divine language, but he can stoop, if he chooses, to talk to us in our language and to deal humanly with mankind. When, for example, for us men and for our salvation ...'

On hearing these dogmatic words, Philosophy muttered, 'We will hear thee another time on this matter,' and faded away to tea, followed by the Stoics and Epicureans. Theology was left addressing the empty Areopagus, except that I could see the Areopagite Denys skulking behind a column, and a woman called Damaris looking over the wall.

'Won't you come in, my dear?' said Theology to Damaris. Damaris entered, pulling on a commoner's gown. She produced a pencil and notebook as though from nowhere, but on being assured that the subject in hand was of no Schools value she was persuaded to put them away again and converse like a human being. She had, in fact, thought of an Intelligent Question: 'I think I see what you mean,' she began, 'when you say it doesn't matter so much our not being able to talk straight about God, so long as he talks straight to us. You would say he does that specially in the Gospel?'

Theology assented. 'But,' Damaris continued, 'doesn't that make God talk a terribly incorrect language? I mean, the Jews knew nothing about it really, did they, and they mixed up their logical types like anything. And we find Christ talking just like a Jew. And it isn't only the language, it's the ideas. He said he was Messiah, and you can't understand what that means without a whole lot of Jewish history. And it's the same with everything else, for instance, how he meant the sacrament would be his body and blood.'

'I know,' said Theology. 'But we can't have it both ways, can we? If God comes down to our level and talks to us in our speech, it will have to be the speech of some one time and place. When he was fully grown he had the thought-forms of a bible-minded Jew; before that, he had used the broken speech of childhood.'

'That sounds all right in theory,' said Damaris, 'but the Jews' ideas were so queer, and it is all so far away now.'

'Queer, if you like,' said Theology, 'but expressive for the purpose. You could talk vividly about divine things and be understood in the streets of Galilee, just try at our street corners, or – or here in our Areopagus. And as to your 'Far away' – two thousand years are two thousand years, but there is always a bridge. For those ideas you speak of have lived on and partly moulded, partly adopted the forms of every age from then till now.'

'What should we do then?' said Damaris. 'Should we try to strip away the Jewish stuff as much as we can?'

'No, I don't think so,' said Theology: 'my business anyhow is to understand the Scripture in its ancient dress and see what is signified to us through it. You don't understand Shakespeare by stripping away Elizabethan England: and it is a more weighty matter to understand God. Yet understanding Shakespeare is no unreal dramatization of yourself as an Elizabethan, and to understand Christ is not to dramatize yourself as an ancient Jew.

'Now here is a book,' said Theology, rummaging in her brief-case, 'called *Revelation and the Modern World,* which I have been given to review. Dr Lionel Thornton does not get round to saying much about the modern world. He opens his readers' eyes to the way in which Apostles and Evangelists thought. He describes, in our language, systems of imagery and implication which the ancients never dreamt of describing, because they lived in them. After doing this for us, Dr Thornton does not bring us back to our modern world. He does not need to. We are in it all the time, and if we have been seriously grasping the ancient speech under our author's guidance, and taking it to ourselves, we shall have been making the modern translation for ourselves – if, indeed, it is right to say that we do anything quite for ourselves in the sphere of revealed truth. May I recommend Dr Thornton as Lent reading for the intelligent? The effort required will be penance enough for the season, and the profit derived an assistance to the enjoyment of Easter.'

Denys, feeling these remarks to be unfair, came alive and carried Theology and Damaris off to tea.

Faith and Evidence

Published in 1964 as the first chapter of Saving Belief: A Discussion of Essentials. *This book was reprinted in 1994 but this chapter was unfortunately marred by the omission of an entire page. A brilliant, deceptively simple discussion of the proper relation between faith and reason (evidence), which also brings in all sorts of other considerations, including imagination, ethics and the question of truth. Farrer says, 'A God could show himself through his creation, and it is the simple conviction of believers that God does. But if he does, he shows through the evidence more than hard-headed calculation could build out of the evidence; and the readiness to accept that "more" will be faith, or the effect of faith.' And he concludes the chapter with the provocative claim that 'God doesn't limit us by being limited; he only limits us by being true.'*

Approaching the Christian religion from without, and wondering how people get in, one meets the strange assertion that the key of entry is faith. Those who have faith (it seems) can turn the lock; those who have none stay outside. The assertion sounds baffling to would-be entrants, and fishy to detached critics. A great deal has been said and a great deal written by the keepers of the door, to explain how keys can be cut, and how the lock can be lubricated; but it never seems quite good enough, and so we find ourselves trying again.

What are we to say? First of all, that faith is not any sort of instrument, or tackle, with which we can arm ourselves beforehand; nothing like a key or, to change the figure, nothing like a fishing-line with which religious convictions are hooked and drawn to land. We must provide ourselves with tackle before we can usefully think of fishing a pond; but faith is not a tackle, but (shall we say?) an attitude of mind, and it is an awkward job to take up an attitude, until you are face to face with the object which calls for it. When we want to make fun of the more portentous Germans, we say they are the sort to take up attitudes of welcome or of distrust, of mastery or of reverence, towards existence, or towards things in general, without first considering whether the objects they encounter are such as to call for the attitudes they adopt. The accusation is probably as unjust as other generalizations about national characteristics; we are less concerned to accuse the Germans than we are to flatter ourselves. We, of course, are men who appreciate our objects, and let our objects determine our attitudes. We think it silly to treat animals (for example) as if they were persons, and imperceptive to treat them as though they were machines. Only if we appreciate them for what they are, shall we react to them as they deserve. Is religious faith the appropriate attitude to deity? If it is, we cannot talk much sense about it, until we first have some perception, or conception, of God.

It does not look as though we should get faith first, and the object of faith second; nor do we in fact. What does happen to us, and how is it that we get round to raising the issue of faith? It begins with our hearing about God or, if we are clever enough, thinking thoughts about him for ourselves. If anything of importance is to follow, the thought we think, or the tale we are told, must be initially persuasive. We must feel, as we say, the force of it. At least part of our mind must be saying, Yes, surely there *is* a first creative cause, surely there is a supreme directive will, a saviour of men, a bestower of grace, or whatever it be. But presently, being reasonable people, we ask ourselves what is the basis of our feeling or persuasion that such things are at all true. In answer to our own question we may state plenty of reasons for believing such things. In spite of all the subtleties of the philosophers, I still think there must be some exterior cause or maker of the world; or I tell myself that the virtue of the heroic saints is something which irreligion does not produce, and which goes above human nature; and I am not prepared to brush aside these men's own account of what it is that has happened to them. Here are reasons, reasons of a kind; and for a while we may be highly pleased with them. But it will not be long before we become aware of opposing reasons; and there seems to be no simple logical method for deciding conclusively between the *pros* and the *cons*. No simple logical method, no, nor any advanced logical method, either. For only look at those famous philosophical twins, Russell and Whitehead, the co-inventors of mathematical logic and the joint authors of an epoch-making book. One of them turned out an atheist, the other a theist; and neither could show the other the error of his ways. Russell now has the advantage, in the continued opportunity to propagate his ideas; but Whitehead has the advantage (let us hope) of now knowing conclusively that Russell is wrong.

Met by such facts as these, we are driven to ask what it is that decides our minds for, or against, religious conviction. Since it is not sheer logic, or plain evidence, what can it be? What but the faith which one man has, and another has not? The believer gives his confidence to the positive reasons, as a voter gives his confidence to the Liberals. The voter knows perfectly well that the practicability or the usefulness of the Liberal proposals can be plausibly contested; but still, on balance, he decides to support them. He has a faith in Liberalism. And so, we may suppose, a man has faith in God.

There is some merit in the political comparison; it brings out the practical character of the decision. If we say to the ardent politician, 'Why not leave the issue open? After all, you can't be sure,' we know very well what he will reply. 'The country's going to the dogs; we can't sit with our hands in our laps. If we do nothing, we are for it, anyway. It may be there are better remedies than those we propose, but meanwhile things are going from bad to worse and we can't wait everlastingly for Royal Commissions to send in reports.' And so a believer may say, 'I've only seventy years, if that, to make anything of my life; I can't indefinitely postpone the question whether I have a God or whether I have to be God to myself.'

But we must not exaggerate the role of practical urgency. It justifies acting upon faith; it does not make the faith. If a man says, 'It's urgent that something should be done and I've a vote; so I'll spin a coin between the Liberals and the Socialists,' then even if the penny comes down on the Liberal side of the argument, the voter cannot be said to have faith in Liberalism. Faith implies genuine persuasion; and persuasion is not genuine unless it comes from the thing which persuades us. It cannot be got going by stoking up the furnaces of the will.

The believer in Liberalism, like the believer in God, is first captured by a story. It is only afterwards that he becomes aware of the faith-factor in his being so captured; and that happens when he becomes aware of counter-persuasions, yet persists in his Liberal conviction. The counter-persuasions make him aware of the faith-factor; they do not create it. Faith becomes self-conscious in exerting itself against the counter-persuasions; but it was there already. It was, in fact, built into the persuasion from the start. Liberalism is, as we say, a political faith.

We see, then, that faith is neither an attitude we adopt in looking for an object of conviction, nor an attitude we work up to bolster a conviction already lodged in our minds. Either we are persuaded or not persuaded, that is the starting-point. If we are persuaded, some element of faith is there; it is a matter of its maintaining itself or not maintaining itself against rival persuasions.

The difficulty about faith is not a difficulty about faith in general, or about the enormous part that it plays in every department of life. The difficulty about faith is a difficulty about religious faith in particular, because it is so unlike other examples of faith; not because it resembles them. And so we shall cast no great light on the question, by plugging trivial parallels such as that of the political vote. The difference is, after all, so startling. Belief in God is belief in his existence; belief in the Liberals involves no such affirmation. The Liberals exist, in any case; 'Worse luck!' you may add, if you deplore the splitting of the white-collar vote – for it takes a whole white collar to meet round the neck of an English prime minister. What the Liberal voter affirms is that the Liberals are worthy of trust; that is the subject of debate. Whereas no one who is not hysterical or deranged debates whether God or the devil is to be trusted. God is trustworthy, by definition, always supposing that he exists.

The difficulty of religious faith may be put in a nutshell. How can an attitude of trustfulness, evidently appropriate to God if he exists, be appropriate to a decision whether he exists or not? I can trust him if he exists, how can I trust him to exist? Imagine saying to the Horatio in Shakespeare's play, 'Horatio, you are such a trustworthy man, I am sure we can trust you to exist; you wouldn't go and let us down by never having existed.' Either he exists, or he doesn't – either Shakespeare invents him, or draws him from the life.

The absurdity we have expressed is so flagrant, that it has led to the denial of any faith-element in a conviction of God's existence. This used to be almost the official Roman Catholic view. We believe in God (it was said) by force of reason; by faith we trust the promises he gives us through accredited channels of revelation, once they are accredited; our acceptance of the channels as authoritative cannot itself repose on faith. Such is, or was, the high and dry scholastic doctrine. As a positive account of the matter, it is utterly useless, and we have already shown why. It is useless, because it involves us in accusing all well-informed atheists either of mental imbecility or of intellectual dishonesty, or of both. As though their disinclination to believe in God were on all fours with the bias I feel against the tax-inspector's estimate of my liability. I tell myself that it cannot come to so much; but facts and arithmetic will persuade me. If they will not, then I am a wilful self-deceiver, or an incapable reckoner, or both. Now I am simply not prepared to bring an accusation of this kind against my godless friends. Since I myself believe, I must suppose that they suffer from some bias in disbelieving; but it is not the sort of bias that turns away from cogent reasons. It is just that subtle and elusive bias which leads to misjudgment in matters of faith.

So we cannot say with the scholastics that faith only comes in later, when we trust the explicit promises of God. There is some element of faith there from the start. Yet the scholastic formula is correct in drawing a distinction between two operations of faith. We trust God to fulfil his promises; we cannot, in the same way, trust him to exist. Faith does not work in the same way in the two cases. And perhaps it might help to have another word than faith to describe our initial attitude in believing God's existence. But until we can think of a word for the job, let us go on saying 'faith', while trying to distinguish one sort of faith from the other.

The faith we are speaking of is a deeply felt personal attitude, even if it is not exactly an attitude of trust. Let us look for an example which might be in some way parallel.

There is a stock scene of Victorian fiction – I do not know how many times it occurs. The seeming orphan, brought up by a hard-faced aunt, is suddenly confronted by his real mother. The mother does her best not to give herself away; but a sort of warm, pinkish wave of sentimental electricity tingles through the child; he is strangely moved, he knows not why. Nonsense, I say; ten to one, the child would experience nothing. Undisclosed, actual mothers can be encountered by seven-year-olds with equanimity. What cannot be a subject of indifference to them is the suggestion of a possible mother, if it actually comes to mind. Our orphan child, let us assume, has some access to normal families. He knows what a mother is. Then one day he says to himself, 'Goodness! Suppose I really have got a mother! They say she disappeared in the Revolution, when I was brought to America. They say she was killed, but I wonder!' The child's mind alternates between hope and resignation. The suggestion that there might be a mother is not an isolated factual hypothesis; it is a picture of the world, with an attitude built in; it is filial existence in place of orphan existence.

In much the same way, the suggestion that there is God contains built-in attitudes. We are too much inclined to think of a disputed idea as a drawing over there on the blackboard, a bloodless diagram about which you and I are calmly deliberating whether to fill it in with the colours of real existence, or not. Such an account is always misleading, but not always equally misleading. It is supremely misleading in cases like those we are considering. For the child, to think of a possible mother is to experiment in having a mother; to try filial existence. The experiment takes place in the realms of imagination, but it is real enough to the heart. And similarly to think of a possible God is to experiment in having God. The attitude of creature to Creator, of doomed mortal to immortal saviour, is built into the very idea. The heart goes out to God, even to a possible God; whether we should call the attitude 'faith' or something else, is a question of little consequence.

That thought of God, from which faith could conceivably spring, is a contested affirmation; it is not a matter of mere curiosity, or of poetic contemplation, like the figure of a nymph in a dead mythology. If the human mind were absolutely single and unitary, like the mind of God himself, we could not make contested affirmations; as it is, the loose texture of our mental life allows us to do so. I say 'There is God', and a piece of my heart goes with it; I add 'Perhaps', my state of being changes; I go on 'But then ...' and my attitude swings into the opposite. Which of my thoughts, which of my attitudes, is I, or speaks for me? It is notorious that I may be deceived in thinking myself committed in one direction, when I am really committed in another. But so long as I know very well that I am not committed, I do not think of claiming to have faith. Yet the faith attitude is there, if it is no more than one posture among several which I try by turns. To have faith in the full sense, I do not need to bring it from somewhere else, and apply it to the idea; all I need to do is to let it have its way, and subdue its rivals.

But why should I? Why should I let faith have its way? Not, surely, on its own evidence. The orphan's painful interest in the idea of a possible mother is no evidence that he has a mother. His concern is not traceable to telepathic waves radiating from his mother's heart, and agitating his. It is traceable (I suppose) to two factors, the pattern of nature, and the organized environment. Nature brings children from a womb and feeds them at a breast and turns them to their mothers for after-care; social organization gives shape and development to the pattern of nature. As to our orphan, a woman bore him, family life goes on around him. His deep concern over the mother-possibility is no evidence that he *has* a mother; but only that he had, and perhaps that it is a pity he has not.

Never mind (the believer may say); for in the analogous case of concern over the possibility of God, the distinction we have just drawn does not apply. If we *had* a creator, we *have* a God. A child may have lost his mother, a creature cannot, in the same sense, have lost his creator. God may lose his creatures, unless he makes them immortal; he is eternal, they cannot lose their God.

The sceptical counter to this move is obvious. The comparison, as now refashioned, has lost all reality. As it is a question whether we have a God, so it is a question to the orphan, whether he *has* a mother. It never was a question to anyone, orphan or otherwise, whether he *had* a mother. You cannot run a plausible line in ametrist propaganda, to persuade the human race that its members had no mothers, but that they grew on gooseberry bushes. You can run a plausible line in atheist propaganda, to persuade us that nature, without God, is the sufficient cause of our existence. There can be no ametrist propaganda, and why? Because the general belief in maternity has no more to do with faith, or personal concern, than has general belief in the movement of the tides. I could not be a witness to my own birth, but I can be a witness to as many births as I like. My heart may be ice-cold on the issue of general maternity – I may not be concerned in the least; the facts will persuade me, though I may actually loathe the thought of origin from a woman's body. Whereas it seems that without a positive attitude of some kind, I shall not be convinced of God.

Yes, the fact of my birth from a mother, and the fact (if fact it is) of my creation by God, are certainly very different facts. All parables are imperfect, or they would not be parables. Wisdom lies in seeing how far any comparison will take us, and at what point it must desert us. The scholastics liked to reiterate the platitude that while God is all the deity there is, an individual such as my mother is not her whole sort – she is not all the maternity there is. Unable to verify my birth from her, I can turn to the childbearing of other women. If I am unable to verify my creation by my God, I cannot turn to the creative action of other Gods. But neither can I turn to other creative acts of the same God. For God's creativity is all one, and it underlies the whole of finite existence in an identical way. God is all the deity there is, and creation is all the creation there is. I cannot refer from an obscure example to a plain example; and, in particular, I cannot refer from the example of my own creation to the example of any other being's; my own example is likely to be the plainest I can find.

God's creatorship will have to be appreciated if it is to be acknowledged; and it will not be any cause for surprise, if appreciation on our part requires an appreciative, or responsive, attitude; that attitude of initial faith which we are trying to characterize.

There are two points in what we have just said, which we should like to develop a little. First, that God's creatorship is the sort of fact to be acknowledged by some kind of appreciation; and second, that there are examples enough elsewhere of objective facts depending upon an appreciative attitude for their recognition by us.

First, then, that God's creatorship is the sort of fact to be known by 'appreciation'. It is so, because of the way in which God transcends us. Everyone, however little he reckons to be a philosopher, has heard the blessed word 'transcendence'. God, if he is God, must infinitely transcend, or outsoar, his noblest creatures, not merely in power and greatness, but by the sort of being he has. If our finite being is to be evidence for God's infinite being, it has somehow to speak to us of what is infinitely above itself. When Robinson Crusoe saw a naked footprint on the sand of his island, it did not take him half a second to conclude that a man had been there. For, to look no further, he had manhood in himself, and the recipe for footprints in his own familiar knowledge. Suppose we attempt an analogy, and say that we recognize our own existent being as the print of God's creative act. How then are we to say that we achieve the recognition? We have not the divine nature in ourselves, nor do we know the recipe for printing off created beings from an eternal existence. We are bound, admittedly, to suppose in ourselves some faint resemblance of the divine nature, some acquaintance with a recipe for originating what was not there before; else how could we pretend to hold the slightest clue to God or his creative act? Nevertheless, human nature is far removed from godhead, and human creativity (so-called) from that creatorship which is the prerogative of God. If, then, our own being is to act as a footprint indicating our creator, he must have somehow made himself felt in the evidence, or spoken through the sign. And why not, since he is everywhere present if he exists at all, and the very thought by which we think him depends on his power and his will? A God could show himself through his creation, and it is the simple conviction of believers that God does. But if he does, he shows through the evidence more than hard-headed calculation could build out of the evidence; and the readiness to accept that 'more' will be faith, or the effect of faith.

Without the readiness of faith, the evidence of God will not be accepted, or will not convince. This is not to say that faith is put in the place of evidence. What convinces us is not our faith, but the evidence; faith is a subjective condition favourable to the reception of the evidence.

When an unbeliever hears what we have just said, he takes it that faith is an irrational makeweight to turn a scale weighted by reason on the other side. The evidence for God, he thinks, is intrinsically unconvincing; it is made to convince by the introduction of a selfish and infantile prejudice. Faith believes what she wishes to believe. The believer remains unshaken by the accusation. To him, the evidence is intrinsically and of itself convincing, but only under conditions which allow it to be appreciated. Faith supplies the conditions. Seeing is believing; but visible evidence is itself of no force in pitch darkness. If the scene is flooded with cunningly selected rays of multi-coloured light, illumination may provide nothing but illusion. If the scene is lighted with good plain sunlight, it simply gets the chance to reveal itself.

Well, but we are not talking of ocular evidence. No man has seen God at any time. We are talking of intelligible evidence. And again, we are not talking of sunlight, we are talking of a mental attitude.

How then can the parable apply? It may perfectly well apply; and this brings us to the second point we proposed to develop. For we are all familiar with regions of intelligible fact which are only perceptible in the sunlight of a favourable attitude. Sympathy does not create the personal facts it descries, it reveals them; and there are many true facts sympathy appreciates, to which suspicion closes our eyes. I am not denying that sympathy lies open to imposture, or that suspicion is a necessary guard. I am saying what everybody knows – that the place of suspicion is secondary and subsequent. Without the initial venture of sympathy, suspicion has nothing material to criticize. I may justly suspect my own sympathies; but I must have them first. To speak of sympathy for God would, indeed, be an impertinence; we may however dare to speak of openness, or acceptingness towards God.

The comparison between knowledge of God by faith, and knowledge of mankind by sympathy, is like other parables; nothing is more instructive about it than its inadequacy. Only consider the dissimilarity of the matters compared. We understand our neighbours through our common humanity; we are the same sort of animal, we are reared in the same culture. Failure of understanding through lack of sympathy can never be entire. We cannot fail to see that, behind the phenomena of their actions or utterances, they are men to themselves, as we are. We cannot fail to understand the plain sense of much that they say, or the plain intention of much that they do. We may fail to see the soul, the charm, the kindness, the subtlety – our picture may be cruelly impoverished, but an outline will remain.

Whereas God is not the animal that we are, nor an animal at all. We do not share an identity of nature with him, but are the remote offprints of his likeness. To acknowledge the infinite Creator in the facts of finite existence requires therefore a positive attitude, an incipient faith, from the very start. What is required for an appreciation of the godlike in our fellow-beings is required for any recognition of God whatever. The blind eye of suspicion may reduce our neighbour to a cunning beast; it can utterly shut out the being of God.

But is it not a cruel and an unjust fate which makes the acknowledgement of God depend upon the forthcomingness of faith? If this is the knowledge supremely worth having, how unreasonable that the lack of faith should preclude it! Yes, if faith were a capricious visitant; no, if faith is natural. The knowledge of humanity which is supremely worth having is denied to cynicism and mistrust; no one calls this an injustice, because sympathy is natural, mistrust and cynicism are vicious. That is not to deny that some men are so warped by circumstance, that they are cynical or mistrustful by no fault of their own. And so it is true that many men are incapable of faith. They can be cured, however, and God will cure them, whether in this life or hereafter.

In the sense required by the present argument, faith is natural, for it is no inexplicable or occasional visitant of the human mind; it is built into our human predicament. But there are so many senses in which we would not call it 'natural', that we had better list them if we are to avoid misunderstanding. First, and most obviously, it is not natural to the human *animal;* it is natural to the human spirit at a certain level of development. Until there is the capacity to think of a sovereign Power, it would be foolish to talk of natural faith in any sense that concerns us. Second, it is not natural in the sense of effortless, as resentment of injuries is called natural in contrast with magnanimity. It is natural as certain virtues and duties are said to be natural; the acknowledgement of them arises out of our common predicament, though the exercise of them requires what is called 'character' in a man. Third, it is not 'natural' as lying on one level with our concern for the natural (that is, the created) order. Faith is no more a natural attitude, in this sense, than theology is part of natural history. Faith cuts across that obsession with the natural world which has the name of 'naturalism'; it breaks into another dimension, the rootedness of the natural order in God. Compared with the dimension of nature, we may fairly call this dimension 'supernatural'. Yet it is not unnatural to man, since man is no mere part of nature. Through reason and free choice he partakes of the divine likeness, and has a 'natural' concern with the Creative Will.

Faith seems, in the only possible sense of 'natural', supremely natural to herself; and, if she is to claim validity, must claim to be natural to mankind. Since she is felt to be unnatural by numbers of men, she is bound to view them as the victims of an unnatural habit, which has become in them a 'second nature': an ingrained prejudice, a subconscious resolve to count God out, an unacknowledged voluntary blindness. If it be asked how such a distortion can have taken hold, heaven knows there is no lack of explanations. The corruptions of faith herself are so many and so appalling as to allow atheism to pass for illumination. The evidence of faith is that it convincingly shows us things in their true colours; having once seen man in God, we know that we have seen man as he is; we can never again believe another picture of ourselves, our neighbours, or our destinies. But superstition and bigotry can so darken and blind the eyes, that nothing is visible in its true colours, or, indeed, with any colour at all; superstition is a night in which everything is either black or else invisible; and atheism or so-called humanism is the very break of day compared with it. But the aversion from faith need not be motived by faith's corruptions. Men turn from faith, because to acknowledge God is to acknowledge *my God,* and men either hate, or fear, to admit that they have a God, or that there is any will sovereign over their own. If they do not fear God, they may fear to be deceived, in wagering their existence on uncertain hopes.

Both the scandal of faith, and the force of it, lie in the fact that the (possible) God of our belief must be *my God* to each of us. Apart from the implied relationship, there is no field in which the peculiar action of faith can be deployed. It is this that makes the absurd banality of the common comparison between faith in God, and the readiness of a scientific investigator to assume a hypothesis. The action or being of God can actually be handled as a hypothesis in a scientific argument; but then, so long as a scientific level of treatment is maintained, there is no place for the attitude of faith. And why? Because the God of the hypothesis does not appear in the guise of 'my God'. If, for example, an act of God is tried as an explanation for the beginning of the world process. Then the name of God is a mere pawn in the game of cosmological chess. The God-pawn may keep its place on the board, or it may lose it, being captured by the forces of the rival argument. The man is interested in working out the game, he is not interested in one piece more than in another; he is not experimenting in the faith-attitude, he is solving a problem according to the rules. The God-hypothesis is maintained, and proceeded upon, to see what it is good for in a given field of explanation; there is no flicker of faith towards God. And why? He does not appear in the guise of 'my God', but only as the possible explanation for a train of events.

What I have just written is, as I can see, terribly indiscreet; I give myself bound into the hands of the Philistines. Everyone is going to exclaim, that we cannot hope to think fairly or to think straight, so long as we are engaged with a disturbing and emotionally charged idea, the idea of 'my God' – the possibility that I have a God, or rather, that God has me for a creature. Whether the idea attracts or alarms, the emotional racket is equally loud; I can't hear myself think. The first move must be to disinfect, to objectivize the idea; and that means considering it in a context which isolates it from all this 'me' and 'mine'.

By all means (we will reply) let the evidence for religious beliefs be stated as objectively as it allows of being stated. But how objectively is that? God alone has access to the life of God in God; his creatures will scarcely claim to know anything of him, but through the part he plays in creaturely existence. God cannot be known simply as God; he must be known, if at all, as the God of ... 'Very well,' you may say: 'but why as the God of *me*?'

At this point I find myself driven to make an avowal which will, I dare say, be regarded as utterly discrediting. I am going to admit that all genuine evidence for God's existence reckons in the quality of human existence, and that if we take ourselves out of the picture, the evidence vanishes. Take the most abstract argument that can be stated for God as the cause of the world. You would say, would you not, that if the argument is valid, it would be just as valid, had there never been men at all. It professes to take the form 'No God, no galaxies' or, if you like, 'No God, no gas – no God, no anything.' What have the special qualities of human existence to do with the issue?

I reply, that however abstract, however scientific, such an argument is made to sound, the scientific colouring is largely irrelevant to the theological conclusion. The argument really is, that nothing can exist in the finite, changeable way without depending upon an eternal and boundless existence. We can narrow the issue still further: the whole argument is about the single word 'exist'. How can I know that to *exist* (in the changeable and finite way with which alone we are directly acquainted) is to require a changeless and infinite Cause? I shall need to have some insight into *existing* before I can argue like that. And where shall I find it, but in my own case? We credit existence to the galaxies, and rightly; we experience existing in ourselves.

We can argue to God from the galaxies – certainly we can; we can endeavour to show that, impressive or far-spreading as they are, and unimaginably old, they need God in order to exist, just as much as we do. 'As much as we do' – that is it; unless we could extend to the galaxies, by however remote analogy, the existence we have in ourselves, we should not even know what we mean in saying that they exist. To prove the God of the galaxies is to prove the God of existent creatures, and of existent creatures I am the type. I cannot prove the God of the galaxies without proving my God.

If we say that the base of the argument for God's existence is an argument drawn from man's existence, we make ourselves an easy target for ridicule. Aren't we taking ourselves a little too seriously? The God we need to prove is the God of the world; and what is man's place in the world? Pre-human history was ten thousand times as long as human history has been; and post-human history may be ten thousand times as long again. Even while we are here, what is our part? Are we not dust upon the star-dust of illimitable space? And how is it that we come to be here at all? We are the most casual of by-products. As fungus grows in rotting trees, so life is parasitic on energies breaking down. Here we have a splendid theme of stock rhetoric. I could keep it up for hours, and so could you. But enough is enough. For all these sounding rhetorical buffets are aimed at shadows.

If we argue to divine existence from human existence it is not because we take man to be the crown, glory and end-product of the universe. It is the weakness of our faculties, not the strength of our position, that leads us to take ourself as standing instance of created being. It has, of course, to be admitted that we have one privilege: we can raise the question about God's existence. Mountains and hurricanes, suns and planets cannot. Not even dogs, nor dolphins even, though high claims are being advanced for their discursive powers. Are they not being kept in tanks on the other side of the Atlantic, and trained up to talk to the Man in the Moon? But however it may be with dolphins, we at least can reflect upon our existence. We cannot, on the other hand, get outside our own skins, there lies the infirmity of our condition; so when we philosophize on the world's existence, we must be content to take our own for sample.

Yes, theology is about man and God; about God as the creator and saviour of man. But man is not so slight a basis for theological belief, either, if, along with man, you reckon in his roots. What I am directly aware of, what I acknowledge as dependent upon God, is my existence. But it will be silly of me indeed if I credit myself with existing in unitary isolation. I may be a mushroom sprung up in a night – as we said, like the fungus on a rotten tree. I might not have grown; the tree could have done without the fungus; but not the fungus without the tree. No tree, no fungus; and no soil, no rain, no sunshine, then no tree. If you know God as your Creator, you know him as the creator of everything in which your being is rooted. To make you or me, God must make half a universe. A man's body and a man's mind form a focus in which a world is concentrated, and drawn into a point. It may be in that point that I know existence; but it is an existence which involves the world. And so, as we said, to argue from our existence as man to the existence of God is not to take so slight a basis, after all.

The qualifications are important; but, however qualified, the statement stands; theological belief is concerned with the creator of man. That this is so is obvious, if we consider what God is taken to be. One of the silliest of all discussions is the question whether God is personal – it would be as useful to enquire whether ice is frozen. The theological question is not, whether the world depends upon some sort of exterior cause utterly undefined in nature; the very question would be meaningless. The question is, whether the world depends upon a supreme creative will; and that is the same thing as supreme person. Now if God is inevitably and always thought of as supreme person, he is no less inevitably thought of as the supreme archetype of man; for where else, I should like to know, are we to look for personality, if not in ourselves? We have not yet learnt to talk to the Man in the Moon, nor even to the dolphins in the tank.

To sum up: it is in ourselves that we sample that existence, of which we see the cause in God; and in ourselves that we sample that personality which furnishes the idea of God. The basis of theology comes down to this: human existence has a superhuman creator; the God of my belief can only be my God, and the attitude of faith is necessary to any genuinely theological contemplation. We may be wise, rational, or calm in the exploration of this, as of any other relationship; but unless we open ourselves to it, we shall not be convinced of him to whom it relates us.

In conclusion, let me recall that the faith I have been attempting to describe or to define is that initial faith, which ought not perhaps to be called faith; that attitude of openness or responsiveness through which we move towards an acknowledgement of God's existence. Of such faith we may say, that the mere fact of our moving towards belief is a sufficient sign of its presence in us. But such initial faith is not the faith that saves; it is not enough to believe the existence of God; 'the devils also believe, and tremble'. It is not even enough, to make belief predominant, to commit ourselves to it, to enthrone it above rival attitudes; we must honour our belief in God by giving God his due; and God's due is our life. Indeed we shall not achieve full intellectual belief unless we live by it. Who can go on believing in a supreme Good which he makes no motion towards embracing?

Union of will with God is the subject-matter of revealed religion; we may believe in God, but how shall we walk with him unless he comes to walk with us? Here is a topic which we cannot open in this present chapter.

The practical element in belief is so vital, it has led Christians to say that faith is a purely practical matter, a willingness to trust God and to do his will; and that consequently all worries about the objective truth of theology are a waste of time. This, however, is an exaggeration so absurd that it is amazing it should impose on intelligent men. Say, if you like, that what is asked of a learner-alpinist is that he should obey the guide's instructions and put his weight on the rope; say that these are practical matters; say there is no need for him to have a theoretical understanding either of weights and stresses, or of the way ropes are made, or of the principles on which the guide takes his decisions. Very well; but he must take the rope to be a rope, that is to say, a flexible cable of sufficient strength; and the guide to be a guide, not an impostor or a criminal lunatic. The factual correlates of a practical attitude may be simple, but they are no less essential for that reason. In the matter of religious belief they are, indeed, more important than my mountaineering parable would suggest. Religion is more like response to a friend, than it is like obedience to an expert. It is enough to know that an expert is an expert; it is not enough to know that a friend is a friend. Response, by definition, aims at being appropriate; the more understanding we have of the object, the better we can respond.

If the practical demand is what gives reality to belief, it is also what adds goads to fear. The horror of God is the horror of being enslaved. Like so many positions on both sides of the theological debate, it begs the question. If God is the creative spring of all being, and the inexhaustible fountain of all newness – that is, if God is God – one is no more enslaved by dependence on him than one is enslaved by the habit of breathing. If, on the other hand, God is an idol of the human mind, one is enslaved by obsession with so tyrannical an idea. What is a *free-thinker*? Not, I suppose, a man who maintains freedom of mental manoeuvre by refusing submission to true facts. Freedom can only be freedom to embrace and explore the world; not even the humanist can create his universe; he must respond to realities according to the demands they make on him; and it cannot surprise him that, in the eyes of a believer, the supreme freedom should be freedom to know God and to respond to him. 'How cramping, to shut oneself in to the God hypothesis!' Yes, if God is a hypothesis; but if you think so, you are assuming that he is not God. To the believer God, like man, is a reality about whom all sorts of hypotheses have been, and can be, entertained; the variety of the hypotheses does not debar us from practical response to their object.

Is the acceptance of God as my God a cramping acceptance? Well, is the acceptance of my neighbour as my neighbour a cramping acceptance? X married a wife, kind and clever and better than he deserved. X deserts her in the midst of her second pregnancy. His wife cramps him; he wants to be off with a fascinating blonde. She cramps him, for she puts a limitation on his freedom of action. But she exists, and so do her children. She loves him (blast her!) and the children need a father. Besides, he gave his word. Reality is a nuisance to those who want to make it up as they go along. But then, while every wife is actually limiting – she is a finite good; there are charms she doesn't possess, and another will – God does not limit us by being limited; he only limits us by being true.

Narrow and Broad

Published in 1960 in Said and Sung, *reprinted in* The Essential Sermons. *A sermon on the same theme as the preceding chapter, presenting many of the same thoughts from a different angle. 'The narrowness of spiritual truth is seen in the field of evidence,' Farrer says, and then pays special attention to the role of saints in providing such evidential support of faith: 'the saint is our evidence'. But the breadth of spiritual truth is the entire field of divine action: 'For no piece of this most rare and precious evidence can be understood by itself, but only as a detail in the vast divine action it subserves.'*

Living in a university as I do, and even venturing from time to time to hear essays from beginners in philosophy, I cannot help being aware of the sort of tortures faith suffers from contemporary criticism. No doubt it would be more suitable for a theologian to be absolutely pickled in devout reflection and immune from all external influences; but wrap ourselves round as we may in the cocoon of ecclesiastical cobwebs, we cannot altogether seal ourselves off from the surrounding atmosphere. A tail protrudes from the envelope for the twisters of tails to twist, and it hurts a bit sometimes. But it must be confessed that one gets used to it, and it does not hurt so much as it did. After twenty years of having one's tail twisted into several variations of the same knot, one begins to appreciate how the tail is constructed, and why it is that, though twisted, it does not break. I will venture to offer a few observations based on experience of the anatomy of this resilient organ. To speak without metaphor, I will mention two characteristics of spiritual truth, which those who criticize it seem sometimes insufficiently to notice. I will call them its narrowness and its breadth.

The narrowness of spiritual truth is seen in the field of evidence. It is very wicked indeed to call saints (as people will call them) by the boastful name of religious geniuses. But there is this point of truth in the comparison between sanctity and (let us say) poetical genius, that it is rare, and that the instances which most fully reveal its nature are the rarest. Is there such a thing as poetical creation? Then produce me an instance under laboratory conditions. Well, I will find you a verse-maker who will do his entry for the *Sunday Times* competition epigram under laboratory conditions; though I fear that under those conditions I cannot hold you out much hope of his winning the prize.

What do you mean by the evidence of divine presence and action? Where will you look for it? In the field of prayer? Though how we are to pray, when we are watching ourselves to see what happens, I really don't know. By good luck, however, we forget about the laboratory conditions, and we just pray. It is almost sure to be one of those days when we can do nothing but remember our God and our friends, put the two together, and identify our will with our duty. But perhaps it is an exceptional day. 'Sometimes a light surprises the Christian while he sings'; the world turns over in our heart, like a capsized boat recovering its true position; the throne of Mercy is seen, planted victoriously upon it; and the rays which stream from there kindle our dead affection for heavenly things.

Well, but even so, isn't that just a dream? What importance attaches to such a scrap of abnormal psychology? While you were praying, it looked to you as though the world had turned inside out; but is that a reason why I should turn my world inside out and (what is even more serious) turn myself inside out? That instead of drawing my life out of the well of my own decision, I should strike the shaft deeper, deeper than the brain can think, deeper than creation, and draw my life henceforth out of the fountain, from which all things always have their first unimaginable origin? You must give me better reason for that than the dream you dream, the prayer you pray, for half an hour one day in twenty. Are the foundations of the world uncovered then? Does omnipotence look through? How am I to know it?

If you address such questions to me, I fear that you will merely throw me into the unfashionable posture of repentance. By my fault, by my great and inexplicable fault, the God whose face is unveiled in my heart is obscured in my life. The almighty lovingkindness shapes a fragment of my thought; I do not let him wield the engine of my action. My assurance of him is in my repentance, in the miracle (as it is to me) that he renews my fresh beginnings with inexhaustible patience. But how are you to see that? I must give you better evidence. Somewhere a life wielded by God in a way that could not be mistaken, a life lived out of God, not out of self.

And indeed I knew a man whose name, though uncanonized, I shall always silently mention when I recall at the altar of God those saints whose fellowship gives reality to our prayers; a man who sacrificed in the prime of his age a life which he had never lived for himself; a man whose eyes sparkled with all the passions, pity, indignation, sorrow, love, delight, but never for himself; unless it is more proper to say, Yes, for himself; since he had made God's loves and God's concerns his own, and had no others you would greatly notice.

Such a life, then, is evidence; and what other evidence could you hope to find? We have no inspection, no insight into the works of nature, which could conceivably let us through them to a vision of anything that lies beneath; all we can study is the diagram their movements draw in space. The only being we can know from within is our own; we are forced, however inadequate it may be, to take it as a sample of the rest, and judge the world from man. And man knows God only by yielding to him; we do not know the fountain of our being, so long as we are occupied in stopping it with mud. So the saint is our evidence, and other men, of course, for the glimpses of sanctity that are in them.

There, then, is something about the principle of narrowness. The unknown God reveals himself; but revelation is not something which tends to occur; apart from heroic charity, it is something that tends not to occur. Jesus Christ rose from the dead, but men do not tend to rise from the dead, as water tends to reach a level. Neither do men tend, deserted by their following and rejected by their nation, to die, with their eyes open, for a cause which they alone are left to sustain, praying for their assassins and offering themselves for their friends. Men do not tend to do so, but Jesus did. And I hope that when you next hear spiritual reality discussed as something which must be generally diffused if it is genuine at all, you will not be greatly moved. The evidence of faith is incorrigibly aristocratic.

But now something about breadth. Those who scrutinise evidence like to chop it into convenient slices, so that they can slip it on a slide and put it in the microscope of exact inquiry. This saint of ours now, what can you do with such a confused lump of data? Good heavens, the very unity of the human person is an unsolved logical problem. 'Give me something manageable, some single proposition he enunciated, some single decision he made, some single act he performed.' Well, you may take your specimens if you like, but I am afraid you will learn nothing from them. How much can you learn about dramatic art from half a line of Hamlet? Nothing, unless the half line carries the overtones of the whole drama; and how will you pile those on to the microscope-slide? There are those who rub the texture of verse between their fingers, like women at a handkerchief counter; but there are many things that such criticism is incapable of testing.

The acts and words of saints will not fray between your finger and thumb, but you will not take God between your finger and thumb, the supernatural will have escaped you. The acts of saints are but brush-strokes towards a picture; and the picture is not even to be found in the rest of their own biographies. The picture they are painting is God expressed in mankind, God entirely and worthily served and adored. The saint paints his picture over and over, effacing his former work and aiming at perfection; and just when he has painted everything out and prepared for a fresh delineation, he dies. And in any case the piece he is busied with painting is only one corner, in itself meaningless, of a picture where Christ born, living, dying, raised and glorified holds the centre. That friend of mine, for example – except as serving the divine mission of Christ, his life was meaningless; and it was meaningless except as directed to that great goal or consummation, where all things shall be fulfilled in the light of the countenance of God.

Here then is the principle of breadth, to set beside the principle of narrowness. Spiritual truth is narrow, in the sense that the sort of spiritual evidence which will carry weight fills a minute area. But again, and in another sense, spiritual truth is broad. For no piece of this most rare and precious evidence can be understood by itself, but only as a detail in the vast divine action it subserves. Our weak prayers and weaker virtues are understood in the saints, and the saints on earth are understood in Jesus Christ; while Jesus Christ, the saints and our own Christian existence are understood in that end alone towards which they strive, and in assuring which the love of God to us is love indeed.

There light spills evermore from the fountain of light; it fills the creatures of God with God as much as they will contain, and yet enlarges their heart and vision to contain the more. There it is all one to serve and to pray, for God invisible is visibly portrayed in the actions he inspires. There the flame of deity burns in the candle of mankind, Jesus Christ; and all the saints, united with him, extend his person, diversify his operation, and catch the running fire. That is the Church, the Israel of God, of which we only exist by being the colonies and outposts, far removed and fitfully aware; yet able by faith to annihilate both time and distance, and offer with them the only pleasing sacrifice to God Almighty, Father, Son and Holy Ghost; to him ascribing, as is most justly due, all might, dominion, majesty and power, henceforth and for ever.

On Credulity

Published in 1947 in Illuminatio, *Volume 1, Number 3, and reprinted in* Interpretation and Belief. *An early but important essay in which Farrer wrestles with balancing the demands of both faith and reason. Looking at two ways of thought which normally co-exist in our minds, he says, 'Unless our minds in fact function in these two ways: unless we sometimes see God as truth and evasion of him as credulity, at other times the proved facts of the special sciences as truth, and the outrunning of them as credulity – unless this is so, we are not confronted with the specifically religious problem of truth.' In seeking to understand this particular problem, he outlines four different sorts of 'truth': (1) science, (2) personal understanding, (3) formal ethics, and (4) religion. He goes on to argue that 'as (1) is related to (2), so (3) is related to (4)'.*

There are various ways of offending against truth, and different environments stress different types of falsity. In the nursery they punished us for evasive lying: in the world of practical affairs evasive lying is considered in many circumstances to be a duty, but you must not enter into engagements that you do not propose to fulfil, or go back on those you have made. In universities, the crime is credulity: you must not believe, still less assert, what evidence does not warrant. What is the use of studying anything – history, science, what you will – if in the end you are going to make up the answers, and believe what you choose? Every society will punish by penalty or contempt the vice which frustrates its peculiar aims, and credulity will get short shrift in universities.

And Christianity appears to be credulity. The Christian believes, as faith, general truths which he must suppose to be the concern of philosophy, and particular facts which cannot be exempted from the scrutiny of history. He does not live long in a university without discovering that what passes there for philosophy does not oblige its practitioners to believe in God, and that history indeed obliges us to reckon with the Christian movement, but not necessarily to accept the Christian's account of the facts in which it originated. The Christian comforts himself for some while with the reflection that nothing, anyhow, has been proved *against* him; and then goes on to ask whether to believe without compelling evidence is not, after all, credulity.

At this point, perhaps, he picks up the New Testament, to see whether the apostolic writers have anything to say in their own defence. Not a word. Defence, indeed! They are putting their opponents through it, asking how men can look truth itself in the eye, and turn away to believe and practise lies. And this is plainly not the pose of propagandists. It is the only way in which these Christians can see things. And our perplexity is not simply that apostolic men once felt like this, but that a part of our own minds has often shared their view. We have often just seen (so we have thought) the inexorable truth that we are rebellious creatures under the eye of our Creator, and that our Creator has come upon us in Christ. Credulity, here, is the crime of pretending to believe that there is any way out of this situation but one – to reconcile ourselves to the truth of our nature, which demands our submission to the God who made us.

Unless our minds in fact function in these two ways: unless we sometimes see God as truth, and evasion of him as credulity, at other times the proved facts of the special sciences as truth, and the outrunning of them as credulity – unless this is so, we are not confronted with the specifically religious problem of truth. If we do feel the problem, the most reasonable attitude to start with is that two ways of thinking which exercise an undoubted sway on the truth-seeking mind both have their rights: it is a matter of finding the proper relation between them, not of allowing one to oust the other.

So it seems natural to ask whether there are not more sorts of truth than one. At the first brush we must answer that there is only one sort of truth, if by truth you mean 'being true', in the sense in which our acts of mind can be true. To be true is to conform to fact, and we know what we mean when we say that an act of mind so conforms to facts as to be true about them. Professional philosophers can write volumes about the sense in which the statement 'There is a lamp-post in the High Street' is true, because it is their business to sharpen the wits of boys by the dissection of trivial questions. But unless the result is to make them and their students better fitted to attack questions which are not trivial, they will not have used their time well. Truth is the conformity of thought to fact, and that is all there is to it. When we suggest to ourselves that there may be various sorts of truth, we must mean something else, for instance, that there may be facts of different sorts. Well, but that's a platitude: facts can be classified in all sorts of ways. Yes, but what we mean is something more special, there may be several classes of fact which are differently related to our faculties, so that what our minds can 'do' about them is different. If our minds do it right, the result will be truth; and truth will be conformity to fact, and fact will be the way things are in themselves: nothing will differ except the way in which our minds deal with these different classes of fact.

To put the same point differently: the word 'truth' is used in three senses, and only one of these is meant when we talk about 'different sorts of truth'. 'Truth' is used to mean:

(a) the facts to which true thinking corresponds;
(b) an act of thought which is, as it happens, true;
(c) the truthfulness of an act of thought.

We are talking about *(b)*. There are various sorts of 'truths' (truths of science, history, etc.) because the subject-matters of several disciplines oblige them to use different sorts of thinking. It is not the *truth* of these thinkings that differs, it is their nature as thinkings: the difference between erroneous scientific thinking and erroneous historical thinking is just the same as the difference between true scientific thinking and true historical thinking. Naturally, it is only because scientific and historical thinkings are *capable* of truth that we are interested in their differences, but the difference between them lies not in their truth but in the way they are thought.

So much for generalities; and now, unless our indiscreet scorn of certain professional philosophers is to topple back upon our own heads, we shall have to put our definitions to some use, and make a division of sorts of 'truth' which may help to clarify the religious problem of truth from which we started. Four sorts will, for our purposes, be plenty. So we will list the truths of (1) science; (2) personal understanding; (3) formal ethics; (4) religion. We will try to show that as (1) is related to (2), so (3) is related to (4).

(1) Science of all sorts obtains precision by artificially limiting its subject-matter. Modern physics began to get under way when it began resolutely to refuse to consider anything but the *measurability* of physical process. Not that physical process can possibly be nothing but its own measurability, but that the question of its measurability is a tidy question which leads to exact answers. The same artificial limitation has been brought into the study of human affairs. The economist may concentrate on man in so far as he is an economic agent, but if the economist concludes that *because* it is possible to get sound results this way, man is nothing but an economic agent and all the rest of his apparent action is economic activity under a disguise, then the economist is a fool. So, again, with the psychologist's study of man's subrational impulses, or any other limited inquiry.

(2) As soon as a man stops asking tidy questions about a single aspect of things and asks the very untidy question 'What *whole* reality is confronting me here?', science stops. Science may lay down the lines within which the answer can be found; but it cannot supply the answer. If we ask our question about *physical* realities, we shall not get an answer, anyhow. No one is going to know, or guess, what the whole being of physical substance is. But if we ask it in the human field, we do get some sort of an answer. I may consider very scientifically a man's economic relationships and the probable psychology of his instinctive urges, but the answers I shall get will do no more than point to what it is I am up against in dealing with this man. I have just got to know him through interacting with him. That is personal understanding.

(3) Science is true when it conforms to certain abstract patterns which real things or processes exhibit, and personal understanding is true when persons are (or, in history, were) as we understand them to be (or to have been). It does not matter whether the facts are such as to be approved or deplored, whether the persons are acting a lie or living sincerely. As long as we get the deplorable facts right and understand how insincere the insincere agents are, our science and our personal understanding are true. But we open up a completely new dimension

of questions when we ask what is that true essence of man which the insincere betrays and the fool misses and the callous ignores and the perverse distorts. This time we are up against an object which is quite differently related to us from the objects of science or personal understanding. It isn't *out there,* it is, so to speak, *within;* not 'within' as our states of mind are within, for our states of mind, worse luck, are not the standard of the just and the worth while. The standard of the truly human is something even more deeply 'within', which our states of mind ought to be expressing, but very likely they are not.

Now there are two ways in which the mind may relate itself to this essence of the truly human which it is our life's work to express. We may think about it abstractly, and that is ethical philosophy: we may think about it whole and in the round, and that is religion. The ethical philosopher is like other scientists of human nature – like the economist or the psychologist. He limits the issue and picks out a tidy question. He says: 'I do not propose to allow myself to be bemused by anything so overpowering or confusing as the attempt to see my whole human nature in its place in the world of real beings, and how I, as a mind and will, am related to it. I shall limit my scope. Anyhow, I shall say, men do feel themselves to be under obligations; and they habitually codify them in moral rules. And they, less clearly perhaps, but nevertheless effectively, build up ideals which outrun the letter of the rules. So let us talk about the limited fact of moral thinking – the recognition of obligation, the attempt to make moral rules consistent, the problems of particular duty.' All right, then, let's.

(4) But, say we, that cannot be the end of the matter. The ethical philosopher remains the master of his subject-matter by limiting his question. But in the end there is something more important than remaining the master of your subject-matter, and that is that you should undergo the impact of the whole fact. Just as you cannot become aware of the personal reality of your friend by trying on him preconceived questions of psychological or economic science, but only by undergoing the impact of his existence, so it is with awareness of your own being and destiny, and of its demands on you. You cannot say: I propose to open just a crack of my mental door and admit only those facts to which I have already issued blue tickets. You have to throw the door open, however mysterious, or terrifying, or overwhelming the body of fact may be that tumbles in.

Now when the New Testament writers said that in Christ they had met the truth, they meant that in him they recognized what was demanding admittance through this door. It is of no use, of course, for Christians to pretend that on this ground everybody is bound to agree with them straight away, but anyhow on this ground their position is immensely strong and need fear no antagonist. There is no constraint, no embarrassment here; here we can take on all comers. We do not need to worry whether all philosophers agree with us, for the philosophers are for the most part discussing carefully limited questions and their opinion on the total question may be of little interest even if they are prepared to plead guilty to having one. Certainly it is up to us to think as clearly and philosophically as we can about our own beliefs; but what sort of logical structure belongs to theological propositions is a very complicated and special question, and I do not propose to start upon it here.

As to the historians, we shall have to treat them with great respect, because it is vital to us that Christ was, in the field of history, what we say he was. We must have no bogus history. But at the same time many historians are limiting their scope to the search for 'truths' of the (1) and (2) type; such men are not going to see truths of the (4) type breaking out at them through the façade of history, for they have discounted them from the start. There is no question of proving the Christian view of what happened in the year AD 30 out of 'mere' history. Indeed historians who take the precepts of their own art for the laws of being, and decide that what 'mere' history does not prove cannot reach the human mind, are the men of all others least likely to admit the Christian fact. But the historian whose mind is open to the fourth type of truth, and who has some awareness of the abyss of divine being which underlies his own existence, may meet a voice and a visitant out of that abyss, when he weighs the strange history of the year 30 as it is mirrored in the witness of those who most intimately responded to it.

Double Thinking

First published posthumously in 1970 in A Celebration of Faith, *reprinted in* The Essential Sermons. *In debate with an atheist philosopher, Farrer says that 'since God has shown me a ray of his goodness, I cannot doubt him on the ground that someone has made up some new logical puzzles about him. It is too late in the day to tell me that God does not exist, the God with whom I have so long conversed, and whom I have seen active in several living men of real sanctity, not to mention the canonised saints.' However, this does not mean that Christians and their faith are immune to criticism. Atheists accuse Christians of 'double thinking' – of not really believing what they say they believe – and so of being, in fact, 'sentimental atheists' themselves. In reply, Farrer admits a certain justice to this accusation: 'For which of us Christians is there, whose conscience does not reproach him bitterly with the crime of double thinking, or as Christ himself called it, the crime of hypocrisy?' But again, as in 'Narrow and Broad', Farrer finds cognitive value in the example of the saints: 'The saints confute the logicians, but they do not confute them by logic but by sanctity.'*

It is a very ancient and mossy platitude, that men throw away priceless opportunities for self-improvement by resenting criticism instead of taking it to heart. And what is true of men is true of doctrines and systems. If only we could seriously consider what the communists say about us, instead of blasting them with cries of 'You're another!' And if only the Church in every age had been as concerned to see what had driven the heretics into heresy, as she was to condemn and suppress them! For the heretics were as serious men as the orthodox, often more serious. Well, it is easy to be wise after the event: our fathers burnt the heretics and we touch up the crests on the Martyrs' Memorial. But cannot we, in our own time, show a little more wisdom and listen seriously to our own heretics?

Two nights ago I was so rash as to let myself be put up in a sort of public match or verbal cock-fight with an unbelieving philosopher. He was to attack theology, I was to defend it. Neither of the birds (needless to say) achieved a kill. I had heard all the arguments before: so, I expect, had he. He argued kindly and temperately. He had no need to get excited, he was so entirely convinced of his own position. But how strange it is, that two men so different inside should present the same placid face to one another, and exchange little neat verbal arguments about the two different universes in which they respectively live! There is no God in his world: he has yet to be convinced that belief in God has any serious meaning or can be discussed on a respectable level. Whereas I – I, like you, make it a rule to spend a certain part of every day conversing with this God, whom my fellow philosopher more than suspects of not existing. I put a good part of my available nervous energy and a fixed ratio of my time into the endeavour to hold my existence in a focus which is for him a spot of moonshine.

Meanwhile, a room full of young philosophers or would-be philosophers watch the cock-fight. If they took it seriously, I suppose their world ought to turn upside down with every apparent swaying of the battle. Fortunately, the young men don't take argumentative dons as seriously as that.

But I must take seriously what my colleague thinks: not, that is, to call my faith in doubt, for since God has shown to me a ray of his goodness, I cannot doubt him on the ground that someone has made up some new logical puzzles about him. It is too late in the day to tell me that God does not exist, the God with whom I have so long conversed, and whom I have seen active in several living men of real sanctity, not to mention the canonised saints. But there must be much in our teaching of Christianity and our living of it which is at fault, if good men react in total disbelief of it. So let us open our ears to what they say, and take the implied criticism to heart. This Chapel is no place in which to argue against the unbelieving philosophers: it would be ungenerous, for this is not a place where they can argue back. But this is a fine place in which to take their criticisms to ourselves, and examine our own consciences.

Let us take, for example, the accusation of 'double thinking' which is brought against us Christians. Allow me to remind you how that accusation comes in. You have to suppose first that the critical philosopher has proved to his own satisfaction that religious beliefs can have no meaning at all in terms of real life. Religious beliefs and ceremonies are just superfluous decorations. In fact all religion in a scientific age is fundamentally of the same character as the religion practised by a couple of sentimental atheists getting married in church because it sounds more comforting. But, you and I object, we are not sentimental atheists: we really do believe. To which the answer is given: You *think* you believe; but you are deceived. You are a double thinker: you have two systems of thinking which in fact you keep apart – you think, as people say, in watertight compartments. And when you switch from one system of your thinking to another, that is, from your religious thinking to your practical thinking, you turn a blind eye to the transition, the passage from the world of reality to the world of fantasy. In the world of reality you think like anyone else (unless, of course, you are a lunatic or a fanatic). But when you turn to your devotions, or read pious books, you enjoy a fantasy picture of the world as subject to God's goodness and governed by his providence. And in this fantasy picture of the world there is a fantasy picture of yourself as a Christian, mysteriously incorporate with Christ and serving his cause, with only occasional lapses and deviations. Whereas in fact you are just an undergraduate or a business man, or some other type of worldly man, a serious man, perhaps a virtuous man, but one who does not take the will of God into his practical calculations, or experience his life as conducted by God. That is just a story you amuse yourself with while you are worshipping or praying or talking pious talk.

Well, now I think you will see what the accusation of double thinking amounts to: and I think also that you will see how deeply the accusation bites into our consciences, and how important it is that we should lay it to heart. For which of us Christians is there, whose conscience does not reproach him bitterly with the crime of double thinking, or, as Christ himself called it, the crime of hypocrisy? For hypocrisy, as attacked by Christ, does not mean self-conscious humbug, it means just 'play acting', that is to say, that the religion of the hypocrite no more enters into the rest of his life than the part the player acts on the stage enters into his life off the stage. In fact, Christ meant by hypocrisy what is now called 'double thinking', the endemic disease of religion everywhere.

Notice that our critics make the substance of religion what we reject as the vice of religion and its most deadly poison. How does this come about? Are not we the men who have brought it about? Am I not, perhaps, the Christian don who is just like any unbelieving don, except that I sometimes talk theology for professional reasons? And are not you, perhaps, the undergraduate who is just like any other unbelieving undergraduate, and proud to be, and whom no one would suspect of being a Christian unless they found you in Chapel? Are we just as ready as anyone else to join in the enjoyable game of slander (called gossip); just as determined as anyone else to make our worldly fortunes, whatever the needs of the Church or of unfortunate men may be? I could go on making up a lot more unpleasant questions like this, but I will forbear.

To return to the main point. To the clever logicians, Christianity is amiable and harmless hypocrisy. But we take the thing more seriously. Christian hypocrisy is not amiable or harmless at all. We are all hypocrites, indeed, because we are all sinners, but God is saving us out of our hypocrisy, if we are faithful to him: he is forcing the two parts of our thinking together. That is the whole issue in the religious life, not to be a double thinker, or anyhow, to be less and less of one.

It is obvious that our blessed Saviour was not a double thinker at all. He just lived God, or God lived him, it does not matter which we say, though the second is better – I mean, that God lived him. And I have known some men – living men, breathing with us a common air, men with whom I have talked and worked – who were single-minded Christians and simply followed the will of God step by step in this life, without any seeming regard for their own fortune or happiness or life, even. But what visible happiness God gave them in this world! and what happiness he has given them in that other world, eye has not seen, nor ear heard, nor has it entered into the heart of man once to conceive the least part of it.

When the logicians say that there is a certain inevitable division between spiritual thinking and natural thinking, they are in a certain sense right. We can't reconcile the spiritual picture of things and the everyday picture of things completely on the intellectual level. If we claimed to be able to do it, we should claim to comprehend the ways of God as well as we comprehend the ways of this world, and that would be an exaggerated claim. We see God in pictures, in images only, reflected in a glass and riddlingly says St Paul: and we cannot fuse our picture of God perfectly with our picture of the natural world. There always remains a certain discontinuity, a certain incoherence on the intellectual level.

The saints confute the logicians, but they do not confute them by logic but by sanctity. They do not prove the real connection between the religious symbols and the everyday realities by logical demonstration, but by life. *Solvitur ambulando*, said someone about Zeno's paradox, which proves the impossibility of physical motion. It is solved by walking. *Solvitur immolando*, says the saint, about the paradox of the logicians. It is solved by sacrifice. I can offer my life to the God who has shown me his face in the glass of riddles. The God who is seen in the sphere of religion takes control in the sphere of conduct, and there he gives me, unworthy, the help of his holy spirit.

You can live your religion if you like; you can know the reality of God if you like: for God will rejoice to assist and infinitely over-reward whatever effort you will make. *Resolution* is the crucial point. That is the link by which religious contemplation passes into practical action. From your prayers form simple resolutions – not, like the absurd resolutions of New Year's Day, resolutions for the next twelve months; but resolutions for the next twelve hours. Make them few enough to be practicable, and obey them for the sake of God himself. If you break them, repeat and renew them. What does God ask of me? is a part of every sincere prayer. By resolutions kept, men turn religious fantasy into the substance of living. By resolutions broken, men learn their weakness and are driven back on God. By resolutions renewed and kept they learn to live by him who says: 'My strength is made perfect in weakness' and 'my grace is sufficient for thee.'

Emptying Out the Sense

First published posthumously in 1970 in A Celebration of Faith, *reprinted in* The Essential Sermons. *A (literal) sequel to the previous sermon, dealing with the persistent problem of analogical language in theology. By the time we've qualified our language about God by saying that we are not using the terms literally, is there anything meaningful left for us to say?After a searching discussion of this problem, Farrer shifts from logic to theology: 'The discarding of the literal sense of God's promises is a trivial jest to the unbelieving philosophers, but to us it is nothing less than the crucifixion of Christ.' And, once again, in reaching the very edge of reason, Farrer finds recourse in faith: 'There is no short cut to the understanding of God's promises. You cannot do it by the wisdom of this world, or by logical sleight of hand. You can do it by active faith alone, by believing in God who has promised, by persevering in purity of life, in constant prayer, in Christ's sacraments, in obedience to every showing of God's will. Then God will reveal to you his excellent things.'*

Eye hath not seen, nor ear heard,
it hath not come over the heart of men
what God prepares for them that love him.
1 Corinthians 2.9

I was being told the other day about a former Principal of Brasenose who preached to his College once in twelve months, and this is how he would begin: 'The Greek word *allotrioepiskopos*, as I was saying last year', and so on. It is almost as foolish for me to go on where I left off a month ago, for which of you is going to remember? After all, you are not proposing to do a schools paper on your chaplain's sermons.

Nevertheless, I shall commit this absurdity, because we hit on a good vein a month ago, but we did not properly exploit it: so it seems a good plan to revisit the site and see if we cannot dig something more out of it.

The idea, if you remember (but of course you don't) was this. The unbelieving philosophers have been putting up a powerful line of criticism lately against our Christian beliefs, and it seemed that we ought to see what light their criticisms cast either on our beliefs or on our unworthy way of holding our beliefs. We found, for one thing, that they supposed us to be double thinkers, that is, to think one thing on our knees, and something quite different on our feet: and we had to agree that this was only too true, and we spent the sermon reflecting upon that most insidious spiritual disease of double thought. Today we will take up another point of accusation, of which the title is not 'double thinking' but 'emptying-out'.

The point about 'emptying-out' arises like this. You must imagine a theologian – it might be your unfortunate chaplain himself – brought to bay by a ring of savage and keen-scented logicians. 'You say' (thus they begin to bark at him) 'that God is active for your good, that his love makes all things work together for your advantage. But the other day your bicycle skidded and threw you against the wall of a house, and bruised you properly; and today you suddenly got an idea into your head and forgot an important engagement in consequence. Was divine benevolence making the bicycle work for your good when it skidded, or what you call your memory work for your good when it failed you so humiliatingly?' I begin to feel unhappy under such questioning, but (I say) God does work everything for my good, but not in the simple way you seem to expect. He is a very subtle worker, and we cannot always see what sort of good he will achieve for us by his management of events. 'Ah,' the philosophical critics reply, 'God's management of events seems to be management in a highly special sense, almost a Pickwickian sense, mightn't we say? It isn't much like the sort of management we would expect from a good human manager who was really in control. A human traffic manager, for example, who (to suppose the absurd) happened also to be omnipotent, would eliminate nasty accidents. But it appears that God does not do so, either for those who love him, or for those who do not. Some prayer books contain forms for blessing cars; but you do not, I take it, suppose that the proportion of accidents in blessed cars is lower than in those unblessed?' No, I hasten to assure them that I do not suppose anything of the kind. Perhaps, as a matter of fact, I do not hold much of an opinion of the blessing of vehicles. There is a good deal of rust in my car but none of it is due to the sprinkling of holy water.

'Where, then,' they reply, 'is your alleged faith in providence?' I look down my nose, and wonder how much longer this ordeal is to last, and I say, 'My believing in providence means that whatever happens it will be all right: not that one thing will happen rather than another.' 'Then why,' they retort, 'call it a faith in providence, governance, or management? The words sounded quite full-blooded and real when you began, but in the course of discussion you have been emptying the sense out of them bit by bit, until there is no more meaning left: or if there are still a few drops in the bottom of the cup, we could make you empty them out too, if we pressed you a little longer.'

Now I think we have sufficiently recalled what is meant by the accusation of 'emptying-out'. It means that religious language sounds quite full-blooded and ordinary, but when you press the religious believers they empty more and more of the meaning away, until they seem to be saying nothing at all.

Well, I did not do very well against the logicians, because they got me rattled, but you are my kind friends and fellow-Christians so I will relax and take a deep breath and try to explain myself a bit better. After all, it never was much good trying to explain spiritual things to unbelieving men. When I say unbelieving men, I don't mean humble enquirers, whose hearts God has touched. That is another thing.

Well then, about 'emptying-out'. God wants to give us the best thing in the world, a perfect and supernatural good. How is he going to make it known to us? He has to talk to us in the language we already know, the language of earthly things. If he talked to us the language of heaven, how would we ever understand? God takes our words, and uses them: Jesus spoke the dialect of the Galilean peasantry. Inevitably, the earthly words do not fit the heavenly things. The result is a good deal of initial confusion and disappointment. When we begin to learn our religion, we are told that God will answer us in our prayers: that sounds like the promise of a conversation. But when we try to pray, of course we find it is not like that. And how God's Spirit does touch us in our prayers, is a thing no number of words can properly describe beforehand: only God himself can show us that, if we go on faithfully in our prayers, until we find out something of what it is.

Or again, we are promised happiness in our religion. We soon learn to see that we are not assured by religion of the external means to happiness, such as health and wealth. But we may still expect emotional contentment, peace of mind. Yet even these things are not assured to us in the common sense of the words. The greater the saint, the more he feels the burden of the world's suffering and of his own sin: and yet (most strange) in his very suffering, in the opening of his heart to every assault, he is most blessed so.

What shall we say, then? Are the words 'converse' as applied to prayer or 'happiness' as applied to sanctity emptied out by God's actual dealings with men? Emptied out? Are the words emptied out? What was it Christ said of the words of the ancient law? I came not to dissolve but to fulfil. Not to dissolve, to melt away, to empty of sense, but to fulfil, to make full, to pack with all the meaning they could bear.

God promised many things to the Israelites in their ancient religion, things which seemed as human and literal as the promises we give in his name to Christian children now. If they would be good, they should be blest. His presence should go with them, and defend them from their enemies. Their cause was the winning cause, for he was almighty, and in his name they should rule the world.

The Israelite nation outgrew the religion of childhood, but did they pass off the promises of God with bland philosophic indifference? They did not. They adhered to the promises of God, they were crucified upon the promises of God, and in that national crucifixion they crucified the literal sense of the promises in order that God might reveal to them the true and spiritual sense.

The discarding of the literal sense of God's promises is a trivial jest to the unbelieving philosophers, but to us it is nothing less than the crucifixion of Christ. Perhaps that is why we could not answer the philosophers: for how could one say in such a company, 'that's the issue you are talking about: you are talking about the crucifixion of Christ'? Christ did not take the promises of God to be a jest because they could not be literally fulfilled. He did not say 'In the face of Roman power we can found no messianic kingdom here.' He said: 'In the face of

Roman power, which excludes our messianic kingdom in the literal sense, we will see what sort of messianic kingdom God will make.' He kept the words, and God changed the thing, and so we still call him Christ, Messiah, King, but not in the pre-crucifixion sense. He kept the words, and when Caiaphas asked him, 'Art thou the Christ?' he said, 'I am'; and when Pilate asked him if he were King of the Jews, he did not deny. But God changed the thing. The body of Jesus, first living, then dead, was trussed up and crucified as the Guy of literal messiahship, but God placed his true Messiah on the throne of heaven and in the hearts of his believers.

Well, they say, we empty out the professions of our religious faith. And I suppose we do. Not only do we give away too much in debate with the philosophers: we empty away too much in our own minds, we are content to think that God promises us something or other which is good, but there is no need to press very closely the sense of the words in which he gave his promises to us. Not so Christ: he pressed the sense of the words, those words 'Messiah' and 'kingdom' for example, he pressed them so, that he ran them clean through his heart; and that was how he discovered what they meant, both for himself and for all mankind. He did not empty out the meaning of the words, he lived it out, and found it wonderful; he died for it and found it transfiguring. His fulfilling of the words was not a matter of scholastic exposition, but of death and resurrection.

There is no short cut to the understanding of God's promises. You cannot do it by the wisdom of this world, or by logical sleight of hand. You can do it by active faith alone, by believing in God who has promised, by persevering in purity of life, in constant prayer, in Christ's sacraments, in obedience to every showing of God's will. Then God will reveal to you his excellent things. For, says Christ's apostle, when in the wisdom of God the world failed by wisdom to know God, it pleased God by the folly of the gospel to save believers. Not but that we speak a wisdom among the fully grown, but a wisdom not of this world, nor of the princes of this world who came to naught. But we speak God's wisdom in mystery, the hidden wisdom which God appointed before the ages for our glory; which none of the princes of this age understood, for had they understood, they would not have crucified the Lord of Glory: but as it is written, what eye hath not seen nor ear heard, what hath not come over the heart of man, the provision God had made for them that love him. And our Saviour says, 'I thank thee Father, Lord of heaven and earth, that thou hast hidden these things from the wise and prudent and hast revealed them to babes, for so it seemed good in thy sight.'

Does God Exist?

A paper delivered to the Socratic Club in Oxford on 13 October 1947, published in The Socratic Digest, *Volume 4, that same year, and then reprinted in* Reflective Faith. *An early essay which outlines two basic arguments for God's existence – the cosmological and the moral – and suggests a way of thinking about God's nature in meaningful terms. Farrer is not here actually trying to prove God's existence, but to sketch out the way in which he thinks such theistic argumentation must proceed.*

INTRODUCTORY REMARKS

I am asked to state an argument for the existence of God which appeals to grounds of general reason. I will do what I can, even though it is my experience that such arguments are about as likely to weaken as to strengthen belief. For, even granted that the argument is convincing in itself, its force lies in many presuppositions which cannot themselves all be stated, still less established, except in a big book. These presuppositions are (in the theist's opinion) natural, and so he puts forward his argument, hoping that the presuppositions will awake in his hearer's mind. But he knows that they may be buried, lost, or distorted: and in that case the argument will fall flat and discredit theism by so falling.

In any case, theistic arguments are not formal demonstrations. Since the Divine Being is unique, he can only be known by a sort of acquaintance: he must impress us *in and through* finite things, very likely without our fully conscious appreciation of the fact. We can never know the unique by mere inference from other things, nor God by mere inference from the world. What we suppose, is that finite-things--

enacted-by-God form the proper object of a fully awakened understanding. For a thousand practical purposes we neglect, we abstract from, the God-dependence of things: we may never, even, have become distinctly aware of it. But because it is there for us, we can make ourselves aware of our neglect of it, by making ourselves see that a Godless account of things is incomplete. The incompleteness is not logical: what it falls short of is the ideal completeness which is, in fact, present to our minds, however neglected or misunderstood – the activity of God everywhere supporting and inworking his creatures.

So without more ado, let us set forth an argument through which the dependence of the world on God may make itself felt by our minds.

THE ARGUMENT

The world, so far as I can see, appears to be made up of systems of active process. My conscious being is a system of active process anyhow, a wonderfully balanced interplay of willings and reactings and doings. The existence of living things, my own body for example, is also an interplay of active processes: my body lives as a body only in so far as the heart beats and the blood circulates and the lungs expand and contract and all sorts of other rhythms of digestion and distribution go on, such as physiologists study. There are living bodies of all kinds in the world, vegetable as well as animal, and all are systems of active process. But, if we are to believe the sciences, active process is not the being of living things alone. The apparently solid and stupid lumps of physical matter are, in fact, nothing of the sort: they are really made up of infinitely complicated, minute rhythms of active process, without which process, nothing would exist at all.

Active process, then, is a sort of common denominator of all existence known to us, from the lowest to the highest. It seems to be capable of existing at various levels, and in various forms: moreover, it is capable of passing from one level and one form to another level and another form. I am a living and active process when I am half awake, but it only requires someone to apply a suitable stimulus to me, and the slumbering activity which was me a minute ago becomes the highest degree of active attention and perhaps the highest energy of physical action. Lazy day-dreaming may transform itself into philosophical contemplation in a moment, so that the active process which constitutes my being may vary its form, for example from thought to action, and it may vary its level, for example from feeding to reasoning.

These transformations take place within my own conscious life; but consider the transformation by which my conscious life itself arises out of the elementary active process shut up within a germ, or the transformation by which, according to the evolutionists, the rudimentary system of action called an amoeba becomes at last a mammal. We must not, of course, imagine that the transformations are all for the better. On the contrary, species of animals degenerate, individuals die, moral character decays, and as I awake out of sleep into consciousness, so I fall away out of consciousness back into sleep.

I have two points to make here: first, that the common and basic something, active being, takes on an infinity of forms; and second, that all these forms appear to be in a sense arbitrary. None of them is the form of active being as such: they are all particular forms, and they might have been otherwise. We might have had a universe in which physical matter was not organized in the manner in which the atomic theorists say it is, in which there were no oak trees or daisies, no dogs, horses, or men, but completely different systems of active being.

Thus we seem to require an explanation for the fact that existence has taken the shape that it has. In the ordinary way, when we ask for explanations, we simply go one step, or several steps, back into the history of the process; if we want to know how there came to be those active systems which we call giraffes, we take for granted antelopes, a habitat providing the best fodder on the tops of trees, and the fact of chance-variation. From a certain state of affairs we can see another state arising, and we call this 'explanation': but the explanation is limited, for there is always some state of affairs presupposed. If we presuppose no state of affairs, no organization of active existence already operative, we can explain nothing. We cannot say: let it be supposed that *active existence as such* is loose in space, and you will get a world. You have to suppose, not active existence as such, but active existence already organized in a particular way: but why in such a way? We always have to suppose active existence running on certain lines: what put it on those lines? If we say, some other finite organization of active existence, the same question crops up about that. We can arrive at no answer which gives final satisfaction, except one. We must step right out of the finite sphere altogether, and conceive of a being who is not just one possible form of active existence, for then we should have to ask 'why *this* form rather than another?' – but who realizes in himself the fullest possibility of active existence, in whom Reality has the full stature of which it is capable. The notion of such a being is self-explanatory: we do not ask why he is *so*, rather than otherwise: he is just himself. Such a being it must be, therefore, who has laid down the particular lines on which active existence runs in the world we know. He has, to use an ancient phrase, *ordained* it thus. The processes which make up the world cannot be what they are, they are not capable of existing at all, without an infinite ordainer who wills that they should be so.

The argument which I have sketched is based on a survey of everything in general, it argues from the most general facts we can state about the whole range of existing beings in our world. I will now support it by an argument drawn from one very special sort of being, the being that we ourselves are. We can become aware of a whole universe of creatures objectively, but there is only one creature we can experience subjectively, and that is ourself. I can become aware through outward experience of the patterns of activity which make up many levels and sorts of being, for example, a biologist can examine the activity-pattern of the body of a frog. But one cannot taste what it is like to be a frog, one can only taste what it is like to be a man.

Therefore, when we have concluded on grounds of general reason that an infinite and absolute being must have ordained or appointed the forms of finite being, we naturally turn to our own being, in order to ask whether, in our own case, finite being tastes as though it had been appointed or ordained: whether we experience our own existence as something for which the lines have been laid down by a higher power. And, I maintain, this is in fact the case. I shall argue as follows:

We experience our own existence as an activity of self-determination. To be a man is to be the architect of one's own life. We do what we choose to do. The astonishing and almost terrifying fact of our own freedom only throws into higher relief the fact of its limitations. These limitations are of two kinds. On the one hand there are limitations imposed by brute fact. I may try as hard as I will to see into the essential nature of physical being, but I can get hardly any way at all, and never shall, because my faculties don't allow of it: I am a man, and not an angel. I may try as hard as I like to think as well as Aristotle or Kant, but I shall not do it, because I am only Austin Farrer and I haven't got it in me. I may do my best to be in Trinity College to keep an appointment at 10.00 a.m., but even if I defy the traffic lights I can't do it, because it was 9.59 a.m. when I mounted my bicycle in Manor Road. I may resolve to remember and do something at a given hour, but for all my resolution an intervening train of thought washes the memory out. All these are cases of brute fact limitation, and they really add nothing to our argument, for we have already seen that every finite existence is limited by the hard fact of its nature and its place. When I find how many things I cannot do, I am simply realizing that I am Austin Farrer, and not God Almighty, not even the Archangel Gabriel, nor even Immanuel Kant, nor even the captain of university athletics.

But there is another set of limitations which are of more interest here. My free activity is not merely limited by the things I can't do: it is limited also in the doing of the things I can do. All serious men know that they are limited not only by what they are, but by what they are *called to be*: not by what the human race has attained (which isn't, on the average, anything very grand) but by what the human race in general, and they themselves in particular, are *called* to attain. *Called* to attain: and who does the calling? It is, fundamentally, as simple as that. There is a pattern of our true destiny to which we know that we are called, and to which we are bound to show a measureless respect. Now the more evolutionist we are, the more sceptical about any fixed form called human nature, the more ready to admit that all the forms of finite existence are mere temporary phases in the process of the world – the more we admit these things, the more we ought to be bothered by the question, who or what calls us on into one destiny rather than another? It is vain to talk about 'ideals', as though ideals somehow floated about in space or inscribed themselves in the colours of the sunset. Ideals are made by men, or else they are evoked by God. If they are made by men, why cannot we make them what we choose? But we cannot. Old-fashioned philosophy based the stern call to the quest for perfection on a fixed form called human nature, the same in all men from the beginning of the world and on to the end of time. Darwinianism and Historicism have knocked that on the head fairly effectively. Human nature is the form of one particular emergent process. Yet we all know that we are called – not by what man just essentially always was and always will be, nor by what in fact he is going to become in this world, for he may be going to become something not very creditable. Then by what, or rather, by whom, are we called?

Are we not here experiencing God's ordaining in its actual happening? We were previously arguing that it was necessary to suppose that all finite existence is ordained, because it is finite. Then we turned to our own existence, the only existence which we can taste from within, to see whether being a man feels like being under divine ordinance, or no. And it seems that it does, even in our most human, most independent, most godlike aspect, our free will. Precisely at this point at which we are able to make the experiment of playing at being God Almighty, and decreeing what we choose, we find that we cannot, but are under mysterious ordinances. Our free will certainly has great play, it can even reject its true destiny: but that, we know, is a sort of suicide.

Now what can we say of the nature of the being who ordains for us the perfection after which we have to strive? We can say that he is a being to whom none has (in turn) measured out a perfection after which *he* has to strive: he is one who has caught up with his own perfection, who is all the good he sees, and sees all the good he is.

I have put forward these arguments with extreme crudity, and without any of the philosophical caution the matter requires. But I think that some such crude statement may suffice for my immediate purpose, which is not so much to prove God, as to show you what the method of argument for God's existence is. They simply show how the incomplete and Godless view of the world is supplemented with what it needs by that which believers think God to be. I am well aware that unbelievers can get rid of the whole force of the arguments by denying the meaningfulness of the whole basis from which the arguments start. It is easy, for example, as you very well know, to challenge the whole account of our free will and the claim of our true destiny upon us, which I have so roughly sketched. To which our only reply is, that serious men are forced to think like that in practice, whatever they may pretend to hold in theory. Still, if you deny, you deny, and there is nothing to be done about it, except to cultivate the power of contemplating your own spiritual being, a power which in some otherwise very clever men remains at a rudimentary stage. Cleverness will not take us to the knowledge of God, but wisdom will, and wisdom is a rarer gift.

But the most serious sceptical objection to all arguments for God's existence is that we have no intelligible notion whatever of God, nor therefore of the way in which the world depends upon him. To return to our first argument: if we argue that finite existence as such is an arbitrary sort of fact requiring explanation, we are tacitly comparing finite existence, to its disadvantage, with some other sort of existence which would not be an arbitrary fact. But this other sort of existence can be none other than the existence of God. The argument cannot stand at all, unless we are catching a glimpse of the Divine Nature out of the corner of the mind's eye. We are really saying: since Divine Nature is the standard of what one might expect being simply to be, how does it arise that what our senses meet on every hand is not God, but finite things? And the argument goes on to answer: it is because the finite things have been ordained by God.

This is perfectly true. If you feel the force of the argument, it is because you are catching sight of the Divine Nature out of the corner of your mind's eye. So much the better for us: that does not help to discredit the argument: it rather helps to suggest that God is there in fact.

Still, if the most rudimentary analysis can show (as many people say) that the idea of God is completely bogus, a piece of unintelligible nonsense: if 'infinite spiritual activity' is the description of God, and if 'infinite spiritual activity' is a piece of contradictory nonsense like 'square circle' or 'perfect wickedness', then, of course, the whole argument collapses.

I mention this question because it seems only honest to do so, but I can scarcely handle it here. The most subtle point of theist philosophy is the definition of the sense in which we can think about God. The theistic philosophers are well aware that all our thinking about God is infinitely short of his real nature, and yet they have thought it possible to find a middle position between adequacy and complete frustration. I will not enter into the subtleties of this question: but I will just put before you a train of thought which makes a great appeal to my own mind, and which may show you that the thought of an absolute spirit is far more natural and usual with us than we are inclined to suppose.

I ask you simply to reflect for a moment about your own understanding and will. Simply ask yourself, what you mean by understanding, and what you mean by willing. And I think you will find that the first and simplest thing you tell yourself about understanding is that it is a sort of seeing with the mind of how other things are in themselves. But when you turn to look at your own understanding, you will find that it never is in fact this, but at the best, a distant approximation to it. When have you understood any being as it is in itself? So you have to say, 'My understanding is not a pure or proper understanding; it is a limited or diluted understanding.' What have you done? You have found it natural, when you begin to think about understanding, to start with what believers suppose the Divine Mind to be: then you have gone on to make the surprising discovery that your mind isn't the Divine Mind. An odd way of thinking, but one which suggests that the idea of absolute or perfect mind is not so completely foreign to us as we were inclined to suspect. So again with will. What is will? A power freely to frame projects seen to be good, and to execute them because they are seen to be good. What could be simpler – and what could be more divine? We have hardly, ourselves, more than the shadow of such a power. Our rational choice is invaded in every part by irrational impulse, so that we can never perfectly separate the two: we never fully understand the business that we bring about; and we cannot choose what is simply good, but only the best of the possibilities that circumstances open for us. It is because our will is only half a will, that the determinist case has any plausibility. So natural it is to us to measure the modicum of will we possess by the standard of this absolute, creative freedom which is what we mean by God.

What I have been saying about understanding and will is no sort of proof that God exists: it is only some indication that the notion of such a being as God is believed to be, plays quite a natural part in our common thinking. If this is so, then we must be overdoing it if we say that the idea of God, or of his creative act, is just meaningless. We measure ourselves by our approximation to the divine. That does not mean that God exists: but it should mean that the idea of God isn't nonsense.

On the other side we must not overdrive the argument. We haven't got 'a clear and distinct idea of God' or anything approaching it. If you take the notion of a pure understanding or an absolute will and try to work it out, to conceive such a being in the round, you will quickly fall into an abyss of darkness. But after all, that is what we have to expect. If God might be comprehended, he would not be God. An over-confident dogmatism is as fatal to theistic belief as scepticism itself: it pretends to prove and to define, only to discover that what it has defined and proved is not its Lord and God. You can no more catch God's infinity in a net of words, than (to misapply Housman's poem) you can fish out of the sea the glories of the dying day.

How Can We Be Sure of God?

A sermon preached in 1967 (the year before Farrer died and the same year as his last book, Faith and Speculation*), published posthumously in* A Celebration of Faith, *and reprinted in* The Essential Sermons. *Farrer begins with the example of his mother's faith: 'a more unphilosophical thinker it would be difficult to find'. But in so doing Farrer is not advocating anti-intellectualism, for 'faith perishes if it is walled in, or confined. If it is anywhere, it must be everywhere, like God himself.' The universe raises a question about itself that it can't answer, and the only way to avoid the question is to 'Split the evidence [for God] up, and keep it apart.' But if, on the contrary, you think holistically and consider everything we know about the universe and human nature, then faith presents itself as a real and living option.*

There is something absurd, or almost indecent, in the task I have been given this morning. We are here before God's altar, pledging our souls to him: we are considering what his holy will lays upon us, to make our self-oblation an actuality; we are to receive at his appointment the body and blood of his incarnate Son under a mystery of bread and wine; we are to give thanks to him for infinite and inexpressible acts of mercy in our creation and in our redemption. And now in the midst of this we are to pause, and ask ourselves how we can be sure of God at all. What is our predicament like? I will tell you what it is like. Yesterday I had to replace a lamp at a height of fourteen feet in the clear middle of the ceiling: and my stepladder wouldn't reach. For the first time I found a practical use for the bound volumes of the *University Gazette* bequeathed me by my predecessors in office; and balancing a pile of them on top of the steps, I reared myself gingerly up. I had just unscrewed the globe when I asked myself whether I was securely placed. No sooner the question asked, than I trembled at the knees, and came near to losing my balance by thinking of it. Pull yourself together, I said, get on with the job, that way safety lies – and so I did; and so I remain in one piece, to come and address you this morning. I hardly need to draw the moral of the comparison. It is not in looking at our faith that we have conviction of God, but in looking at God, and in obeying him. God can convince us of God, nothing else and no one else can: attend the Mass well, make a good communion, pray for the grace you need, and you will know that you are not dealing with the empty air.

Think of my mother, now – you have known women like her, though few, perhaps, as good – a more unphilosophical thinker it would be difficult to find. Now suppose that in the heyday of my adolescent intellectualism I had told her that she had no right to her fervent evangelical faith, not being able to put together half a dozen consistent sentences in justification of her mere belief in God. What would she have said? She would have told me that admired intellects had bothered themselves with such enquiries, and been able to satisfy their minds: for her part, God had given her faith, and God had never let her down except it was by her manifest fault.

Well, but surely the Warden of Keble isn't going to preach you sheer anti-intellectualism – no, he isn't: you are perfectly right. The centre of your Christian conviction, whatever you may think, will be where my mother's was – in your exploration of grace, in your walking with God. But faith perishes if it is walled in, or confined. If it is anywhere, it must be everywhere, like God himself: if God is in your life, he is in all things, for he is God. You must be able to spread the area of your recognition for him, and the basis of your conviction about him, as widely as your thought will range.

And now today, on Septuagesima [third Sunday before Lent], we think of God's illimitable creation; so let me say something about that. Can I honestly claim to see this mighty spread of galaxies as God's handiwork – as needing him for their existence? I think it is best here to be very modest in one's assertions. I will even begin by something with which a candid atheist ought to agree. It is this: the world raises a question which the world doesn't answer: you can't find within the world an explanation why the world's the way it is. All explanations come back to the laws of Nature: but we can't account for the laws. We must say they are what they are, and there it is. Again, all explanations of a present state of affairs carry us back to a previous state of affairs; we never come to a state of affairs which explains itself, or has to be the way it is. Why are Nature's laws as they are? And why are brute facts the way they are? There is no answer within the world.

I say that a candid atheist should agree with us. But only up to a point – he will say that the question the world raises and the world doesn't answer is an empty and fantastic question, since it admits of no answer, and we can do nothing with it: it is like those silly questions little children go on asking beyond all meaning and all sense: Mummy, why is that a dog? Don't be silly, darling, a dog is a dog.

So the atheist thinks, poor man, because he is an atheist. Not that we are to pretend that we believers can get behind the scenes of Nature, and see God making things be the way they are. Of course we can't. Indeed, if we *could* press behind the scenes of Nature, there'd be nothing for us to see. God acts by simple will; and we cannot see the will of God except in what that will has created. There is only one point at which we can possibly touch the nerve of God's creative action, or experience creation taking place: and that is in our own life. The believer draws his active Christian existence out of the wellspring of divine creation, he prays prayers which become the very act of God's will in his will. Because we have God under the root of our being we cannot help but acknowledge him at the root of all the world's being. So it is that, where the atheist sees the search for an ultimate explanation of things as a meaningless 'Why', we see it as the searching out of God's creative power.

I will tell you how to disbelieve in God. Split the evidence up, and keep it apart. Keep the mystery of the world's origin carefully separate from your experience of God, and then you can say that the cosmic facts are dumb: they raise a question, they give no answer. Keep the believer's experience of God by itself, and away from the general mystery of nature; then you can say that it's so peculiar, so odd a little fact in this vast indifferent universe, that to attach universal importance to it is too absurd. Then on the other side, be careful to keep the barriers up between the God in you and the God in Christ. Then you can say of your own Christianity (as you must indeed confess) that it's too slight a thing to support the towering edifice of faith. Meanwhile, shutting

Christ off in a separate compartment of your mind, you can say that the idea of a God-Man is a mere erratic streak, with nothing to support it in the whole range of experience.

I have told you how to disbelieve. Now I will tell you how to believe. Just do the opposite: pull all these mental barriers down. Where can I be sure of God? In Christ, yes, of course, in Christ: if Christ was not the breakthrough of God showing his hand in a part of the world, where are we to look for it? But is not God-in-man too great a stretch of miracle to be believed? No indeed, for God-in-man overflows from Christ and shows many shining tokens in the saints; and even the clue to what it is, it reveals in our own poor lives. Poor they are, and too thin to bear the weight of evidence: but then they do not stand alone. We see clearly enough that what we have an inkling of, the saints apprehend, and Christ simply achieves. Ah, but is not this whole phenomenon of life invaded by the divine a mere freak in the vast material solid of the universe? Nonsense, the universe isn't solid at all: it is, as a totality, unexplained and subject to the appointment of creative will in all its infinite detail.

We believe in One God, One not only in the unity of his substance but in the unbroken wholeness of his action. All the work of God is one mighty doing from the beginning to the end, and can only be seen in its mind-convincing force when it is so taken. It is One God who calls being out of nothing, and Jesus from a virgin womb, and life from the dead; who revives our languid souls by penitence, and promises to sinful men redeemed the vision of his face, in Jesus Christ our Lord.

Griefs and Consolations

Published in 1961 as the concluding chapter of Farrer's extended book on the problem of evil, Love Almighty and Ills Unlimited. *Here Farrer struggles with the theoretic understanding of – and also the practical response to – pain and suffering. How do they relate to the enterprise of thinking rationally about religious faith? In developing his reply to these issues, Farrer places great emphasis on the Christian hope for the general resurrection and future life. And again his exploration takes him to the very limits of reason: 'Peasants and housekeepers find what philosophers seek in vain; the substance of truth is grasped not by argument, but by faith.'*

. . . If we wish to study the ways of divine Wisdom, or to see in any detail how God brings good out of evil, the first clue to the windings of the maze must be the appointed goal. Nor is it enough to know that the goal aimed at is good in general. Why, there are as many sorts of good as there are forms of existence, and as widely different. Unless we are bold enough to ask what particular good God intends in any case, we dream in vain of understanding his particular providences.

We can always ask; we cannot always answer, or even conjecture; and that is why we have often to acquiesce in a blind faith. Yet sometimes we can conjecture, and sometimes we can have a reasonable assurance. And there is, anyhow, before our eyes that last and universal end which God has disclosed and, by disclosing, has conferred on our present state the highest blessing he could bestow, or we receive.

Indeed, if we are speaking of the ills that are peculiar to man, we can say nothing of God's purpose in regard to them which has not some reference to that one ultimate and revealed end. The old women, nodding their heads and sighing over their neighbours' misfortunes, offer pious-sounding consolations which are the merest nature-lore. In so far as they express any truth, it is a truth belonging to the animal level. 'Poor dear Mary, she died, but it was a happy release; she had suffered so much pain, and there was no other way out ... Poor old John, crippled with the rheumatics; but he's more comfortable tied to his chair than breaking his back at the digging; that garden of his would have been the death of him. God knows best.' What do these sentiments express, but the general balance of animal life; the effect of pain in economising exertion, and of death in putting an end to pain?

The old wives' reflections tread closer to Christian ground when they bear on the correction of faults, or the formation of character. 'Don't you know about young Harry? He hurt his spine and kept his bed eighteen months, just at the age when boys grow strong and daring. But it all turned out for the best; it made him so much more thoughtful than other lads ... It was hard luck on Tom, his great plans coming to nothing; like all these contractors, he was bursting to expand. Only before his disappointments he was so pleased with himself, he'd no time for anyone; while now he listens to you quite civil-like. These trials are sent to teach us.'

The other old ladies assent to their gossip's moralities, like a flock of ducks quacking in chorus. They specialise in being wise after the event; and in such a field, indeed, there is little other wisdom to be had. No one can be sure beforehand how a man's character will be affected by the trials he undergoes. Tom's business disappointments may not make him gentle, they may make him morose. So Tom, in turn, becomes a trial to his mother and his wife. These women, perhaps, rise to the level of their opportunities and edify the old ladies by an exemplary cheerfulness. But then, again, they may not. The whole family, a prey to ill-temper and mutual irritation, becomes a trial to the neighbourhood. It will be admirable if it brings out the best in the neighbours; but very likely it brings out the worst.

The evils of our life have an alarming tendency to spread, and to breed other evils. Every extension of the trouble is a possible occasion of good, through the challenge it throws down to character, or the appeal it makes to kindness. But how far the evil may have run and multiplied, before the appeal is heard or the challenge taken up! And even where the virtue is forthcoming to meet the opportunity, in how many other directions the evil may be answered with evil. The good Samaritan, by his kindness and resource, broke the barrier of prejudice and made a neighbour of an enemy. The priest and the Levite, passing by on the other side, confirmed themselves in their self-righteous egotism.

The old women like to say that what happened was all for the best. They are probably wrong. Good, even animal good, such as physical health or a moderate plenty, is a more fertile breeder of good on the whole – yes, even of moral good – than distress of any kind can be. Were it otherwise, we should be faced with an intolerable dilemma. We should be bound to fear that in consulting our friends' natural happiness, we should be imperilling their spiritual salvation. Like certain truly fiendish monastic superiors and novice-masters, we should feel called upon to arrange artificial mortifications for our juniors, and to twist the tails of our fellow creatures for the good of their souls.

Good breeds more good than any evil can. It is a special revelation of God's divine power that he is able to bring some good even out of evil. But his use of evil for good ends does not immediately sterilise it; it continues to breed after its own kind. What perhaps most offends us in the old women's talk is a suggestion implied, rather than stated; the suggestion that the evil they deplore finds its characteristic or dominant effect in the redeeming feature they fix upon. The boy's motor-cycle slipped, and he was smashed against the wall. The effect of the bereavement on his father's heart may have been truly edifying; from a besotted, possessive parent he changed into a general philanthropist. But it is almost indecent to mention the fact; still more, to dwell upon it with any satisfaction. Who cares about the old man, anyway? He has had his life. The young man, alas! was cut off in his prime. His promise was unfulfilled; he never married the girl who loved him; he had no posterity. Nothing that happened to his father can make any difference to so absolute an evil.

Of all consolations the most glib and the most indecent in the ears of unbelievers is the promise of an invisible and an eternal good. 'The boy was smashed against the wall, his life ran out in blood and soaked away into the grass; but his soul is saved and treasured, every drop; all will be poured back into immortal veins, it will animate the body of his glory; he will see the face of God, and enjoy a happiness in comparison with which the best pleasure of his golden youth was the shadow of a shade.' The offence here is not that the compensation is either inadequate or irrelevant, but that it is fantastic and unproved. Anyone can spin phrases about a world hidden from sight, where all journeys end, and from which no traveller returns.

And yet there is no other consolation but this which carries any force. The issue is all or nothing; either we believe, or we do not. The half-believing moralities of the old women fall flat, so long as they equivocate on this single point. Has the boy perished as though he had never been, and is his father to go the same way in a few years? Then how trivial it is that the old man should sublimate his disappointed parenthood in an enthusiasm for the reclamation of young gangsters! He has begun his charitable work somewhat late in life; it is not to be thought that he will make much of a showing at it. But once admit that the characters of the tragedy are immortal souls, and the balance alters. The boy's premature death, though an undoubted flaw in the order of nature, and a wound in the body of human affection, is not so blank a loss as to make the mention of redeeming consequences an indecency; while the opening of the father's narrow heart, being the preparation of a soul for glory and a beginning of heaven on earth, obtains a weight which may fairly tell in the scale of compensations. Even the old-man's ill-practised philanthropy begins to have an incalculable radiation. He may not appear an effective agent in his chosen work, but divine charity once lighted in him will kindle his fellow-workers, or awake a response somewhere. And all charity, visible or invisible to human eyes, is everlasting life.

Yet however believing we may be, we hesitate to offer open consolations, unless we have an equal right to grief. Let the father console the fiancée with immortal hopes, or she him. The friends of both hold back, for either they do not feel the grief with equal force, or if they think they do, cannot expect to be believed. It may give them some title to speak, if they have a comparable and acknowledged grief of their own; they too have lost lovers or sons. Why should this help? Because it is not a matter of seeing a consequence, it is a matter of feeling grief and hope. You may see that present evil lies in the path to an immeasurably greater good, and yet you may feel present grief with immeasurably greater force than future hope. And it seems no consolation to say that good will one day come. You must be able to say that divine hope can temper human grief. Any Christian can say the first; only a sufferer can venture the second.

It is indeed the common character of grief, as also of pain, to be obsessing; and we ask too much, if we demand that the saving action of God should not only redeem us from sorrow, but should make the redemption to be felt by us in the moment when the sorrow seizes us. But then it is not on feeling that Christians plant their feet, it is on faith; and faith is an act of the will. The Christian sufferer will scarcely lay hold on future hope by an imaginative delight in blessings still unrealised. But he may have a practical belief in the present work of God, through which Providence prepares good things beyond the grasp of our understanding. He may adhere to the divine purpose, and co-operate with it.

It is this practical aspect of faith which makes the riddle of particular providence appear so urgent a question. The Christian sufferer need not know why the blow was struck. He wants to discover what God is doing in face of it, so that he may do it too. He cannot set about directly to alter his feelings. He can only consider what to do with himself, or what to do for his fellow-sufferers, in the destiny which has fallen so heavily upon him. And being a Christian, he will want to do what God is doing.

And yet, as we said above, it is hard to be wise in the tracing of particular providences, except after the event. Looking back over a tract of time, we can see how circumstances have shaped us, even in spite of ourselves, and regret that we have put so many obstacles in the path of a mercy we failed to discern. Yet we probably do ourselves an injustice if we suppose that we could have seen the way plain in front of us. We could only have found it by letting ourselves be led up it. This manner of proceeding is not so mysterious as it sounds. We become sensitive to the leading of God by a faithful attention to common claims, and an obedience to his revealed will. The Christian sufferer goes on quietly with his duties, and embraces his opportunities of well-doing, sustained by the general belief that through these things God will make suffered evils fruitful of good. He needs a faith in the working of particular providence, not a detection of it.

Pain, grief, and every sort of discontent put a drag on action and drain the colour out of enterprise. Merely to resist the deadening influence, and go on with life at all, may be an effort almost too great. Half the sufferer's business is to suffer bravely, to endure and not give away. In such a state of being, he will find it the most direct consolation to know that his suffering has itself a place in the redemptive action of God. And this is the gospel of Christ's Passion – that God saves us not only out of suffering, but by suffering. The world is redeemed by the sufferings of Christ; and his sufferings work out their divine effects through the sufferings of Christians.

There is nothing morbid or masochistic about the doctrine of redemptive suffering. It does not teach that God is pleased with the costly effusion of blood, with the torture of brain or of nerve, rather than with the health and happiness of his creatures. The suffering he approves, and himself undertakes, is redemptive. Redemptive of what? Of evils which are in any case there, and which will not be overcome by our running away from them. It is our faith that in standing against them we can vanquish them, through our union with the heroic and all-conquering Passion of Christ.

But that is not all. Our religion teaches us that suffering is one; our endurance assists the endurance of other men, as theirs assists ours. The suffering endurance of the individual man may not seem to him important; he does not want to think of achieving holiness in his own person, or of acquiring the virtues. He would much rather that a merciful Providence should shorten his painful life. In such a mood it is something for him to be reminded that his endurance supports those in a position to feel it, and through them, others unknown and uncounted. His patience is an unspoken prayer; it will only gain in force if it finds utterance in intercession.

To live is to do; while we have something fruitful to do, we are commonly content. The sufferer finds his action, in the ordinary sense, cramped or enfeebled. The mere supporting of his trouble uses up such energy as he has. He is to learn that this mere supporting is a doing, an action of great power, a co-operation with almighty Love. It was thus the martyrs endured their deaths. They did not see themselves as passive victims of pagan malice. They died willingly, to honour and to implement Christ's victory. They were his soldiers, and they fought a battle they could not lose, except by their own treason. For though they were weak in their own strength, they had the grace of God; and nothing could be stronger than omnipotence. . . .

Goods and evils, then, are known where the shoe pinches, or where the heart dilates. In like manner God's creatorship is perceived when we ourselves are the beings created, and dependent on his will; or if not ourselves, then neighbours who concern us; and others only afterwards, and by analogy. Since I do not know except in the remotest way what it is like to be a snail, or an oak tree, and not at all what sort of existence an atom of iron enjoys or exercises, how can I think what it is for any of these to have their being from God? Whether we choose it or not, we must stand to ourselves as our sample of creaturehood, just as we must stand to ourselves for our sample of a being that is subject to good and evil. Indeed, experience of creaturehood and experience of value are intimately linked; our sense of God is dependent on our sense for evil and good. God is felt as the source of good; or, if you say he is felt as the source of existence, you must acknowledge that the existence which is known as something bestowed by God has a positive character; it is itself a blessing, and enriched with blessings. In this fact lay the root of Job's agony. He had known God as the author of blessing; and the blessing had turned to a curse. Where, then, was God?

The same issue faces Christian sufferers, though their resources for meeting it are infinitely greater than Job's were. Associating themselves with the sufferings of Christ, they find the soul of good in the heart of evil. They identify themselves with the will of a God who raises the dead.

The inquiring mind is not to be turned back from its chosen path. Speculative questions deserve speculative answers; and so in this book we have tried to satisfy those whom the riddle of providence and evil intrigues or torments. But the value of speculative answers, however judicious, is limited. They clear the way for an apprehension of truth, which speculation alone is powerless to reach. Peasants and housekeepers find what philosophers seek in vain – the substance of truth is grasped not by argument, but by faith. The leading of God through evil out of evil and into a promised good is acknowledged by those who trust in his mercy. The balance of the world is good to them, though in the eyes of onlookers their misfortunes go beyond endurance. I remember the happiest man in a hospital, lying broken-backed forever in pain on a water bed, overflowing with gratitude to those who tended and those who visited him, and blessing us all by his prayers.

There are those whom the sight of unassisted misery in others chiefly appalls, and leads them to curse or to deny the Author of the Universe. They are seldom those who yield to the natural pressure of sorrowful scenes on a compassionate heart, and give themselves to the work of relief. An overmastering sense of human ills can be taken as the world's invitation to deny her Maker, or it may be taken as God's invitation to succour his world. Which is it to be? Those who take the practical alternative become more closely and more widely acquainted with misery than the onlookers; but they feel the grain of existence, and the movement of the purposes of God. They do not argue, they love; and what is loved is always known as good. The more we love, the more we feel the evils besetting or corrupting the object of our love. But the more we feel the force of the besetting harms, the more certain we are of the value residing in what they attack; and in resisting them are identified with the action of God, whose mercy is over all flesh.

The Country Doctor

A Christmas Day sermon preached in the Cathedral of Christ Church Oxford and published in 1960 in Said and Sung. *Farrer begins with the fact of suffering in order to reflect on God's answer for it: 'God does not give us explanations; he gives us a Son.' This leads to a meditation on the role of Mary in the life of Christ and in the life of a Christian, and from that to the indwelling of Christ in the Christian. In short, this brief sermon takes the three concerns of this entire reader, and indeed of Farrer's life – Scripture, tradition and reason – and brings them together into a concluding, and convincing, doxology.*

Once upon a time there was a country doctor, a pompous and unimaginative man. He was summoned to attend the wife of the squire. After the affair was successfully over, the woman, still only half alive, moaned that it was unbearable – why, she asked, does one have to suffer such pain? The doctor showed his learning. 'My dear lady,' he said, 'if you had looked as I have looked into the workings of nature, you would perceive that the nobler the animal, the more developed must be its condition when it separates from its parent; and the more developed the condition of the offspring, the greater the wrench to the parent must be. Now man is the noblest of the animals. The pain of human childbirth is the price of man's nobility.' The doctor's voice trailed in the woman's listless ear: 'That makes it no better,' she murmured, 'it hurts just the same.' At that moment her mother came into the room and showed her her son. And she began to think how it would be when she suckled him; and suddenly she remembered no more the anguish, for her joy of that little man, who was born into the world.

The Word of God brings upon human pain and strife the consolation of eternal love. It is often thought that the Christian preacher is called upon to imitate the doctor in my fable, and somehow to prove that the intolerable evils which ravage the earth are only the price of greater good. But the answer naturally provoked by such explanations is that of the suffering woman: 'That makes it no better; it hurts just the same.' Or even: 'If this is what God's love does, then for God's sake let me have a taste of his wrath.' No, God does not give us explanations; we do not comprehend the world, and we are not going to. It is, and it remains for us, a confused mystery of bright and dark. God does not give us explanations; he gives us a Son. Such is the spirit of the angel's message to the shepherds: 'Peace upon earth, good will to men ... and this shall be the sign unto you: ye shall find a babe wrapped in swaddling clothes, and lying in a manger.'

A Son is better than an explanation. The explanation of our death leaves us no less dead than we were; but a Son gives us a life, in which to live. The mother revives, as her thought attaches itself to this new life. And Mary of all mothers is most blessed, as her thought ranges forward over the happy tasks of which her life hereafter must consist, the nurture and protection of her Son. Here is a Son in whose life she can always more richly live; for he is life itself, and to live in him is to live in life everlasting. If we live in our own children we live in what must fail and disappoint us; we may even be so unhappy as to outlive them. But if we live in the Son whom God has given we have a life which will not fail, but always deepen and extend. This is the peace, this is the joy God gives: our joy is swaddled in the cradle, our peace is crucified, our glory rises from the tomb.

Mary was most blessed, because for her the natural love of parenthood could run on unbroken into the love of that Son whom God had supernaturally given. And so Christians have desired to have her prayers, not because special virtues are recorded of her, but because she has a path of incomparable simplicity into the heart of God's love. In company with her, we too have desired to find access; we have followed her through the stages of her journey. First, Jesus is in her arms, and has no life independently from her; she carries him to the temple, she presents him before God. Then, even in his childhood, he shows a mysterious life of his own. Now he walks into the temple on his own feet at his mother's side, and there detaches himself; he remains hearing the doctors, and asking them questions. She misses him, and seeks him sorrowing; she finds him about a business of his own, or of his heavenly Father's (it is all one) in his Father's house. Now he is something that she has not made him, his heart and mind are not under her hand; yet he returns to Nazareth, and is subject to her, for he is a child still. The day comes when he is no longer subject, but she is subjected to him: 'Whatsoever he bids,' she said to the servants at Cana, 'do it.' And so, from a mother, she came to be a worshipper; she lived in him – not in what she made him, but in what he made of her.

How blest was she, above all women; and how happy are we, if, following her progress with devout imagination, we can come to live, even for the short period of our prayer, in that Son whom God has given to us, caring for his concerns, and not for ours! For what else is it to pray, but this: that we live for a little while in the Son of God, and share in some measure the love he has for all the men with whom we have to do? That we deeply care for the fulfilment in them of his saving work, and worthily prize the work of his mercy in our own souls?

It is written 'Unto us a Son is given.' And elsewhere it is written, 'God sent forth his own Son.' 'Unto us a Son is given,' that is, he is given to be our Son, the Son of human race; that Mary might have him for her own, and we with her might grow from a natural to a supernatural love. But he who is so given to be our Son, is God's Son everlastingly: 'God sent forth his own Son.' He is our Son, and so we can come to live in his life, as Mary did. He is God's Son, and therefore, as we come to live in his life, we come to partake in the love with which the eternal Son loves the eternal Father.

The Philosopher says that the love of friendship involves some equality between the friends who love; and it is difficult to resist the truth of the saying. Between Infinite God and us there is no equality or proportion at all; and the more I dwell upon the greatness of God, the more inconceivable I find it, that there can be any friendship between him and us, or any interchange. And it seems cold comfort, and a mere fiction of words, to be told that though I can give him nothing that is of worth, he is pleased to set a worth upon it; as the whim of a stamp-collector sets a value on a slight tissue of dirty paper. That God is infinitely good, infinitely generous to my unworthiness, that he creates and sustains me not for his sake but for mine, this I can believe;

but that he can so trifle as to delight in my poor and inconstant affection, this is a thought that carries no conviction with it.

But now, if he has given me his Son; if he has placed me in his Son, and his Son in me; his Son, who is the equal of himself, and in whose love his heart delights: then what matters the triviality of my response to the Eternal Father? For beneath my heart, inspiring its weak and intermittent motions, there beats the heart of the eternal Son of God. There the Father is loved; in that love he rejoices; and that love is in me, and in you; for the Son of God has put us on as a garment; he bears us on his heart, as he goes in to minister in the tabernacle of heaven. Therefore we can be content, when we pray, to let the love of the eternal Son go out in us towards his Father; we can be content to know that it is so, that it happens, and that our triviality is carried on the surface of it, like foam upon the tide.

It is not, then, that the Eternal Father has fixed an artificial worth upon us, to value us for what we are not. He has put a real and infinite worth into us, that he might value us for what we are; for he has incorporated us into his Son. There are no fictions with God, not even in his generosity. He does not turn a blind eye to our shallowness; he turns a seeing eye on the infinite depth with which he has underlaid it, the love of Jesus Christ his only Son; whom he gave to be born for us this happy morning, of the Virgin Mary, by the Holy Ghost.

Her virgin eyes saw God incarnate born
When she to Bethl'em came this happy morn.
How high her raptures then began to swell
Only her own omniscient Son can tell.
All Saints are by her Son's dear influence blest:
She kept the very fountain at her breast.
The Son adored, and nursed, by the sweet maid
A thousandfold of love for love repaid.[1]

So now for the one eternal Son, Son of God and Son of Man, Jesus Christ, be ascribed to the Father in the Holy Ghost, all honour, glory, thanksgiving and praise, this day and ever.

---

1. Thomas Ken.

Further Reading

This collection should be a beginning rather than an end. Farrer published fifteen books before his death in 1968, and several posthumous collections of essays and sermons have since been added. Because of the profound integration of Farrer's mind, assigning specific genres to his various books can be difficult, and in particular the distinction below between 'Theology' and 'Philosophical Theology' is only a matter of degree. However, readers may find these seven categories useful as one way of identifying Farrer's books according to their basic themes, methods and genres. Within each category, they are listed chronologically according to their original publisher and date. Some have since been reprinted by different publishers. A comprehensive bibliography of Farrer's published works may be found on pages 277–87 of Charles Conti's *Metaphysical Personalism* (Oxford, 1995).

Philosophy

Finite and Infinite: A Philosophical Essay, Dacre Press, 1943; second edition, 1959.

The Freedom of the Will, A & C Black, 1958; second edition, 1963 – the 1957 Gifford Lectures at the University of Edinburgh.

Biblical Studies

A Rebirth of Images: The Making of St John's Apocalypse, Dacre Press, 1949.

A Study in St Mark, Dacre Press, 1951.

St Matthew and St Mark, Dacre Press, 1954; second edition, 1966.

The Revelation of St John the Divine: Commentary on the English Text, Oxford University Press, 1964.

Theology

The Glass of Vision, Dacre Press, 1948. The 1948 Bampton Lectures at the University of Oxford.

Saving Belief: A Discussion of Essentials, Hodder and Stoughton, 1964.

Philosophical Theology

Love Almighty and Ills Unlimited, Doubleday, 1961. The 1961 Nathaniel Taylor Lectures at Yale University.

A Science of God?, G. Bles, 1966. The Bishop of London's Lent Book for 1966, published in the United States as *God is Not Dead* by Morehouse-Barlow.

Faith and Speculation: An Essay in Philosophical Theology, A & C Black, 1967. Containing the 1964 Deems Lectures at New York University.

Devotional Works

The Crown of the Year: Weekly Paragraphs for the Holy Sacrament, Dacre Press, 1952.

Lord I Believe: Suggestions for Turning the Creed into Prayer, first edition, Faith Press, 1958; second edition, revised and enlarged, SPCK, 1962.

The Triple Victory: Christ's Temptations According to St Matthew, Faith Press, 1965. The Archbishop of Canterbury's Lent Book for 1965.

The One Genius: Readings Through the Year with Austin Farrer, edited by Richard Harries, SPCK, 1987.

Sermons

Said or Sung: An Arrangement of Homily and Verse, Faith Press, 1960, published in the United States as *A Faith of Our Own* by World Publishing Company.

A Celebration of Faith, edited by Leslie Houlden, Hodder and Stoughton, 1970.

The End of Man, edited by Charles Conti, SPCK, 1973.

The Brink of Mystery, edited by Charles Conti, SPCK, 1976.
The Essential Sermons, edited by Leslie Houlden, SPCK, 1991.
Words for Life, edited by Charles Conti and Leslie Houlden, SPCK, 1993.

Collected Essays

Reflective Faith: Essays in Philosophical Theology, edited by Charles Conti, SPCK, 1972.
Interpretation and Belief, edited by Charles Conti, SPCK, 1976.

In addition, a number of books have been written about Farrer. Those who wish to know more about his life should read Philip Curtis, *A Hawk Among Sparrows: A Biography of Austin Farrer* (SPCK, 1985). Those who are interested in the spiritual or theological aspect of his work should read Charles C. Hefling Jr, *Jacob's Ladder: Theology and Spirituality in the Thought of Austin Farrer* (Cowley, 1979); David Hein and Edward Hugh Henderson (eds), *Captured by the Crucified: The Practical Theology of Austin Farrer* (T & T Clark International, 2004); and Robert Slocum, *Light in a Burning Glass: A Systematic Presentation of Austin Farrer's Theology* (forthcoming from University of South Carolina Press).

Those who are more interested in Farrer's philosophical legacy should read Jeffrey C. Eaton, *The Logic of Theism: An Analysis of the Thought of Austin Farrer* (University Press of America, 1981); Jeffrey C. Eaton and Ann Loades (eds), *For God and Clarity: New Essays in Honor of Austin Farrer* (Pickwick, 1983); Brian Hebblethwaite and Edward Henderson (eds), *Divine Action: Essays Inspired by the Philosophical Theology of Austin Farrer* (T & T Clark, 1990); and Charles Conti, *Metaphysical Personalism: An Analysis of Austin Farrer's Theistic Metaphysics* (Oxford, 1995).

For an extensive bibliography that includes journal articles, dissertations and significant discussions of Farrer within more general books, see the 'Bibliography of Writings about Austin Farrer with Other Research Aids' in Hein and Henderson (eds), *Captured by the Crucified*, pp. 197–208. Most of Farrer's books do not have indexes, but for 'Indexes to the Main Works of Austin Farrer', see Hebblethwaite and Henderson (eds), *Divine Action*, pp. 230–81.

Finally, for relevant essays by the present editors, see Ann Loades, 'Austin Farrer on Love Almighty' in *For God and Clarity*, pp. 93–109; 'The Vitality of Tradition: Austin Farrer and Friends' in *Captured by the Crucified*, pp. 15–46; 'Farrer, Austin Marsden' in *The SPCK Dictionary of Anglican Theologians*, edited by Alister E. McGrath (London: SPCK, 1998), pp. 120–3; and Robert MacSwain, 'Above, Beside, Within: The Anglican Theology of Austin Farrer' in *Journal of Anglican Studies* (Volume 4, Number 1, June 2006), pp. 33–58.